Macho Medicine

To my wife,
Susan Presley Taylor,
for everything she is
and will be.

Macho Medicine

A History of the Anabolic Steroid Epidemic

by

William N. Taylor, M.D.

McFarland & Company, Inc., Publishers
Jefferson, North Carolina, and London

British Library Cataloguing-in-Publication data are available

Library of Congress Cataloguing-in-Publication Data

Taylor, William N.
    Macho medicine : a history of the anabolic steroid epidemic / by
William N. Taylor, M.D.
        p.   cm.
    Includes bibliographical references and index.
    ISBN 0-89950-613-5 (lib. bdg. : 50# alk. paper) ∞
    1. Doping in sports — History.   2. Anabolic steroids — History.
I. Title.
RC1230.T42   1991
362.29 — dc20   91-52506
                                                                    CIP

Manufactured in the United States of America

McFarland & Company, Inc., Publishers
  Box 611, Jefferson, North Carolina 28640

Contents

Acknowledgments

I would like to thank the following persons for their major contributions:

Robert O. Voy, M.D., former Chief Medical Officer for the United States Olympic Committee Drug Control Program, for allowing me the opportunity to serve as Physician Crew Chief under his guidance during the 1985–1988 quadrennium, and for his decision to be the first medical doctor to support my proposal to have anabolic steroids reclassified as narcotics under federal law.

Thomas C. Namey, M.D., Director of Sports Medicine at the University of Tennessee, for his timely suggestions and continued friendship.

The pharmaceutical representatives, district managers, and regional managers of Pfizer Pharmaceuticals, who promoted and supported my lecture series "Drug Issues in Sports Medicine" for the continuing medical education of the nation's physicians.

The Hon. Joseph R. Biden, Jr., Chairman of the Committee of the Judiciary of the United States Senate, for the legislation he introduced to reclassify anabolic steroids as narcotics under federal law. This designation increases the penalties for illegal anabolic steroid trafficking, gives the Drug Enforcement Agency responsibility for investigating anabolic steroid cases, and provides for anabolic steroids' incorporation in federal substance-abuse education, prevention, and treatment programs.

William N. Taylor, M.D.

Preface

This book summarizes a decade of my research, clinical observations, and personal convictions on the most controversial topic in the history of athletics—the anabolic steroid epidemic. Although there have been many influential scientists and policymakers who have attempted to tackle this issue (and I know most of them personally), few have had a great deal of insight on how to solve or curb this form of drug abuse. Others working in this area have fallen by the wayside because of their perpetration of false dogma which failed to convince the millions of users over the long haul. Still others, to protect their corner of the sports scene, have contributed to the overall cover-up and minimized the extent and severity of this problem.

Throughout this decade my personal and professional credibility have been thoroughly challenged, often resulting in temporary setbacks and near defeats. Through hard work and perseverance, I helped accomplish a task that all others felt was impossible: the reclassification of anabolic steroids as dangerous narcotics under federal law. When I first recommended this proposal in lectures, previous books, and articles that appeared in the lay and scientific press, the "good old boys" responded, "Young man, don't you know that this would take an act of Congress!"

The postwar period ushered in a new era of biologic research, spurred by the discovery of antibiotics. Suddenly there was both enthusiasm and money for biology, and a torrent of discoveries poured forth: tranquilizers, steroid hormones, immunochemistry, the genetic code. . . . A crisis is made by men, who enter into the crisis with their own prejudices, propensities, and predispositions. A crisis is the sum of intuition and blind spots, a blend of facts noted and facts ignored. Yet underlying the uniqueness of each crisis is a disturbing sameness. A characteristic of all crises is their predictability, in retrospect. They seem to have a certain inevitability, they seem predestined. This is not true of all crises, but it is true of sufficiently many to make the most hardened historian cynical and misanthropic.

—Michael Crichton
The Andromeda Strain (1969)

Introduction

Anabolic steroids are a group of molecules that include the male sex hormone testosterone and synthetic analogs of testosterone. Simply put, *anabolic* comes from a Greek verb meaning to put on, or add, and thus anabolic steroids tend to influence many of the body's mechanisms in a constructive fashion. One of the more obvious of these mechanisms deals with the increase in muscle mass of the steroid user, especially when the user combines the steroid use with a weight-training program.

Anabolic steroids are made synthetically and are powerful drugs that function as steroid hormones within the body. In many ways they tend to mimic the functions of the male sex hormone, although each of the 20 or so varieties currently on the market may produce a slightly different effect on any given user.

Continuing controversies have plagued the scientific research and medical use of these steroids ever since the initial discovery of testosterone over 50 years ago. Testosterone was labeled "medical dynamite" and "sexual TNT" by premiere physicians of the mid–1930s. There were claims of testosterone-induced rejuvenation that lead to affixing the name "Dr. Ponce de Leon" to the early scientist who pioneered the clinical uses of the male sex hormone. Even the pharmaceutical industry that synthesizes and sells these anabolic steroids couldn't avoid using tempting promotional phrases in the past such as "the lure of the Land of Bimini," which caused a medical uproar. Furthermore, the temptation to take these steroids seduced a few medical researchers into self-use and self-experimentation.

Recent evidence suggests that there may be over 3,000,000 regular anabolic steroid users in the United States. Most of these users buy their steroids illegally on an estimated $4,000,000 annual black market without a prescription from a licensed physician. Many of these users are school-age boys who may begin to take these steroids in middle school or high school. Surveys have shown that steroid use may afflict about 10 percent of all high school boys nationwide and that about 40 percent of the first-time users progress to hard-core steroid use. For many first-time users, anabolic steroids may be the first drug ever tried, and many users do not perceive

1

steroids as a "hard" drug. Steroid use by high school girls, although currently much less than that by boys, is perhaps the fastest-growing segment of total steroid use. Some of the users are athletes, but most take these steroids to enhance one or more of the many ingredients of body image, ego, and sexual desire and performance.

Older steroid users have begun to enter into a cross section of society. Muscular men and women have become superstars in a number of athletic and entertainment arenas. Anabolic steroids have become "the drugs of choice" for competitive powerlifters, and strength athletes in professional and college football. There has been significant use by some major track and field athletes and power hitters in professional baseball. A few major movie and television stars have also gained great fame through steroid use to obtain imposingly muscular bodies. Steroid use is also gaining popularity among police officers and armed forces personnel. The muscular body obtained by months and years of steroid use is transmitted by the press, commercial television, television advertisements, and the cinema, and has had a major impact of today's youth. In many cases, these overly muscular "heroes" portray very violent roles, which may translate to the true picture of a steroid user's personality. Young men take steroids and lift weights to mimic these "heroes" to participate in sports, or simply to "strut their stuff" on the beaches.

The anabolic steroid epidemic did not occur overnight, and neither have the suggested solutions to the problem. It has been an issue that the medical community, including the American Medical Association (AMA), would rather ignore, and the sporting organizations have fumbled for years. In fact, steroid use is so deeply engraved in the record books of modern sports that it took the Steroid Trafficking Act of 1990, reclassifying steroids as narcotics, to redefine the illegality and dangers associated with steroid use. The pages that follow contain a historical treatise of the steroid epidemic in the United States, from the discovery and synthesis of testosterone to the reclassification of anabolic steroids as Schedule III substances under the Steroid Trafficking Act of 1990.

1
The First Fifty Years

The continuing controversies and mistakes that have plagued the scientific advancements associated with anabolic steroids is perhaps unparalled in medical history. In this chapter an overview of the early history of the medieval experimentation with organ extracts and the history of the discovery, isolation, synthesis and some of the early clinical uses of testosterone will be presented. This historical approach is important for several reasons. First, no other hormone parallels the history of the development of medical endocrinology better than that of the male sex hormone. Second, it reveals how important *timing* is for the discovery and use of drugs. Third, it reveals some of the pitfalls in attempting to thwart scientific inertia by the promotion of false dogma. Fourth, it uncovers some of the medical antipathy associated with drugs or hormones that significantly alter sexual desire or sexual performance. Finally, it sets the stage for remaining chapters.

The Era of Medieval Organotherapy

Since recorded time, the customs of primitive societies provided for the use of human and animal organs in treating disease conditions. This type of therapy, organotherapy, was based on observation, speculation, and a smattering of science. For instance, some medieval physicians suggested that warriors eat animal or human hearts to enhance bravery, or that rulers and philosophers ingest animal or human brains to enhance intellect. During the Dark Ages, organotherapy perhaps reached its peak, for the people of this period indulged in consuming such bodily substances as bile, blood, bones, brains, feathers, feces, animal horns, intestines, placenta, testicles, and teeth.[1] Reviewing the theories of the ancient and medieval scientists, it seems that they may have had considerable comprehension regarding the presence

3

and function of the body's glands. In practice, though, organotherapy was a composite of mysticism, religion, philosophy, and customary dogma. No critically appraised theory could be adequately tested.

Organotherapy, although today it seems quite silly, still has some modern remnants. Organ extracts have been used in modern medicine to treat disease conditions in humans, especially when other, more scientific methods have yet to be devised. For instance, until very recently, brain extracts (pituitary glands from human cadavers) were used to treat dwarf children and allow them to grow to an acceptable adult height. Today, through the development of genetic engineering techniques, scientists have learned to isolate and synthesize from the human pituitary gland unlimited amounts of synthetic human growth hormone to treat short-statured children.

Other organotherapy remnants include the self-use and prescription use of glandular extracts, which are sold in the nation's health-food stores. These glandular preparations are usually available for oral consumption and may contain extracts from animal or human adrenal glands, ovaries, pituitaries, livers, or testicles. The effectiveness of these extracts in treating disease conditions remains controversial, and scientific studies are certainly needed to determine the safety and effectiveness of these over-the-counter products.

Another remnant of organotherapy that relates to athletic performance is the use of extra blood (blood doping or hypertransfusion of red blood cells) by endurance athletes such as marathon or middle-distance runners and long-distance cyclists. This practice, proven scientifically to enhance aerobic capacity in elite athletes, is being phased out due to the genius of genetic engineering techniques. Now available is synthetic human erythropoetin (EPO), which is a recombinant human hormone that can stimulate red-blood-cell production within the cardiovascular system to a much greater extent than normal. The use of synthetic EPO by endurance athletes remains undetectable by even the most elaborate drug-testing procedures and certainly may enhance aerobic capacity and endurance.

The early roots of the discovery of many hormones began with crude, experimental organotherapy. Whether it is eating wild animal hearts for bravery or blood transfusions for endurance or the use of testicular extracts for strength development and vitality, organotherapy has deep roots in society and in athletics. These brief remarks introduce organotherapy and serve to begin the tracing of the male sex hormone from its earliest recorded history and to build a foundation for the following chapters, which deal with anabolic steroid use in more modern times.

The earliest empirical knowledge regarding the male sex hormone comes from the ancient accounts of castrated animals and men and observing the subsequent effects this castration had on the body. But even before these observations, in about 1400 B.C. a physician from India recommended the use of testicular extracts as a cure for impotence in men.[2] Prior to 300 B.C., the Greek philosopher Aristotle documented the effects of castration in many species of animals in his *Historis Animalium*.[3] The earliest documented correlation between testicular function and the aging process is found in the works of Aretaeus the Capadocuean in A.D. 150.[4] In one chapter he wrote:

> For it is the semen, when processed of vitality, which makes us to be men, hot, well braced in limbs, well voiced, spirited, strong to think and act. For when the semen is not possessed of its vitality, persons become shrivelled, have a sharp tone of voice, lose their hair and their beard, and become effeminate, as the characteristics of eunuchs prove.

It was several centuries later (about A.D. 800) that Johannes Mesue was reported to prescribe testicular extracts as an aphrodisiac and for the treatment of pulmonary tuberculosis.[5] Centuries later, Willis published the following:

> The blood poured out something — through the spermatic arteries to the genitalia — and that it received in turn certain ferments from these parts, — that is, certain particles imbued with a seminal tincture and carried back to the blood — which makes it vigorous and instills into it a new and lively virtue.[6]

It was about a century later that anatomist-scientist John Hunter, during the Enlightenment, attempted to approach the functioning of the testicles in a scientific experiment in 1792. He attempted to remove the testicles from cocks and transplant the testicles into the abdomens of hens and observe the subsequent changes in the hens. However, due to infection and an apparent rejection of the testicular implants, he failed to observe the expected "masculinization" of the hens.[7]

About a century passed before the landmark work of the German scientist Berthold was reported in 1848. In his experiment, he removed the testes of four roosters and surgically replaced one testis into the abdomen in two different capons (castrated roosters). After this surgical implantation of the testis, he allowed the experimental capons (with implanted testis) to live for six months, observed them, and then killed them. He reported that "these animals remained male in regard to voice, reproduction instinct, fighting spirit, and growth of comb and wattles ... is maintained by the productive influence of the testicle."[8]

There was a lengthy interim following this fundamental "rooster science" of Berthold before other scientists would attempt to experiment further with the testicular substance in humans. According to the historical record of his era, Brown-Sequard epitomized the French scientific world, and many of the syndromes he described for human disease conditions still bear his name in modern medicine. He had been a keen-thinking physiologist, and he was acutely interested in developments for the infancy of the science of hormones. Yet he was aging, and at the end of his career at 72, he made the quantum leap from the pages of the "rooster science" to self-experimentation. There was much more work he wanted to accomplish, but his health was fading quickly.

Brown-Sequard began his experiment by removing the testicles of dogs and guinea pigs. He then smashed these testicles and brewed them in a salt solution, giving rise to a sort of "testicle stew." He then began to inject himself with this crude testicular extract, and with a new fire in his eyes, he lectured to the premier French physiologists that these testicular extracts had rejuvenated him. He claimed a remarkable return of physical strength and endurance, a rejuvenated bowel system, and enhanced mental capacity.[9]

Never before had there been such a powerful report on how to attain a new lease on life by such a prestigious scientist. Unfortunately, Brown-Sequard's fountain of youth lasted for only a few months, and he died shortly thereafter of apparently unrelated causes. Even with all of the other important discoveries Brown-Sequard made in the medical field, he died one of the most discredited scientists in the history of medicine. The response of the scientific world was to break into a laughter that can still be heard occasionally in some medical circles today. The very idea of testicular extracts affording such strength, endurance, and vitality! And for his perceived scientific blunder, Brown-Sequard had critics who have tried to wipe him completely off the scientific map. But what the critics of his era had forgotten was that Brown-Sequard had a unique ability to think keenly and that he had dedicated nearly 50 years of his life to science.

By jumping into human experimentation too soon, Brown-Sequard handed down a message that still has meaning today. If you are going to experiment with the secret of vitality hidden within the testicular substance, you had better be correct. Brown-Sequard had attempted to make a new man of himself during his elderly years, and this Dr. Ponce de Leon imitation resulted in a blunder that would place the study of and search for the male sex hormone in the scientific "doghouse" for many years. For nearly four decades, the early endocrine scientists didn't forget Brown-Sequard's apparent failure. The medical world was disappointed and somewhat furious about it.[10]

The quest for some sort of drug or elixir that affords perpetual life or a fountain-of-youth effect has been with mankind for a long time, and perhaps it has intensified with the progress of medical science. If not the male sex hormone, then perhaps some other hormone? The most modern hormone that may be perceived to delay aging or reverse some aspects of aging has been recombinantly produced human growth hormone. One of the first scientific papers on the potential powers of human growth hormone in the antiaging process was published in 1989,[11] but other supportive reports have been published since. But the manner in which the press perceived these scientific articles portraying human growth hormone as a possible youth drug resulted in physicians nationwide being bombarded by phone calls from their patients requesting treatment to delay aging.

The Isolation and Synthesis of Testosterone

Following the fate of Brown-Sequard, it seems that research in the area of testicular extracts took a few steps backward to reevaluate some of the earlier findings. Then, after piddling about for nearly four decades, attempts to extract the male sex hormone from animal testicles was begun.

In 1926, Professor Fred C. Koch and a young medical student, Lemuel C. McGee, flirted with being called the laughingstocks of the scientific world by reopening the search for the male sex hormone. With money donated from Squibb Pharmaceuticals, these University of Chicago scientists began their search by castrating enough bulls to obtain 40 pounds of bull testicles. And by utilizing some of the extraction techniques afforded them by the advances in organic chemistry, they stewed these bull testicles in benzene, alcohol, and acetone solutions. Out of the 40 pounds of bull testicles, they ended up with a measly 20mg of a fat-soluble extract. They presumed that this resulting testicular substance had male-sex-hormone capacities, and to prove it, they had to utilize the old "rooster science."

Koch selected a capon with its combs and wattles mere remnants of its former proud roosterhood for the experiment. They then divided the scanty amount of testicular substance they had previously extracted from the bull testicles and began injecting the capon daily with a dose. Within two weeks, the capon's combs and wattles turned redder and brighter, like a rooster's.[12] But prior to publishing their results, Koch sent McGee back to the laboratory to repeat the entire experiment, from the bull testicles on up. The results were the same. This became the first documented proof of the existance of a male sex hormone derived from the testicles, and thus Koch and McGee became the first of the great hormone hunters.[13]

Three years later, Koch and Dr. T. F. Gallagher, aided by a modest sum of research money from the Committee for Research in Problems of Sex of the National Research Council, began with a half ton of bull testicles and refined Koch's earlier extraction technique.[14] With this version of testicular extract, Gallagher and Koch, along with Dr. A. T. Keynon, performed the first documented human experiment on a human eunuch to prove the efficacy of the male sex hormone in humans.

Now the momentum was gathering in the scientific world to further isolate, identify, and perhaps synthesize the male sex hormone. There was now no doubt that it existed, at least in a crude form. Utilizing the procedures of Koch, in the summer of 1935 organic chemists in the laboratory of the German-Jewish pharmacologist Ernst Laqueur in Amsterdam extracted a few milligrams of pure male sex hormone, named it *testosterone*, and precisely determined its chemical structure.[16] Then, within the same year, two different scientists, Ruzicka (Yugoslav chemist) and Butendandt (German chemist), synthesized testosterone from cholesterol.[16] Both of these groups were later awarded a Nobel prize for the independent synthesis of testosterone, but only Ruzicka actually accepted the award; the Germans declined, apparently due to the influence of World War II.[17]

During this period of science, organic chemistry was burgeoning, and it was greatly influencing the powers of medicine. Such drugs as the sulfa antibiotics, or "God's powder," and drugs to fight malaria had been discovered by organic chemists. But the first great hormone hunter was Dr. Fred Koch, who overcame the previous decades of medical antipathy to extract the male sex hormone and open the gateway for others to isolate and synthesize it. Prior to Koch's work, the general feeling was that there was no such thing as a male sex hormone. In an obituary published in a 1948 issue of the *Journal of Clinical Endocrinology* are the following comments:

> His [Koch's] diversified contributions to endocrine research are well known to all. He will best be remembered, however, by his influence on the development of our understanding of testicular function . . . the details of biological relations to male hormone and hormone-like substances were described.

Dr. Koch had taken the warning of old Brown-Sequard, and when Koch "tinkered" with the testicular substance, he was correct. But as it turned out, it didn't keep others from tinkering with the male sex hormone and its analogs, and some of their "research" was behind closed doors and dehumanizing, as will be briefly covered in the next section.

The Era of Early Clinical Experimentation

In the records of World War II are numerous accounts of hormonal manipulation and experimentation with human prisoners by Nazi scientists. After all, a group of German scientists pioneered the synthesis of testosterone and other hormones to follow. Several publications also suggest that testosterone and its analog, anabolic steroids, were given to Nazi troops to make them more aggressive in battle. But perhaps one of the first and certainly the most famous anabolic steroid user was Adolf Hitler. From the records of Hitler's personal physician, it was reported that Hitler was given injections of the "derivatives of testosterone" for a variety of presumed mental and physical ailments.[18] In fact, besides the "derivatives of testosterone" (anabolic steroids), Hitler's physician reported that Hitler took methamphetamines and several other drugs now considered narcotics during his last few years of life. Who will ever know how much these psychoactive steroids and other narcotics affected Hitler's judgments and dehumanizing tactics?

Putting ethics and morals aside, the results of the experiments believed to be performed by Nazi scientists were never published and will be lost forever. But if we take the stairs down to the basement of one of the many major medical libraries in the United States and blow the dust off journals of the late 1930s and early 1940s, we are able to recap many of the early (and often forgotten) experimental work with testosterone on both normal and ill persons. In reviewing these published articles, it is important to reflect briefly on some of the differences in scientific modalities, design, and freedoms that were in vogue during this early period of experimentation compared to more modern times. First, the code of ethics was certainly much more relaxed during the 1930s and 1940s. Second, much of the research would not be accepted by today's standards for publication due to the relatively low numbers of patients, the lack of a strict scientific methodology, and the lack of control groups. And for these reasons, as well as others that will be discussed in a later chapter, these published findings have essentially been erased from the scientific and medical maps.

Use of Testosterone in Treating Hypogonadism

One of the obvious therapies utilizing testosterone would be in those men (or women) who lacked or had a relative lack of the normal production of testosterone. Such a condition in males would manifest itself by sexual underdevelopment or a delay in the normal maturation process (hypogonadism) or by the loss or lack of testicles. The first case report in the scientific literature using testosterone in the treatment of sexual underdevelopment of a 27-year-old white male medical student was published in 1937 by Hamilton.[19] The following are exerpts from Hamilton's paper:

> The patient was a 27-year-old white medical student. . . . The general body picture was that of a pre-puberal castrate with a feminine emphasis in the wide hips, genu valgum, girdle distribution of fat, protruding mammae, and retarded development of larynx, genitalia and hair. . . . He was engaged to be married. The genitalia were somewhat smaller in size and degree of development than those of a small boy of 3 or 4 years of age.

The patient was given a total of 550mg of testosterone acetate in 14 injections, 3 injections per week, for a period of one month. . . . At the end of these injections, the patient received oil which, unknown to him, did not contain the potent male hormone substance he had been receiving.

The effect of the hormone administration was seen within 60 hours after the first injection, when the patient experienced pronounced penile erections . . . at times reaching a state of priapism. . . . The patient was more energetic than usual, self-assured and in higher spirits . . . a lowering of the pitch of the voice. . . . Small hairs appeared on the chest in a masculine distribution Acneform eruption was seen on back and chest.

Five days following the last injection . . . hot flashes were experienced . . . erections became infrequent . . . lassitude, some loss of self-assurance . . . the acne gradually disappeared.

In evaluating this study and the quotations above, it is important to make several points. First, the dose of testosterone was quite large; in fact, several times the standard dose used to treat hypogonadism today. But Hamilton had no standard dose to refer to, and there were no laboratory tests to measure the amount of testosterone in the blood. It was certainly experimentation. Second, even the earliest clinical case study points to some of the desired and adverse effects that have withstood the test of time and are accepted today. Testosterone has definite effects on the psychological and physiological balance of its user. Over the next 50 years, the use of testosterone therapy in the treatment of hypogonadism and delayed puberty was refined and studied by dozens of researchers. It is one use of testosterone and anabolic steroids that is still considered primary in modern medicine. Third, this early study, since it involved using such a large dose of testosterone, is the earliest record that may shed some light on some of the adverse effects when athletic persons self-use these steroids in more modern times.

Testosterone Treatment of Male
Involutional Melancholia and Mental Disorders

After Hamilton published his paper indicating that testosterone was a psychoactive substance, Barahal, a medical doctor from Kings Park, New York, reviewed some of the earlier research on the etiology and possible therapies of involutional melancholia in men. During the late 1930s and 1940s, involutional melancholia, also referred to as the male climacteric, presented as one of the complex problems of aging. This syndrome had symptoms that could be listed under four clinical headings: neurocirculatory, psychosexual, genito-urinary, and miscellaneous. These clinical headings in older men with the syndrome may translate into a variety of symptoms believed to be caused by a decreased testosterone level, including anxiety, decreased libido, muscular aches, fatigue, and accumlation of lower-trunk fat. In 1938, Barahal published the first report on the use of testosterone propionate (Breton) supplied by Schering Corporation, indicating that the male sex hormone was of no value in the treatment of this condition.[20] But the dose of testosterone was very low and certainly below therapeutic doses (10mg injections three times weekly) used today of 200–300mg monthly. However, there were several other reports published during this period that showed the efficacy of testosterone preparations in the treatment of the male climacteric, including the study of Goldman and Markham.[21] Several other early studies demonstrated that testosterone had psychoactive properties by showing its effectiveness in the treatment of a variety of mental disorders, including depression, anxiety, and psychosis.[22] Although the success rate of testosterone use in these studies varied, these researchers felt that further study was justified. Also, these early reports pointed to the fact that testosterone therapy was dose-related in its response.

Testosterone Treatment of Angina Pectoris, Hypertension, and Coronary Artery Disease

One of the more interesting areas in which testosterone therapy was considered beneficial in the early clinical period was in the treatment of hypertension and heart disease. Today, however, according to the most current medical theories, testosterone and anabolic steroid use and abuse is believed to be a significant *contributor* to hypertension and heart disease. But before we laugh at the efforts of these earlier physicians, it must be considered that there were few drugs to treat these conditions and that the knowledge of these disease conditions had not evolved very far. About a dozen studies were published during the early 1940s that showed or suggested that testosterone preparations were beneficial in the treatment of angina pectoris, hypertension, and coronary artery disease.

The earliest report on the topic of testosterone therapy and vascular disease was published in 1939 as a preliminary report by a group of clinicians working with J. B. Hamilton.[23] A year later, three instructors of medicine at Ohio State University College of Medicine published a paper containing a study of 23 patients with coronary artery disease in which 22 of the 23 showed clinical improvement with sex hormone therapy (testosterone, estrogen, or a combination of these).[24]

Perhaps the greatest proponent of testosterone therapy for angina pectoris during this period was Maurice A. Lesser, M.D., who was a professor in preventive medicine at Boston University School of Medicine and

Massachusetts Memorial Hospitals. In 1942 Lesser published his preliminary report on 25mg of testosterone propionate injected twice or thrice weekly (supplied by Ciba Pharmaceutical Products, Inc., under the trade name Perandren) in 24 patients with angina pectoris.[25]

> Favorable results were obtained in all cases (20 men and 4 women) in that the frequency, severity and duration of attacks of angina pectoris were diminished, and these patients have been able to increase their physical activities to a considerable degree without precipitating attacks. . . . The beneficial effects of this treatment persisted between two and twelve months after treatment was discontinued. . . . No untoward effects were observed in any of the patients studied. . . . Fluorscopic examinations, serial kymograms and electrocardiograms showed no uniform changes resulting from this therapy.

Lesser believed that testosterone might prove to be a valuable drug in the treatment of angina pectoris and warranted further study. Dr. Hamm, a private physician in Boston, supported Lesser by publishing his findings on testosterone therapy and angina pectoris and hypertension with seven of his patients.[26] Depending of the severity of symptoms and response to treatment, the dosage schedule employed was 25mg injected every two to five days for a total of 5 to 25 injections (testosterone propionate, trade name Neo-Hombreol, supplied by Roche-Organon, Inc.). Hamm concluded the following:

> Testosterone propionate appears to be a valuable therapeutic agent in angina pectoris, the effect of the hormone being mediated through its vasodilating properties acting on the coronary circulation and/or through development of coronary collateral circulation. . . . The undesirability of unduly stimulating the libido in patients . . . is obvious. . . . However, this should be no deterrent to sex hormone therapy provided careful selection of patients and control over dosage is practiced.

Dr. Hamm reported increases in libido in both men and women with testosterone therapy. Also, three of the patients showed a substantial decrease in their hypertensive blood pressure.

A year later, Lesser published further observations with testosterone therapy in patients with angina pectoris[27] and perhaps the most definitive study, on 100 patients in 1946.[28] Ninety-one of the 100 patients (92 men and 8 women) with angina pectoris showed moderate to marked improvement. Fifty-one patients showed marked improvement, and 40 patients exhibited moderate improvement.

Similar findings with this form of therapy were found by other groups.[29] One of the more convincing studies of this period was Waldman's who showed that seven or eight patients with positive electrocardiograms during stress testing responded favorably to treatment with testosterone propionate.[30] Waldman postulated that the metabolic action of testosterone was through increasing the phosphorus and creatine content of the heart muscle, providing an increase in contractility of the muscle.

With so many scientific reports from several countries indicating that testosterone therapy was beneficial in angina pectoris, hypertension, and coronary heart disease, it is certain that droves of patients were treated in this manner during the 1940s and beyond. Today, we know that when a scientific article is published in the *New England Journal of Medicine* regarding a new treatment for a common disease or condition, the major media broadcasts the findings to the public even prior to the reading and understanding by most physicians. And since physicians were much more "experimental" during the 1940s than those of today, there is no question that many patients were given testosterone for various heart conditions. For some reason, the medical literature is void in the later decades on why testosterone therapy "fell from grace" in this form of treatment, and very few of today's cardiologists have ever heard of this form of treatment or have been taught that testosterone was apparently the "drug of choice" for angina pectoris in the 1940s. It is also certain that testosterone and anabolic steroids have effects on the cardiovascular system that may enhance cardiac output and contractility directly that have never been studied with the technology afforded medicine today. A number of elite marathon runners have tested positively for anabolic steroid use, and it is certain that they used the steroids to enhance their athletic performance! It is apparent that the whole area of how testosterone and anabolic steroids affect the heart and cardiovascular system, both on an acute and a chronic basis, is in need of in-depth study today.

One thing certain is that people will use and misuse drugs or druglike substances they believe (supported by medical literature) will help a disease condition or will enhance some area of their lives, such as libido. The widespread distribution and use of glandular products represented as containing sex hormones, including testosterone, presented a problem recognized early by the Food and Drug Administration (FDA). In 1941, a paper was published from the Division of Pharmacology of the FDA conceding the abuse potential of such products and suggesting some early attempts of controlling such abuses, primarily directed at the manufacturing levels.[31] Thus, the misuse and abuse of testosterone and anabolic steroids by the general population had its roots 50 years ago!

Testosterone Treatment on Muscular Performance of Older Men

Another area in which testosterone therapy was shown to be useful in the early clinical period was in enhancement of muscle mass, strength, endurance, and reflexes of normal older men. Simonson and coworkers from the Research Laboratory of Mount Sinai Hospital in Milwaukee, Wisconsin, published the most definitive article on this topic in 1944.[32] Six older men were treated with 30 to 40mg of methyl testosterone tablets (supplied by Schering Corporation under the trade name Oreton-M) for three- to six-week periods. The older men experienced an enhancement of central nervous system reflex time (measured by flicker fusion frequency), back muscle strength enhancement, and increases in dynamic and static work performance. These changes were maintained up to eight months with periodic intervals of drug use and off-drug schedules.

Testosterone Treatment in Other Miscellaneous Conditions

During the period of early clinical experimentation, testosterone therapy was considered beneficial in a number of medical conditions. Many of these uses are listed below, and some of them could still have some benefit in modern medicine today if research were reopened and evaluated by modern technology. Testosterone therapy was shown to be useful in

- treatment of premature boy and girl infants;[33]
- treatment of enuresis (bed-wetting) in children (boys and girls);[34]
- treatment of anemia;[35]
- treatment of male impotence;[36]
- treatment for contraception in men;[37]
- treatment during dieting to spare muscle-mass loss;[38]
- treatment for nephrotic syndrome;[39]
- treatment to enhance suntanning;[40]
- treatment of dysfunctional uterine bleeding in women;[41]
- treatment of the female menopause;[42]
- treatment of premenstrual syndrome (PMS) in women;[43] and
- treatment to enhance sexual desire, sexual pleasure, and orgasmic response in normal women.[44]

Summary: Establishment of Clinical Uses and Abuses

In this first chapter, the first 50 years of the history of testosterone and anabolic steroids has been presented from the apparent blunder and self-use of testicular extracts by French physiologist Brown-Sequard through the early years of clinical experimentation with testosterone in a variety of disorders and medical conditions. Testosterone is a powerful hormone with significant psychogenic and physiologic effects on anyone who uses it or is treated with it. Likewise, in the next chapters, the derivatives of testosterone (anabolic steroids) will be shown to be both powerful psychogenic and physiologic drugs, especially with self-use or clinical abuse.

The background has been laid for the modern anabolic steroid epidemic in the United States, and it becomes more obvious that it is destined to occur as bits and pieces of this chapter begin to seep through the historical cracks and pervade the decades to follow. It is part of human nature to experiment with clinically, and self-use socially, hormones and hormone-like drugs that may alter so many basic human characteristics, such as sex drive, sexual performance, muscle mass and strength, endurance, work capacity, growth and development, and so forth. Therefore, hormonal manipulation for clinical good or for social abuse has been deeply seeded, and as medical science has synthesized and continues to synthesize the full array of powerful hormonal drugs, there will be both an expansion of clinical good *and* societal abuse potentials.

Paul de Kruif, a medical student during the 1920s, published the first book on testosterone in 1945.[45] He had become a reporter and worked closely with *Reader's Digest* during the writing of this book. He also knew personally many of the scientists and medical physicians who conducted the early experimental work with testosterone. In de Kruif's book, *The Male Hormone*, he portrays the known science and medical uses of the early 1940s regarding testosterone and couples this knowledge with what he felt were the prevailing medical thoughts and concerns of that period.

De Kruif wrote that because of its nature, that testosterone *was* chemical manhood, it had two strikes against it from the outset. Because testosterone could enhance the sex drive of both men and women, he wrote that many an eminent physician felt that using this hormone had bawdy overtones. Physicians of this period, according to de Kruif, referred to testosterone therapy as "medical dynamite" and "sexual TNT." He wrote about the pervading medical antipathy and cynicism regarding testosterone therapy by the American Medical Association and other premier medical groups. He felt that scientifically speaking, testosterone would not get a true evaluation by future medical physicians due to the prevailing feelings of the early 1940s. He also cited self-use of testosterone preparations by physicians, and in one case, this self-use allowed an aging professor of surgery at a major medical school to continue to perform surgery because of his new lease on life.

During the early 1940s, many warnings were issued regarding testosterone therapy. According to de Kruif, "Despite the warnings of these highest medical authorities, just the same, many physicians, and more of them all the time, were trying out testosterone on this, that, and almost every disease of the middle and later years of the lives of men."

De Kruif also knew personally about the effects of testosterone, for he was a self-user. He wrote:

Now I'm fifty-four years old, and there's so much left to do. I've grown old much too quickly and smart much too late. . . . I'll be faithful and remember twenty to thirty milligrams a day of testosterone. I'm not ashamed . . . it's chemical crutches . . . it's borrowed manhood . . . it's borrowed time. . . . And who knows, maybe tomorrow, they'll hit on a simple dietary chemical trick that will, to a degree, bring back the power of the glands that make my own natural male hormone. . . . Meanwhile I'll keep taking the methyl testosterone that now gives me the total vitality to go on working.

De Kruif was also aware during the 1940s of many of the methods that athletes would resort to for performance enhancement. He knew that testosterone preparations would quickly filter into the sports industry in a big way:

We know how both the St. Louis Cardinals and St. Louis Browns have won championships, super-charged by vitamins. It would be interesting to watch the productive power of an industry or a professional group that would try a systematic supercharge with testosterone — of course under a good hormone hunter's supervision.

2

The Search for Medical Applications

During the period of early clinical experimentation with testosterone, there was a hint that it was going to have a difficult time becoming medically reputable. This hint gained an official stamp in the late 1930s by the American Medical Association's Council on Pharmacy and Chemistry when the Council declared testosterone "not acceptable for New and Non-official Remedies."[1] And the boundary lines between the medical scientists who were conducting clinical studies and the "authorities" who represented the governing voice of medicine were being drawn, with a paucity of studies published. In other words, the AMA's council was making conclusions about testosterone therapy prior to profound study. This fact always seems to be a basic ingredient for *dogma*, and much dogma, because it is based on opinion and a smattering of science, is eventually proven incorrect and often damaging for further progress. Besides, what appointed "authority" ever discovered anything? Not one. They're too busy politicking themselves into being appointed or elected as authorities.

As dogma began to invade the clinical testosterone studies in the United States, the early scientific fate of testosterone therapy fell more heavily into the hands of medical scientists in other countries. Perhaps the German scientists, who were well ahead of their times partially due to their methods of human experimentation, would have a greater respect for the simple facts about testosterone therapy. But World War II came and dropped a curtain over German medical science, and the pioneering German hormone scientists faded from the scientific picture. German medical science was falling on evil days.[2]

No one seemed to deny that testosterone therapy was indicated in cases of testosterone deficiency, but the quibbling began when it was used outside this obvious indication. This quibbling, and the dogma, had a major impact on the direction of testosterone research, and later, anabolic steroid research. Even today, testosterone and anabolic steroids have been the least studied and least prescribed of the major classes of steroid hormones. Significantly more medical attention has been paid to the corticogenic, esterogenic, and progesterogenic steroids.[3] However, there has been extensive study of testosterone and anabolic steroids on animals, and the use of these steroids on animals, including livestock, show horses, and race horses, is extensive today.

In this chapter, some of the history of testosterone and anabolic steroids over a 31-year period or so (1945–1976) will be examined. A brief section regarding the initial discovery and synthesis of anabolic steroids obtained through the chemical manipulation of the testosterone molecule will be presented. Some of the studies dealing with the proposed medical uses of anabolic steroids, including those examining the effects of these steroids on athletic performance, will follow. Finally, the major factors that play a role in the development of the anabolic steroid epidemic will be ushered in.

The Initial Synthesis of Anabolic Steroids

As documented in Chapter 1, the first synthesis of anabolic steroids was by German medical scientists during World War II. However, credit for the original synthesis of anabolic steroids is usually given to a medical doctor, John B. Ziegler, whose work was supported by Ciba Pharmaceutical.[4] From the early pages in the epic of hormonal manipulation of athletes, Ziegler learned at the 1956 World Games that Russian athletes were using testosterone. When he returned to the United States, he developed the first documented analog of testosterone, the anabolic steroid trade-named Dianabol (methandrostenolone). In Ziegler's unpublished work, he gave 5mg doses of Dianabol to athletes to examine the benefits and safety factors. But very quickly these athletes abused the drugs behind Ziegler's back and began developing "all sorts of medical pathologies."[5] A few years later, on Southern California beaches, bodybuilders wore T-shirts that read *Dianabol, the Breakfast of Champions.*

By 1963, several other pharmaceutical companies synthesized versions of anabolic steroids to go with the already available testosterone preparations, methyl testosterone and Dianabol. The list included Halotestin and Ultandren (fluoxymesterone), Nivelar (norethandrolone), Adroyd (oxymetholone), Durabolin (nandrolone phenpropionate), and stanozolol (Winstrol).[6] About a year later, several more anabolic steroids became commercially available in the United States, including Deca-Durabolin (nandrolone decanoate), Stendiol (methandriol), Oranabol (oxymesterone), Myagen (bolasterone), Maxibolin (ethylestrenol), Genabol (norbolethone), and Anavar (oxandrolone). As the steroid black market is discussed in later sections, it is important to realize that these anabolic steroids became commercially available in the early 1960s and that the patent-life protection for them was 17 years, so by the early 1980s, the patents for anabolic steroids had expired, thus becoming *generic drugs*, and led to further mass production and illegal diversion.

Description of Anabolic Steroids

Anabolic steroids are artificial synthetic derivatives of the natural male sex hormone testosterone. They were originally synthesized to retain and magnify some of the effects that testosterone produced on the body, at the same time reducing or alleviating some of the other effects of testosterone.

Testosterone's effects on the body can be placed into two basic categories: anabolic (constructive metabolism, or simply "to build") and androgenic (characteristics that are man-like). Several bodily functions are under direct or indirect control by testosterone. Basically, testosterone has a stimulative effect on skeletal muscle mass, some visceral organs, the hemoglobin concentration, and the red blood cell number and mass. Testosterone also affects characteristics associated with the development of sexual organs—the pattern, distribution, and amount of facial, body, and pubic hair; the deepening tone of the voice; the percentage and distribution of body fat and other man-like features such as personality and sex drive. Testosterone, however, does not seem to alter one's sexual preference once it has been established.

In order to understand better the reasons behind the synthesis of anabolic steroids and how they may differ to some degree from their parent hormone, testosterone, the following table has been constructed to compare the basic anabolic and androgenic functions of testosterone.

Table 1: Basic Comparison of the Androgenic and Anabolic Functions of Testosterone

Androgenic Functions

initial growth of the penis
growth and development of the seminal vesicles
growth and development of the prostate gland
increased density of body hair
development and pattern of pubic hair
increased density and distribution of facial hair
deepening voice

increased oil production of the sebaceous glands
increased libido and awakening of sexual interest
male personality characteristics

Anabolic Functions

increased skeletal muscle mass
increased hemoglobin concentration
increased red blood cell mass
enhanced activity of certain cells of the immune system, such as
    T-lymphocytes
influence on the distribution of body fat
influence on reducing the percentage of body fat
increased calcium deposition in the bones
increased total body nitrogen retention
increased visceral organ size
increased retention of several electrolytes

The basic idea behind the development of anabolic steroids was to alter the testosterone molecule so that the anabolic functions were enhanced selectively and the androgenic functions were reduced or alleviated. However, the "perfect" anabolic steroid that enhances the anabolic functions of testosterone but is free of testosterone's androgenic functions has never been developed.

Attempts have been made to measure and classify the anabolic and androgenic effects of various anabolic steroids. The ratio of anabolic functions relative to androgenic functions has been termed the *therapeutic index*[7] as determined by investigational studies conducted mostly on animals. The reference point for the therapeutic index is testosterone, which is given a therapeutic index value of 1. Anabolic steroids would generally have a therapeutic index of greater than 1 since they tend to magnify the anabolic functions and reduce the androgenic functions.

An excellent discussion of investigational research conducted on animals to determine the therapeutic index of anabolic steroids has been published containing nearly 40 research articles,[8] and it will not be reproduced here. Basically, the studies utilized a number of methods to measure the genital and extragenital responses that various anabolic steroids produced on laboratory animals.

The basic fact remains that different tissues respond to anabolic steroid stimulation in different manners. Most of the current theories regarding this therapeutic index remain in their infancy, for a number of reasons. Some of these factors that tend to complicate any study of anabolic steroids regarding the therapeutic index are:

1. The solubility of a particular steroid, which gives rise to the availability of the steroid molecules to bind to various receptors in the tissues.

2. The difference in the threshold concentrations of different steroid compounds.

3. The use of a less than ideal method to determine the anabolic versus androgenic properties of a particular anabolic steroid.

4. The rate of absorption from the intramuscular depot in subjects, when an injectable anabolic steroid is studied.

5. The apparent loss of reproducibility when extrapolating the results from animal experiments to humans.

6. The continued lack of scientific studies performed on human subjects.

7. The difficulty in determining accurately the androgenicity of anabolic steroids in man on a quantitative basis.

A comparison of the therapeutic index range for a number of anabolic steroids was published by Dr. James Wright,[9] and an adapted version is presented below in Table 2.

Table 2: Therapeutic Index for Some Anabolic Steroids

Trade Name	Generic Name	Original Manufacturer	Therapeutic Index
Halotestin	fluoxymesterone	Upjohn	2–6
Myagen	bolasterone	Upjohn	2–5
Nivelar	novethandrolone	Searle	3–7
Oranabol	oxymesterone	Farmitalia	4–7
Adroyd	oxymetholone	Parke-Davis	3–8
Anadrol	oxymetholone	Syntex	3–8
Dianabol	methandrostenolone	Ciba	2–7.5
Nortestonate	nandrolone	Upjohn	5–16
Durabolin	nandrolone phenylpropionate	Organon	11–12
Deca-Durabolin	nandrolone decanoate	Organon	11–12
Winstrol	stanazolol	Winthrop	5–20
Primobolan	methenolone	Schering A-G	13–16
Primobolan Acetate	methenolone acetate	Schering A-G	7–9
Primobolan Depot	methenolone enanthate	Schering A-G	10–16
Anavar	oxandrolone	Searle	13
Maxibolin	ethylestrenol	Organon	8
Genabol	norbolethone	Wycth	22
Dostalon	dimethazine	Richer	14–22

The list in Table 2 is by no means an exhaustive one regarding *all* the anabolic steroids that were commercially available for human use during the period of the search for medical applications. But even with the 18 preparations listed, it is easy to conclude that the pharmaceutical industry was banking heavily on the medical future of anabolic steroids for treating disease conditions.

Early Medical Applications of Anabolic Steroids

Despite much of the prevailing medical antipathy generated by the clinical use of testosterone, a number of research groups were willing to experiment with anabolic steroids in a number of disease conditions during the late 1950s through the early 1970s. In most of the studies cited below, anabolic steroid therapy proved to be of some benefit or the results were inconclusive. The designs of some of the experimental work, although more scientific than those used during the early clinical work with testosterone, were often flawed when compared to current standards.

Some of the early medical applications for anabolic steroid therapy were

- underweight patients;[10]
- patients with rheumatoid arthritis;[11]
- surgical patients;[12]
- patients with myelofibrosis;[13]
- patients with various anemias;[14]
- patients with osteoporosis;[15]
- for patients with hyperlipidemia;[16]
- as a growth stimulator for short children;[17] and
- for enhancement of muscle mass, strength and athletic performance.[18]

The clinical studies conducted during this period indicated that although anabolic steroids had some powerful effects on the body, harnessing the positive effects anabolic steroids had would be difficult to mold exactly into treating disease conditions. In other words, anabolic steroids can do this and do that, but what disease are they good for? For this reason, as time went on, there were fewer and fewer true medical indications for anabolic steroids. Also, during this early period of the clinical evaluations for anabolic steroids, many of the research tools that were available had not evolved far enough to permit an accurate and true evaluation. Perhaps if some of the current medical equipment was utilized in new studies today, the results may be different, and more specific indications could be found for anabolic steroids in modern medicine.

Perhaps the greatest reason that clinical research began to slow with anabolic steroids in the 1970s was the bad reputation they were beginning to gain by the situation surrounding athletic use and abuse. In fact, after 20 or so studies were published on the effects or lack of effects anabolic steroids had on athletic performance, the medical and sports-medical worlds constructed and adopted dogma that claimed that anabolic steroids were just short of being mere placebos for athletes. This dogma, as seen earlier with testosterone, proved to be incorrect.

3

The Period of False Dogma

During the period of the search for medical applications, about two dozen scientific studies were published on whether anabolic steroids would alter athletic bodies and enhance athletic performance. About half the published studies indicated that anabolic steroids did not enhance muscle mass, strength, endurance, or athletic performance, and about half of the published studies found that they did. There were strong proponents on both sides of this controversial topic. Within a 15-month period from February 1975 to May 1976, both the British Association of Sport and Medicine and the American College of Sports Medicine held lengthy meetings to discuss the anabolic steroid situation in sports and to develop official position statements on the topic. Both organizations constructed official position statements with their views of the scientific literature combined with incorrect dogma. This marked the beginning of the period of false dogma for the history of the anabolic steroid epidemic, one that lasted until 1984 when the American College of Sports Medicine published a revised official position statement.

In this chapter, the events of the period of false dogma will be examined as well as the scientific and medical literature published on anabolic steroids and athletic performance. Also, some of the sequelae of this period will be used to usher in the anabolic steroid epidemic and how medicine was "caught with its pants down."

1975 British Association of Sport and Medicine Meeting

A symposium, "Anabolic Steroids in Sport," was held on February 19, 1975, in London. Sports delegates from Belgium, Denmark, France, Germany, Hungary, Italy, the Netherlands, Romania, Spain, Sweden, the United States, the Soviet Union, and Yugoslavia were among the attendees.

Ten papers were presented on anabolic steroids by some of the top researchers in the field, on topics divided into the following categories: metabolic effects, practical experience, anabolic-steroid detection methods, and methods for enforcement. Following the formal presentations there was a period for questions and comments; 61 questions, answers, and comments were addressed. At the time of the symposium, it was understood that anabolic steroid usage was confined to a few "heavy-event" athletes, few of course being British! They conceded that little was known of the benefits or dangers of anabolic steroid use by athletes, that there were no drug tests available for detection of anabolic steroid use, and that there were no mechanisms for enforcement of regulations regarding anabolic steroid use.

One of the studies presented, still the most definitive experiment on the subject of anabolic steroids and enhanced athletic performance, was by Dr. D. L. J. Freed, of Manchester University.[1] Freed's study utilized a double-blind crossover, placebo-controlled design and experienced weight-trained athletes. It showed with its scientific design that anabolic steroid use in moderate doses statistically enhanced the muscle mass and strength of these athletes above the effects of weight training alone in just six weeks of steroid treatment.

Another study on whether anabolic steroids would enhance athletic performance was presented by Professor G. R. Hervey, of the Department of Physiology at Leeds University.[2] Hervey's study, which seemed to carry the weight of the evidence for the British Association of Sport and Medicine (BASM) position on steroids, showed that even large doses of anabolic steroids had little effect on the muscle mass and strength of athletes. But unbeknownst to Hervey or the BASM, the anabolic steroids intended to be given to the study group of athletes were stolen by a graduate assistant and sold for profit to other athletes who lifted weights in a nearby gym.[3] Years after this student graduated, he was convicted and imprisoned for anabolic steroid trafficking in the United States.

The BASM's official policy, published after the 1975 meeting, held steadfast to its previous policy and stated that "the only effective and safe way of ensuring optimum performance in any activity is a proper programme of training and preparation. ... No known chemical agent is capable of producing both safely and effectively an improvement in performance in a healthy human subject." In the question-and-answer period that followed the formal symposium, the experts discussed whether it was experimentally ethical to prescribe the doses of anabolic steroids the athletes were self-using (moderate to large doses) and observe the results; also, they felt that education was the major tool to prevent anabolic steroid abuse.

So, let's educate! But how can education be an important tool at this point to discourage anabolic steroid use when the BASM conceded that "little was known of the benefits or dangers" of anabolic steroid use by athletes? One way is just to make up dogma you hope is true and promote it as education. This is exactly what the BASM did, in effect. Let's say that anabolic steroids do not enhance athletic performance, although the most definitive study showed that even low to moderate doses of steroids enhanced strength and muscle mass in weight-trained athletes that were statistically significant! Good luck with that approach. It will not work. So the BASM tried to use dogma to educate athletes, and it backfired; the sports-medicine physicians, scientists, and officials lost credibility with the athletes. Perhaps the feeling was that if their policy was less than truthful, the anabolic steroid problem in sports would just dwindle away. After all, the BASM was trying to protect the "purity" of sports.

The trouble with using dogma as "selective" education in this case was that there were many athletes using anabolic steroids and they knew that these drugs could enhance their performance in a particular event. Ljungqvist presented a paper during this BASM meeting that involved a questionnaire distributed to the ten best male athletes in each track and field event in Sweden in 1973 (144 athletes total).[4] Sixty-nine percent of these athletes responded to the questionnaire. It was found that 31 percent of the athletes had been using anabolic steroids to enhance their performance, and 97 percent of those who had improved their performance believed that their improvement was due to the use of anabolic steroids!

The American College of Sports Medicine Meeting of 1976

The British Sports Medicine officials were not the only ones creating and disseminating false dogma on anabolic steroids. Perhaps the greatest American perpetrator was Allan J. Ryan, M.D., former president of the American College of Sports Medicine and creator and long-term editor in chief of *The Physician and Sportsmedicine*. He lectured to hundreds of sports groups; he generally referred to anabolic steroids as "fool's gold" and said that anabolic steroid's performance enhancement was a "myth."[5] Second only to Dr. Ryan was Dan Hanley, M.D., from Maine, who was on the Executive Committee of the United States Olympic Committee (USOC) and a highly ranked medical official for the National Collegiate Athletic Association (NCAA). In a similar fashion to Dr. Ryan, Dr. Hanley often used his position as a platform to promote false dogma about the effects of anabolic steroids on athletic performance. Both Ryan and Hanley were strong believers that if anabolic steroids had any effect on performance, it was largely due to a "placebo effect."[6]

At the 1976 annual meeting of the American College of Sports Medicine (ACSM), one of the topics that received special attention was the anabolic steroid situation in sports. Several experts and medical scientists presented papers on the subject, and a roundtable meeting followed the scientific session. Two basic groups emerged: (1) those medical physicians and exercise physiologists with advanced degrees who extracted the available scientific literature to support their stand that anabolic steroids were mere "placebos" and (2) those professionals whose collective stand was that anabolic steroids might enhance athletic performance. Dr. Ryan and Dr. Hanley led the former group; Dr. Levon C. Johnson (researcher at the University of Oregon), Dr. James E. Wright (researcher at the United States Army Research Institute of Environmental Medicine), and Dr. Arthur Jones (founder of Nautilus Equipment) led the latter group.

Dr. Johnson presented his paper, the first of its type, showing that anabolic steroids enhanced strength in weight lifters.[7] And in the question period that followed Dr. Hanley accused Dr. Johnson of promoting anabolic steroid use by athletes. The symposium on anabolic steroids became so heated that it resulted in Dr. Arthur Jones' being expelled by the American College of Sports Medicine for his overbearing stance that anabolic steroids did enhance performance. Dr. Jones threatened to take a hundred athletes to South America, at his expense, and design the definitive study to prove that anabolic steroids enhanced performance. His threat was in response to the discussion regarding the ethical issues in prescribing large doses of anabolic steroids (often used by athletes) for athletes as a part of a research protocol; most physicians at the meeting felt that this would be unethical in the United States. The controversy that was a part of this 1976 meeting and the fact that the false-dogma group "won" resulted in delaying the next major symposium on anabolic steroids for eight years!

In retrospect, the professional group that supported the performance—enhancing properties of anabolic steroids had some anabolic steroid users in their midst. For instance, Dr. Johnson was the primary researcher in his 1968 study on anabolic steroids and strength enhancement, but he was also one of the subjects. He has mentioned to me on many occasions that the primary reason he knew his results were correct was that he felt the powers of anabolic steroids on his own athletic performance. And through the years of continuing controversy Dr. Johnson never backed down on this stand; he should be honored for his sincerity and fortitude.

After the 1976 ACSM meeting, Dr. James Wright chose a different route than Dr. Johnson's. Wright also knew of the powers of anabolic steroids on athletes, and in 1978 he published a book that was a comprehensive summary and discussion of the scientific findings of these steroids. Wright worked closely with athletes and knew of their steroid use. He also knew that steroid use was widespread amongst strength athletes. He cited the following examples in his book[8]:

> Information gathered at the 1972 Olympic games indicated that 68% of a large number of athletes interviewed (from: USA, USSR, Egypt, Morocco, Canada, New Zealand, and Great Britain, and who were involved in such diverse activities as throwing, jumping, vaulting, sprinting, and middle distance running to 3000 meters) had used steroids.

> As of 1977, based on personal observations and interviews with numerous athletes in the strength related sports, I [Dr. Wright] would estimate that over 90% use steroids on a regular basis.

Dr. Wright also summarized the prevailing controversy about anabolic steroids during this period:

> Why then, since the athletes using the drugs (anabolic steroids) are so overwhelmingly convinced of the efficacy, do the majority of physicians and officials of sports governing bodies insist that steroids are worthless and have no effect on performance?

Still, another route was taken by the ACSM after the 1976 annual meeting. The ASCM published its official position on anabolic steroids and sports in 1977 authored by Dr. David Lamb (former president of the ACSM).[9] Exerpts from this official position paper echo several of the points made a year earlier by the BASM:

> There is no conclusive scientific evidence that extremely large doses of anabolic-androgenic steroids either aid or hinder athletic performance. ... Serious and continuing effort should be made to educate male and female athletes, coaches, physical educators, physicians, trainers, and the general public regarding the inconsistent effects of anabolic-androgenic steroids on improvement of human physical performance and the potential dangers. ... Administration of anabolic-androgenic steroids to healthy humans below age 50 in medically approved therapeutic doses often does not of itself bring about any significant improvements in strength, aerobic endurance, lean body mass, or body weight.

In other words, let's go educate: Anabolic steroids are placebos, and there are potential side effects from using them, but don't ask about the side effects because we really don't know what they are. Furthermore, we are going to make it unethical to study these effects in the doses that athletes are taking. That just about does it. The anabolic steroid problem now should just go away!

Building Blocks for the Anabolic Steroid Epidemic

After the ACSM and BASM had officially adopted their versions of false dogma, other medical and sporting groups quickly joined in. These included the American Medical Association (AMA), the Federal Drug Administration (FDA) and most governing bodies of sports. For instance, an FDA medical official added the following statement in the *Physician's Desk Reference*: "Warning: Anabolic steroids do not enhance athletic ability." This warning, in italics, is perhaps the greatest lie in the history of modern medicine as will be discussed later.

All the major medical textbooks published during this period basically claimed that anabolic steroids were glorified placebos for athletes. This resulted in the nation's physicians, residents, and medical students being taught incorrectly on the subject. Moreover, the major textbooks published in the area of sports medicine and sports science shared the false dogma. Subsequently the nation's exercise physiologists, athletic trainers, physical therapists, physical educators, and coaches were also taught incorrectly. The use of false dogma as an educational tool was one of the basic building blocks for the anabolic steroid epidemic American society is facing today.

Perhaps the second basic building block for the anabolic steroid epidemic was an offshoot of the BASM's and ACSM's official policies. In effect, these groups felt that since anabolic steroids do not enhance performance, there was no need to fund or publish further research on the topic, especially on the doses athletes were taking. In other words, these organizations discouraged further research, and researchers like Dr. Levon Johnson, who reported correctly the beneficial effects of anabolic steroid on athletic performance parameters, were "blackballed" by the scientific and medical communities. The lack of funding for further studies addressing the effects of moderate to large anabolic steroid doses on athletic performance and overall health characteristics had a devastating impact. The net result of this was an unprecedented void in scientific studies on the topic for nearly a decade.

The third major building block for this epidemic was the formation of a new industry: the health club and bodybuilding industry. Within a few short years, in the United States there were health clubs and weight lifting gyms sprouting up all over the place. The fitness craze was beginning to blossom. Major cities had 20 or more health clubs, and even small farming towns had at least one club. Various bodybuilding magazines and weight lifting journals were on every magazine rack in the United States. The new "macho image" was in full production.

The fourth major building block was the generic drug law passed by the U.S. Congress. Until this law was passed, the pharmaceutical company that initially developed and marketed a particular drug (as a brand name) could retain patent protection for the drug indefinitely. For instance, there was only one Dianabol, and it was made and distributed by one pharmaceutical company, Ciba. What the generic drug law did for the anabolic steroid situation was to allow dozens of generic pharmaceutical companies to mass-produce and sell an anabolic steroid once the 17-year patent protection had expired. As documented in the last chapter, most of the anabolic steroids were commercially available by 1962, and 17 years later (1979) these anabolic steroids qualified as candidates for the generic drug law. Within a year, dozens of generic pharmaceutical companies in the United States were mass-producing and selling generic versions of anabolic steroids to whoever wished to order them, through both legal means and illegal diversion means. This resulted in the 20 or so anabolic steroids being mass-produced by dozens of generic pharmaceutical companies. Millions of grams of these steroids were manufactured and sold (most of them illegally) in the United States at a period when there were few approved medical uses for the drugs.

Where did all these anabolic steroids go? The majority of the millions of grams of anabolic steroids were illegally diverted to the nation's health clubs and gyms for use by athletes and young weight lifters interested in putting on a little muscle bulk. The generic companies offered extensive catalogs of drugs they had for sale, including anabolic steroids. Before long, the athletes in the United States dropped their subscriptions to the sporting magazines and bought subscriptions to the catalogs the generic pharmaceutical companies offered. The net effect of the generic drug law on the anabolic steroid situation was that suddenly there were steroids available everywhere, and no prescription was required to obtain them. This resulted in a major black-market network for anabolic steroids.

The fifth building block for the anabolic steroid epidemic deals with the human desire for a more muscular body, and a portion of the public which is willing to train regularly with weights and take drugs (primarily anabolic steroids) to achieve this altered state of body image. It has been a deep-seated desire, and it will remain one, perhaps forever. So during the period of false dogma, hundreds of thousands of Americans flocked to health clubs and began self-experimenting with muscle-building anabolic steroids. And there was very little medical help available; even if medical help was available, physicians had lost credibility with the steroid users due to the false dogma position that had been established.

A Critical Reevaluation of the Anabolic Steroid Literature

About 20 studies addressing the effects of anabolic steroids on athletic subjects were published the decade from 1965 to 1976. About half the studies indicated that anabolic steroids were of no benefit to various parameters involved with athletic performance, and about half indicated that they enhanced athletic performance. Clearly there seemed to be a need for further studies to unravel this situation.

In 1981, a young weight-trained medical doctor, William N. Taylor, M.D., wrote the first book by a physician on the subject of anabolic steroid use by athletes. Taylor's book, published in 1982, made a clear demarcation of the published studies on anabolic steroids by dividing those studies into two groups: untrained subjects and trained subjects.[10] By utilizing statistical-analysis techniques, Taylor found that the results of the two major divisions (untrained versus trained) were diametrically opposed. Apparently the studies involving the untrained subjects were not able to delineate the gains in muscle mass and strength from *learning* to lift weights and the effects of anabolic steroids. In other words, the athletic subjects were apparently unable to benefit from anabolic steroid use over and above the training effect of the study design itself. On the other hand, if the athletic subject was already weight-trained and then the anabolic steroids were used, the effects of the steroids were seen. The studies with previously weight-trained subjects showed that anabolic steroids enhanced muscle mass and strength over and above the effects of weight training alone. These results are contained in Tables 3 and 4.

Table 3: Summary of Anabolic Steroid Studies with Untrained Male Subjects[a]

Reference	Drug & Dose	Blind Study	Cross-Over Study	Placebo Control	Statistical Increase Mass or Strength
Fowler[b] (1965)	Nibal 20mg/day (16 weeks)	yes	no	yes	no
Johnson[c] (1969)	Dianabol 10mg/day (6 weeks)	yes	no	no	no
Casner[d] (1971)	Winstrol 6mg/day (42 days)	yes	no	yes	no
Johnson[e] (1972)	Dianabol 10mg/day (7 weeks)	yes	no	yes	yes
Fahey[f] (1973)	Deca-Durabolin 1mg/kg 4 injections/9wks	yes	no	yes	no
Win-May[g] (1975)	Dianabol 5mg/day (3 months)	yes	no	yes	yes
Hervey[h] (1976)	Dianabol 100 mg/day (6 weeks)	yes	yes	yes	no

[a]Taylor. Anabolic Steroids (see note 10; this chapter).

[b]Fowler, W. M., G. W. Gardner, and G. H. Egstrom. Effect of an anabolic steroid on physical performance of young men. J. Appl. Physiol., 1965; 20:1038–40.

[c]See note 7, this chapter.

[d]Casner, S. W., R. G. Early, and B. B. Carlson. Anabolic steroid effects on body composition in normal young men. J. Sports Med. Phys. Fitness, 1971; 11:98–100.

[e]Johnson, F. L., G. Fisher, L. J. Silvester, et al. Anabolic steroid: Effects on strength, body weight, oxygen uptake and spermatogenesis. Med. Sci. Sports, 1972; 4:43–45.

[f]Fahey, T. D., and C. H. Brown. The effects of an anabolic steroid on strength, body composition and endurance of college males when accompanied by a weight training program. Med. Sci. Sports, 1973; 5:272–276.

[g]Win-May, M., and M. Mya-tu. The effects of anabolic steroids on physical fitness. J. Sports Med. Phys. Fitness, 1975; 15:266–271.

[h]See note 2, this chapter.

Table 4: Summary of Anabolic Steroid
Studies with Trained Male Subjects[a]

Reference	Drug & Dose	Double-Blind Study	Cross-Over Study	Placebo Control	Statistical Increase Muscle Mass or Strength
O'Shea[b] (1970)	Anavar 10mg/day (6 weeks)	no	no	no	yes
O'Shea[c] (1971)	Dianabol 10mg/day (4 weeks)	no	no	yes	yes
Bowers[d] (1972)	Dianabol 10mg/day (5 weeks)	yes	no	yes	yes
Ariel[e] (1973)	Dianabol 10mg/day (8 weeks)	yes	no	yes	no
Ward[f] (1973)	Dianabol 10mg/day (4 weeks)	yes	no	yes	yes
Golding[g] (1974)	Dianabol 10mg/day (12 weeks)	yes	no	yes	no
Stanford[h] (1974)	Dianabol 20mg/day (4 weeks)	yes	no	yes	yes
O'Shea[i] (1974)	Winstrol 8mg/day (4 weeks)	yes	no	yes	yes
Freed[j] (1975)	Dianabol 10mg/day Dianabol 25mg/day (6 weeks)	yes yes	yes yes	yes yes	yes yes

[a]See note 10, this chapter.

[b]O'Shea, J. P., and W. Winkler. Biochemical and physical effects of an anabolic steroid in competitive swimmers and weight lifters. Nutr. Rpts. Inter., 1970; 2:699–702.

[c]O'Shea, J. P. The effects of an anabolic steroid on dynamic strength levels of weight lifters. Nutr. Rpts. Inter., 1971; 4:363–370.

^{d}Bowers, R. W., and J. P. Reardon. *Effects of methandrostenolone (Dianabol) on strength development and aerobic capacity.* Med. Sci. Sports, *1972; 4:54.*

^{e}Ariel, G. *The effect of anabolic steroid on skeletal muscle contractive force.* J. Sports Med. Phys. Fitness, *1973; 13:187–190.*

^{f}Ward, P. *The effect of an anabolic steroid on strength and lean body mass.* Med. Sci. Sports, *1973; 5:277–282.*

^{g}Golding, L. A., J. E. Freydinjer, and S. S. Fisher. *Weight, size, and strength — unchanged with steroids.* Physician & Sports Med., *1974; 2:39–43.*

^{h}Stanford, B. A., and R. Moffatt. *Anabolic steroid: Effectiveness as an ergogenic aid to experienced weight trainers.* J. Sports Med. Phys. Fitness, *1974; 14:191–197.*

^{i}O'Shea, J. P. *Biochemical evaluation of effects of stanozolol on adrenal, liver and muscle function in man.* Nutr. Rpts. Inter., *1974; 10:381–388.*

^{j}See note 1, this chapter.

The results in Table 4 indicate that anabolic steroid therapy (low doses and short duration) statistically enhanced muscle mass and or strength in eight or ten studies performed on experienced weight-trained male subjects. Therefore, it is safe to say that the use of anabolic steroids by previously weight-trained men who are continuing their weight training while using anabolic steroids can enhance their performance, muscle mass, and strength.

Taylor's findings and conclusions were confirmed by Haupt and Rovere in 1984 as they reported similar results after reviewing the anabolic steroid literature from a statistical-analysis point of view.[11] These critical reevaluations of the literature were the major fuel that burned at the 1984 American College of Sports Medicine's annual meeting and day-long symposium that dealt with the anabolic steroid predicament to be covered in the next chapter.

4

The Period of Enlightenment and Reeducation

After the reviews of studies on anabolic steroids and performance enhancement from a critical perspective, it became apparent to the scientific organizations dealing with sports medicine that they again needed to address the anabolic steroid predicament. And since the original official policies utilized false dogma to conclude that these steroids did not have the capacity to enhance athletic performance, attempting to reeducate persons with a new policy (based on facts) that is diametrically opposed to the original policy became a difficult task to accomplish.

In this chapter the history of the policy reversals by major organizations regarding the effects of anabolic steroid use by athletic users will be presented. Also, some of the historical highlights and problems dealing with the reeducation process will be discussed.

1984 American College of Sports Medicine Meeting

The ACSM's annual meeting in 1984 was held at the Town and Country Hotel on May 23–26 in San Diego. On Thursday May 24, 1984, a symposium entitled "Drug Use in Sports" was held; the chairpersons were John A. Lombardo, M.D., Director of Sports Medicine at the Cleveland Clinic, and Barbara L. Drinkwater, Ph.D., of the University of Washington. This symposium focused on the anabolic steroids and consisted of an introduction, 12 formal presentations, a roundtable discussion, and a postsymposium roundtable discussion regarding the revised ACSM policy on anabolic steroids. The formal presentations were given by a variety of professionals, and the views presented were mixed together like a tossed salad, as indicated:

"Introduction"—John A. Lombardo, M.D., and Barbara L. Drinkwater, Ph.D.

"Biological Actions and Potential Uses for Anabolic Steroids"—James E. Wright, U.S. Army

"Effects of Anabolic Steroids on Performance and Body Composition on Men in Athletic Training"—G. R. Hervey, Ph. D., University of Leeds, England

"Side Effects and Adverse Reactions of Anabolic Steroids"—Thomas Fahey, M.D., DeAnza College, Cupertino, CA

"Physiological Consequences of Anabolic Steroids Specific to Women"—Mona M. Shangold, M.D., Cornell University

"Actions and Effects of Growth Hormones"—William N. Taylor, M.D.

"The Athletes' World"—Laura van Harn, University of California

"Detecting Drug Use in Athletes"—Richard H. Strauss, M.D., Ohio State University

"Ethical Implications of Drug Use by Athletes"—Daniel Hanley, M.D., International Olympic Medical Commission

"The Female Athletes' Viewpoint"—Jane Fredricks, Santa Barbara, CA

"The Male Athletes' Viewpoint"—Paul Ward, Ph.D., Health and Tennis Corporation, Westminster, CA

"The Coaches' Dilemma"—Richard L. Brown, Athletics West, Eugene, OR

"The Clinician's Approach to Athletes on Anabolic Steroids"—John A. Lombardo, M.D., Cleveland Clinic, Cleveland, OH

During and after this symposium it became apparent that the original ACSM position on anabolic steroid use by athletes was in need of some major revision. It was also apparent that the anabolic steroid problem in sports was one of great magnitude with problems noted in several disciplines that dealt with sports.

Perhaps the strongest statements of the symposium were given by Taylor. He referred to the anabolic steroid situation as an "epidemic" and said that these steroids were "addicting as amphetamines" and that "anabolic steroids should be reclassified as controlled substances." He also claimed that anabolic steroids caused personality changes, including violent behavior, influenced body image, and caused withdrawal depression. He insisted that anabolic steroids could enhance athletic performance and presented a critical reevaluation of steroid research with statistical analysis indicating so.

Following the symposium and roundtable discussions there was a dinner meeting that involved Brown, Taylor, Lombardo, van Harn, Susan Taylor (wife of William Taylor), and Robert O. Voy, M.D., chief medical officer for the U.S. Olympic Committee. During the dinner, Brown told the group (corroborated by van Harn) that the majority of the men and women athletes representing the U.S. Olympic track and field team used anabolic steroids and that they were currently using human growth hormone (HGH) and tapering off the anabolic steroids to prepare for the upcoming 1984 Olympic Games to be held in Los Angeles. He expressed concern for the athletes' health since they were using such hormonal manipulation to enhance their athletic performance. He also relayed the athletes' reason for this action: to avoid testing positive for anabolic steroids since HGH had no established drug test.

Imagine the conflicts of interest and the politics of this dinner meeting and the above conversation. Dr. Voy, who represented the U.S. Olympic Committee (USOC) and was the main enforcer of their drug-testing program, was being told by the Athletics West head track coach about the pervasive use of anabolic steroids and the athletes' way to beat the upcoming testing at the 1984 Olympic Games! Of course, the "Olympic movement" is highly political, and it needs to cover up such a problem so that the movement can secure hundreds of millions of dollars from charities and donations to support itself. But to support a flock of cheaters would be a difficult task, so let's not discuss it. But, as will be discussed later, Dr. Voy was not part of the cover-up, and his credibility and ethics as he protrayed them to the public could not be sacrificed. He was much too honest and credible for the cover-up politics of the "Olympic movement," and he ultimately resigned his position a few years later. Meanwhile, both Dr. Lombardo and Dr. Taylor were enlightened by this scenario.

Shortly after this symposium and roundtable discussion, the ACSM revised its official position to state that the use of anabolic steroids in combination with weight training and proper diet may result in enhanced athletic performance.[1]

1984 National Strength and Conditioning Association Meeting

A month following the landmark meeting of the ACSM, the National Strength and Conditioning Association (NSCA) held a similar anabolic steroid symposium at the Pittsburgh Hilton, on June 27, 1984. The symposium consisted of papers presented by six experts and concluded with a lengthy question session. The experts included John Lombardo, M.D. (Cleveland Clinic), Mike Stone, Ph.D. (Auburn University), Jeff Everson (bodybuilder from Los Angeles), Bob Goldman (osteopathic student at Chicago Medical Center), Fred Hatfield, Ph.D. (editor in chief, *Muscle & Fitness Magazine*) and William Taylor, M.D. Shortly after the 1984 meeting, the NCSA revised its official policy statement on anabolic steroids, which now claimed that anabolic steroid use may enhance athletic performance.

1986 Resolution of the American Medical Association

Following the revisions of the ACSM and NSCA regarding anabolic steroids and athletic performance, the American Medical Association (AMA) began a series of scientific affairs meetings to debate the steroid abuse situation in the United States. Two major meetings were held in Chicago to discuss the abuse of both anabolic steroids and synthetic human growth hormone. After the meeting in June 1986, the AMA published a report of the Council on Scientific Affairs in December 1986, "Drug Abuse in Athletes: Anabolic Steroids and Human Growth Hormone."[2] In this report, the AMA concluded that

> anabolic steroids have been used by athletes for more than two decades in the belief that they increase body mass, muscle tissue, and strength. . . . Although studies of these agents have not shown uniformly increased muscular strength, certain benefits to athletic performance seem probable. . . . In a continuing program of intensive exercise coupled with a high protein diet (and anabolic steroids), increased muscular strength may be realized in some individuals. . . . It should be noted that small, difficult-to-measure increments in muscular performance or psychological benefit may constitute the difference between winning and losing, particularly at a professional or world-class level. . . . These changes may be perceived to be critical to an athlete.

The AMA's report also adopted the following actions to cope with the burgeoning anabolic steroid epidemic in the United States:

> Regulatory action: The AMA should continue to endorse current activities of the FDA, FBI, and DOJ directed toward curbing illegal distribution of these drugs. If these efforts are ineffective, the AMA should undertake a study of alternate methods of monitoring and limiting distribution.
>
> Educational action: The AMA should endorse educational activities at various levels including sports group administrators, coaches, parents, and athletes. Activites suggested for consideration area:
>
> a) Preparation and distribution of educational pamphlets on drug abuse in athletes emphasizing the adverse effects and limited benefits of such use;
> b) Development of a nationwide network of physicians who would be available to give presentations on this topic to interested community groups;
> c) Preparation of videotape(s) on drug abuse in athletes for distribution and use by schools, sports programs, parent groups, and community organizations;
> d) Judicious use of the news media and editorials and articles in AMA publications to publicize the AMA's interest and availability to work on this problem.

The initial resolutions proposed by the AMA delegates were to have these drugs reclassified as controlled substances, but the AMA, along with the ACSM and NSCA, refused to endorse this action. And as long as anabolic steroids were in the general prescription category, the powers afforded the FDA, FBI, and DOJ to curb the illegal distribution of these steroids were anemic at best. So in effect the AMA endorsed regulatory actions that were failing and were destined to fail. By not adopting the proposals to have these drugs reclassified as controlled substances, the AMA lost a major chance to support the preventive-medicine side regarding the abuse of prescription drugs.

As far as the recommendations for the educational programs are concerned, the AMA neglected the most important aspect of education, in this case reeducation; that is, the nation's physicians. During this period, most athletes and anabolic steroid users knew considerably more about the effects of these steroids than the majority of physicians did. Remember, the nation's physicians were taught that anabolic steroids were mere placebos for athletes, and the medical knowledge of some of the newly discovered adverse effects of these drugs had not been widely disseminated. In effect, a physician asked to lecture on anabolic steroid abuse to college athletes would be as effective as a choir member lecturing on theology to a group of leading theologians; unless, of course, this physician had true expert knowledge.

Perhaps the best current methods of education dealing with this national drug abuse situation consist of a combination of books, scientific articles, news documentaries, expert witness testimony, and continuing medical education lectures that focus on the fact that anabolic steroid abuse could be largely resolved by a congressional act reclassifying them as tightly controlled substances, thus severely limiting production of these steroids by the pharmaceutical industry and severely curtailing illegal diversion. The one physician who incorporated these methods of education toward this single goal was William N. Taylor, M.D. During a four-year period in the mid- to late-1980s, he delivered over 1000 continuing medical education lectures on this subject to the medical profession nationwide. His lecture series, entitled "Drug Issues in Sports Medicine," sponsored largely by Pfizer Laboratories, provided the concerned physicians enough knowledge to affect legislative efforts state by state and ultimately on the congressional level. The first two references of the Steroid Trafficking Act of 1990 (Appendix 1) are from a book and a scientific article by Dr. Taylor that focused on the proposal to reclassify anabolic steroids as tightly controlled substances under federal law.[3]

5

The Reclassification as
Schedule III Controlled Substances

In order for the reader to gain a better understanding why anabolic steroids have been recently reclassified as controlled substances under federal law, it is imperative to present some historical highlights regarding some of the major federal drug laws that have been passed during the past century. Increasingly complex relationships exist between the scientific, economic, and political aspects of drugs or medicines made available to the American public. These relationships have undergone considerable evolution during the past century.

The formation of federal drug laws as we know them today is not static and will change and tighten in the future. With most of the federal drug laws passed over the decades, precipitating factors played a major role. Some of these precipitating factors included questions about drug safety and effectiveness, the need for defining drugs as prescription, the need for laws dealing with habit-forming and psychoactive drugs, the need for making prescription drugs cheaper for the public with the generic drug law, the need for curbing illegal diversion, and so on.

This chapter presents a history of some of the major federal laws that regulated nonnarcotic drugs to usher in the federal laws eventually passed to deal with narcotic drugs and other controlled substances. Then the more recent federal hearings and laws dealing specifically with anabolic steroids, which lead to passing of the Steroid Trafficking Act of 1990, will be presented.

Federal Regulation of Nonnarcotic Drugs

Within this text, *nonnarcotic drugs* refers to general prescription drugs or drugs which require a prescription from a licensed physician but are not classified as a narcotic or a controlled substance. Examples of nonnarcotic drugs today include antibiotics; steroid hormones (now excluding anabolic steroids) such as estrogens, progesterone, and cortisone; nonsteroidal anti-inflammatory drugs (NSAIDs); most topical prescription creams and ointments; antihypertensive medications; and most other nonaddicting medications considered not to possess strong psychoactive properties. In this section the topics covered include the history of the regulation of nonnarcotic drugs, current regulations that control the marketing of a new drug, controversies in the regulation and approval of new drugs, the brand name–generic controversy, and some of the potential avenues for the illegal diversion of nonnarcotic drugs.

Prior to the 1840s there was no federal regulation of nonnarcotic drugs in the United States. Although nearly every state had passed some laws to address the purity and effectiveness of drugs, there was a paucity of federal regulation dealing with drugs manufactured within the United States. The initial federal regulation of nonnarcotic drugs was the National Drug-Import Law, passed by Congress in 1848 in an attempt to ensure that imported drugs were properly labeled and of good quality. However, the enforcement of this law was ineffective due to the use of unqualified political appointees who could not effectively reject imported drugs for not meeting certain medical standards of the time.[1]

By the end of the nineteenth century, the necessity to regulate the purity of drugs on a federal level and to govern the therapeutic claims of drug manufacturers was supported by the American Medical Association (AMA) and the American Pharmaceutical Association (APA). In 1906 the federal government enacted the 1906 Pure Food and Drugs Act, which not only defined *drug* but also defined *misbranding* of a drug. This act defined *drug* as "any substance or mixture of substances intended to be used for the cure, mitigation, or prevention of disease." *Misbranding* was defined as "any statement, design or device regarding a drug, or the ingredients or substances contained therein, which shall be false or misleading in any particular."[2] This definition basically referred only to the label on the drug container or the drug packaging and not to any promotional materials or general advertising for the drug. Although this law seemed to have some impact on toning down some of the therapeutic claims of some patent medications, there were still no federal regulations directed at the efficacy or safety of drugs. With medical science and quality control still in their infancies, false therapeutic claims and poor safety profiles of drugs were difficult if not impossible to document.

Shortly after Congress passed the 1906 Pure Food and Drugs Act, a major precipitating factor arose that needed federal attention. Hucksters were claiming that this drug or that elixir could cure cancers. So Congress passed the 1912 Shirley Amendment, which focused on curbing the false claims of various cancer cures. This amendment was the first federal attempt designed to remove drugs from the market that were not effective by outlawing therapeutic claims that were false *and* fraudulent.

At this time there were many other violations of the 1906 Pure Food and Drugs Act believed to be related to poor manufacturing techniques and the absence of quality control measures by drug manufacturers. For instance, if the manufacturer of a particular drug believed the drug to be effective, then enforcing both provisions of the 1912 Shirley Amendment was a very difficult task. This situation provided initiative for a collaboration between the newly formed U.S. Food and Drug Administration (FDA) and the pharmaceutical industry to develop assay procedures for various chemicals and drugs. This collaboration produced two reference books that set standards for various medications, *The United States Pharmacopeia* and *The National Formulary*. However, FDA surveys conducted in the mid–1930s indicated that over 10 percent of the drugs studied did not meet the standards of these texts.[3] Still, no federal laws existed to require a pharmaceutical manufacturer to document that a particular drug was safe prior to marketing the drug to the public or to physicians.

During the 1930s, the widespread use of sulfa drugs as antimicrobial agents precipitated concerns by physicians and legislators regarding drug safety. Overzealous use of sulfa drugs was linked to infant deaths. Federal laws did not forbid the use of drugs that could have lethal adverse effects, and sulfa drugs in elixir forms for use in infants remained on the market. This phenomenon prompted Congress to pass the 1938 Food, Drug, and Cosmetic Act, which required the safety of a particular drug to be documented and submitted to the FDA in the form of a "new drug application" (NDA). This act also stipulated that drug labels provide adequate directions for proper use unless the drug was to be sold only as a prescription drug. Prescription drugs had to now carry a label: "Caution: To be used only by or on the prescription of a physician." However, much confusion still existed about which drugs were intended to be prescription medications. If the NDA for a drug met certain criteria, the FDA would allow the application for the new drug to become effective. From 1938 to 1962, approximately 13,000 new drug applications were submitted to the FDA, and about 70 percent of them were allowed to become effective or essentially approved.[4]

The confusion regarding whether a particular drug was a prescription drug or not prompted new federal legislation. The Humphrey-Durham Amendment of 1951 was passed to define further a *prescription (legend) drug*. Three classes of prescription drugs were classified:

1. Drugs labeled "Warning: may be habit forming";
2. Drugs the FDA determined were unsafe unless administered by a physician; and

3. New drugs, which allowed the FDA to determine whether to classify them as prescription drugs.

This amendment allowed the FDA to regulate which nonnarcotic drugs needed to be prescribed by a physician, and it was a precursor of later federal drug legislation regarding habit-forming or addictive drugs. There were still no federal regulations directed at the effectiveness of nonnarcotic drugs in the United States.

The Kefauver-Harris Amendment of 1962 was enacted to regulate the effectiveness of all new drugs and those older drugs marketed since 1938. The most important aspects of this amendment:

1. It required that advertisements for prescription drugs contain a summary of information regarding adverse reactions to the drug.
2. It required that prior to marketing, the drug must be shown to be effective for the illness cited on the drug label or the promotional materials which accompanied the drug.
3. It required the FDA to evaluate the drugs marketed from 1938 to 1962 in terms of safety and effectiveness, and to remove the ineffective drugs from the market.

The evaluation of drugs marketed from 1938 to 1962 proved to be a difficult task. In 1966 the FDA contracted the task to the National Academy of Sciences National Research Council, which established panels of medical and scientific experts in some 30 areas to study the therapeutic claims of marketed drugs. Three years later, in 1969, the final evaluations were sent to the FDA.[5] Approximately 15 percent of the drugs were found to be ineffective, and since multiple claims were made for most drugs, some drugs were approved only for certain uses. The panel also classified some of the drugs as "probably effective," leaving some doubt about true effectiveness. By 1974, the FDA had taken action to remove over 6,000 drugs from the market, manufactured by over 2,700 companies.[6]

In theory, by 1974, federal laws and federal agencies regulated the therapeutic claims of efficacy and safety of nonnarcotic drugs. However, controlling the diversion of these prescription drugs was shown to be a major problem, as exemplified by one study that reported the fact that retail pharmacists honored or created fake prescriptions for nonnarcotic drugs 56 percent of the time.[7] The magnitude and severity of the illegal diversion of nonnarcotic drugs was later demonstrated by a federal sting operation ("pharmoney") in Georgia where several physicians and retail pharmacists were arrested and indicated for illegally diverting and selling nonnarcotic drug samples to the public for profit. This phenomenon prompted new federal legislation regarding drug sampling in the United States in the late 1980s.

Federal Regulations Regarding New-Drug Marketing

In order to comply with the Kefauver-Harris Amendment of 1962, the FDA established regular protocols and standards that must be met by the pharmaceutical companies hoping to market new nonnarcotic drugs. The current expense of "bringing a new drug to market" consistent with these protocols can be in excess of $50 million for drugs manufactured via chemical reactions and over $500 million for certain protein drugs and hormones manufactured via recombinant DNA genetic engineering techniques. Today, both new drugs and established drugs marketed for new indications must be evaluated by the FDA regulations to ensure safety and effectiveness.

Prior to contacting the FDA for use of a new drug for human use, the pharmaceutical company may screen hundreds of chemical compounds for possible utilization as therapeutic drugs. The company then conducts animal studies, and as minimum evidence for safety, the animal studies must include acute one-time administration of several doses of drug to groups of animals of at least two species. Moreover, they must also conduct and submit studies on animals for a period of time related to the proposed use of the drug in humans, which may necessitate a two-year toxicology report. The route of administration in the animal studies must parallel the proposed route of administration in humans.

In addition to research results, the pharmaceutical company must submit a detailed description of the proposed clinical studies of the drug in humans. The competence of the physicians involved with the clinical studies is also judged by the FDA from further information on the physicians submitted by the pharmaceutical company. Furthermore, any information distributed to these physicians by the pharmaceutical companies must be copied and supplied to the FDA. Information regarding the composition of the drug, complete manufacturing information, and the biological preparation source must accompany the animal research information and the proposed clinical trials information.

The pharmaceutical company must also ensure that the humans to be used as initial subjects be told they are receiving an investigational drug and that the subjects sign an informed consent form that states that they know that they are to receive a drug and that this is acceptable to them. When all of these criteria are met, the company then files a Notice of Claimed Investigational Exemption for a New Drug with the FDA. When the FDA authorizes the use of the drug in experimental human studies, there are at least three phases of clinical trials that must be passed. In some cases, a fourth phase of postmarketing surveillance is carried out by an agency independent of the FDA.[8]

A phase-1 clinical trial encompasses studies with small amounts of the drug on a limited number of healthy patients, who may be pharmaceutical company employees, medical students, medical school personnel, or other volunteers who qualify for the study. During this phase, the clinical researchers are primarily interested in learning how the drug is absorbed, metabolized, and excreted by healthy people. They are also interested in any adverse effects of the drug.[9] In this phase, as with the other phases, the pharmaceutical company must inform the FDA immediately (usually within 24 hours) of any adverse reactions that arise during the clinical trials.

A phase-2 clinical study investigates the drug in patients who have the disease condition the drug is deemed to be effective for. These studies are usually performed in over 100 patients, and they may involve as many as 1000 patients in multiple-clinic settings or hospitals.

Phase-3 trials are extensive clinical studies involving patients with the disease condition the drug is intended for. The format of the trial may be guided by the FDA, and for incomplete or inconclusive results, the FDA may indicate a requirement for further studies to ensure the safety and or efficacy of the drug. The FDA must balance the possible health risks of the drug against the benefits for the patient prior to releasing the drug for marketing and sale to the public. A drug that passes the phase-3 requirements set forth by the FDA is usually approved for marketing. In some cases, as with an orphan drug (a drug with a single, very limited indication), the FDA may require certain marketing or clinical restrictions concomitant with its formal release. An example of an orphan drug is synthetic human growth hormone that has the clinical restriction (placed by the FDA) to be prescribed only for short-statured children with growth-hormone deficiency. These types of FDA orphan drug restrictions serve to impede the use of the drug by physicians in an unapproved, unindicated disease or condition. However, further clinical research for orphan drugs may continue in other disease states as an investigational drug. If a pharmaceutical company has been given orphan drug status for a particular drug, it also has exclusivity for patent protection for seven years. In the case of synthetic human growth hormone, where the treatment of a dwarfish child may cost between $10,000 and $20,000 annually, the issue of costs and profits has been examined by special bills introduced by Congress in 1990. These recent bills would basically repeal the orphan drug law, but the initial bill was vetoed by President George Bush in November 1990.

Once the new drug is marketed, the pharmaceutical company must submit reports on the drug's use and efficacy to the FDA every three months for the first year, every six months for the second year, and every 12 months for the following years. This period of postmarketing surveillance has been called phase-4, and recent congressional hearings have been held to consider a more formal type of phase-4.[10]

As one can determine, the federal regulation of nonnarcotic drug control, drug approval, and drug marketing has undergone a considerable evolution. It should be expected, therefore, that significant changes of federal laws that govern drug-related issues would continue to undergo adaptive processes, especially as technology, marketing strategies, and societal values continue to change. It is hoped that any new federal regulations that are passed would be to the benefit of the society as a whole.

Controversies about Federal Regulations of Nonnarcotic Drugs

Two of the current major controversies about the way federal agencies regulate nonnarcotic drugs in the United States is the time-consuming new drug approval regulations and the brand name–generic situation. Each of these topics will be discussed briefly in this section.

One of the major criticisms of the FDA's "drug approval" protocol is that from the viewpoint of the pharmaceutical industry, it takes too long for new drugs to become approved for prescription use. This has been referred to as "drug lag" in the pharmaceutical industry, the time between the drug's submission to the FDA for approval and its final approval for marketing. In the United States, this drug lag is over two years; in Great Britain, the drug lag averages six months.[11]

Pharmaceutical companies have only a 17-year patent protection on a new drug, and they usually apply for a patent on a chemical compound that has the potential to be a therapeutic drug as soon as there is some evidence that the company recognizes. The pharmaceutical companies claim that by the time a drug is approved via the FDA processes for marketing, there is an average of only seven years remaining on the patent protection. This creates a tendency for the pharmaceutical companies to sell a particular drug for a much higher price to recoup their expenses and make a profit over a much abbreviated period. The expenses usually consist of the costs for basic research and the phases of clinical trials, marketing expenses, liability protection, and so on. In the past, the pharmaceutical industry has suggested a seven-year patent extension for new drugs to compensate for the FDA's lengthy approval process. This would allow the pharmaceutical companies a much longer patent protection for a drug, and they could essentially spread the expenses to "bring the drug to market" over a greater period prior to being affected by the generic drug law (discussed below). The net result would be, according to the pharmaceutical industry, a reduction in the price of new drugs.

In 1980 a report by the General Accounting Office (GAO) auditors admitted that there were many reasons for the "drug lag," and most of the reasons the GAO blamed on the bureaucratic rules and regulations of the

FDA.[12] Two years later, in a 1982 report on this issue, the Congressional Office of Technical Assessment found that the time a drug spends in the FDA's regulatory process was not a significant determinant of its effective patent life.[13] This report suggested that if the pharmaceutical companies would organize more efficiently, they could extend the effective patent protection of their drugs by nearly four years.

In 1980 the FDA Commissioner stated,

> Compared to some other countries, our standards are higher or if you will, more conservative or tighter or however you wish to call it. But on the other hand our people have very high expectations and the law is rather clear that drugs cannot be approved by the FDA unless they are safe and effective, and until and unless the law is changed, that's the overriding criterion.[14]

Because of recent generic substitution laws (discussion to follow) this time element for new drug approval becomes a major factor in the cost of new nonnarcotic drugs. In effect, the FDA's rules and regulations for new nonnarcotic drugs provides the American public (via prescription) with safe, effective, and expensive drugs. And because of the burgeoning costs for liability for pharmaceutical companies to protect themselves against legal actions taken due to potential adverse effects of their drugs in patients, these costs will continue to rise. In fact, recent liability cases resulting in major awards for adverse effects of drugs to patients or patient's families have forced some pharmaceutical companies to file for bankruptcy.

Another controversial issue involving current federal drug regulations is the brand name–generic controversy. For 17 years a pharmaceutical company that has discovered and patented a drug can manufacture and sell it without direct competition. Usually, if the drug is a successful one, other pharmaceutical companies will work to discover equally effective drugs with similar but not identical molecular structures. Often the pharmaceutical company that patents a successful drug will be concomitantly working to discover all the other similar molecular structures within that class of drugs to eliminate competition.

Today, when the patent expires on a drug, the molecular structure of the drug becomes free game for any pharmaceutical company to manufacture and market. The drug is initially released by the FDA and the clearance is obtained by the original pharmaceutical company with all of the aforementioned expenses. But at the heart of the brand name–generic controversy is whether it can be assumed that drugs manufactured to meet FDA standards by new companies do not have to go through the time-consuming and costly FDA regulations to demonstrate safety, efficacy, and clinical equivalence. In 1980 the FDA ruled that manufacturers were permitted to sell generic versions of brand name drugs marketed since 1962 whose patents have expired without repeating the costly testing to show that the generic version's safety or efficacy. The generic manufacturers needed only to cite studies in the literature to show that the name brand drug is safe and effective.[15] There were major scandals involving the generic drug companies and the FDA in the late 1980s. FDA officials have admitted to taking bribes from generic companies, and the generic companies have submitted false documents and drugs to the FDA.

The greatest of all scandals in the generic drug industry has been as a major building block for the anabolic steroid epidemic in America. Without the generic drug laws and the generic industry mass-producing and illegally diverting millions of dollars of anabolic steroids annually (while these steroids were still nonnarcotic drugs), there would have been no major anabolic steroid problem in the United States. These generic companies have been unethical, driven only by the profits of selling nonnarcotic generic prescription drugs to unqualified buyers, as if the drugs were potato chips. It could be that the generic drug law has been the worst federal drug law ever passed because of the illegal diversion of nonnarcotic drugs at a low cost.

Early Federal Regulation of Narcotic Drugs

Drug addicton became a major problem in the United States shortly after the Civil War due to three major contributing factors that led to widespread narcotic addiction in the late 1800s.

1. The invention of the hypodermic syringe in 1856.
2. The importation of Chinese workers to help build the rapidly expanding railroad system. These Chinese workers brought with them the habit of smoking opium, which once introduced in the United States, spread rapidly.
3. The widespread legal distribution of patent narcotic medicines dispensed by traveling peddlers and available at local stores, and purchased as over the counter for self-medication.[16]

By the end of the late 1800s, because of these three major factors, it was estimated that one person out of every 500 in the United States was addicted to some form of opium or its derivatives. Perhaps the greatest offender in this category was paregoric (a Greek word which means "soothing"), an elixir of opium and ethanol. Despite the passing of the Opium Exclusion Act of 1909, which prohibited the importing of opium or its derivatives except for medical purposes, it was estimated that by 1914, one in every 400 Americans was addicted to some form of opium.[17]

The Harrison Act of 1914 was the first federal attempt to make it impossible for narcotic addicts to obtain their drugs legally. This federal law mandated for the first time that dealers and dispensers of narcotics (primarily opium, cocaine, and their derivatives) had to register annually with the Treasury Department's Bureau of Internal Revenue. Physicians, dentists, and veterinary surgeons were named as potential legal distributors for narcotics if they registered. The Harrison Act was the basic narcotic-control law in the United States until the 1970 Federal Controlled Substance Act was enacted in May 1971.

By the late 1920s, narcotic addiction had become a major problem for federal prisons. For instance, individuals sentenced for narcotic offenses made up about one-third of the total prison population.[18] The major narcotics of abuse at that time were opium, cocaine, and their derivatives; marijuana; and peyote.

In 1930 Congress passed several bills that culminated in the formation of a separate Bureau of Narcotics within the Treasury Department. This bureau continued in operation until April 1968 when it became part of a new group, the Bureau of Narcotics and Dangerous Drugs, within the Department of Justice.

Following World War II, the illegal narcotics trade increased in volume every year for several years. In 1951 Congress passed the Boggs Amendment to the Harrison Act of 1914, which established minimum mandatory sentences for all narcotic offenses. By 1955, a subcommittee of the Senate Judiciary Committee stated that drug addiction was responsible for 50 percent of crime in urban areas and 25 percent of all reported crimes.[19] With these estimates in mind, Congress passed the 1956 Narcotic Drug Control Act, which raised the mandatory minimum sentence for violation of the narcotic laws.

The first major federal law directed at monitoring legal narcotics for medical needs was the Narcotics Manufacturing Act passed in 1960. This act licensed all medical narcotic drug manufacturers and made it illegal to manufacture or attempt to manufacture narcotic drugs unless the company was registered. It also allowed for annual quotas to be established for the manufacturing and purchase of narcotic drugs. The Bureau of Narcotics set up a four-part system for classifying drugs as narcotics in 1962.

During the 1960s, U.S. citizens were increasing illegal drug use, and there was a shift in the types of drugs being abused. The 1960s drug users tended to use drugs that altered mood or consciousness or caused outright hallucinations. Amphetamines, barbiturates, and lysergic acid (LSD) became the drugs of choice for many drug abusers. Responding to the need for better controls over the manufacturing and distribution of certain legal and illegal compounds, Congress passed the Drug Abuse Control Amendments of 1965. These amendments added to the list of controlled narcotics drugs that had the potential for abuse because of their stimulant, depressant, or hallucinogenic effects.

In response to the Drug Abuse Control Amendments of 1965, the FDA used the following criteria to determine whether a particular drug caused hallucinations, illusions, delusions, or other alterations in personality:

1. Orientation with respect to time or place.
2. Consciousness, as evidenced by confused states, dreamlike revivals of past traumatic events, or childhood memories.
3. Sensory perception, as evidenced by visual illusions, synethesia, distortion of space and perspective.
4. Motor coordination.
5. Mood and affectivity, as evidenced by anxiety, euphoria, hypomania, ecstasy, autistic withdrawal.
6. Ideation, as evidenced by flight of ideas, ideas of reference, impairment of concentration and intelligence.
7. Personality, as evidenced by depersonalization and derealization, impairment of conscience and of acquired social and cultural customs.[20]

In spite of the Drug Abuse Control Amendments of 1965, the illegal diversion of amphetamines and barbiturates continued to grow. For example, it was discovered that 8 billion doses of amphetamines were manufactured in the United States annually and that nearly half of these amphetamines were diverted into illegal distribution channels.[21] Certainly there was a need for federal regulations that could curtail the legal manufacturing but illegal diversion of narcotic drugs in the United States. To accomplish this control, the Comprehensive Drug Abuse Prevention and Control Act of 1970 was passed by Congress and signed on October 27, 1970, by President Richard M. Nixon. This law, also referred to as the Controlled Substance Act of 1970, will be discussed in the section to follow.

The Controlled Substance Act of 1970

This comprehensive federal law dealing with all types of narcotic drugs became effective in May 1971 and is still the basic law of the land today. It repeals and replaces all previous laws concerned with both narcotic and dangerous drugs. Although the law does not eliminate some state regulation, it specifically states that the drugs controlled by the act are under federal jurisdiction regardless of any involvement in interstate commerce. Simply put, it mandates that federal enforcement and federal prosecution is possible in any illegal activity involving the controlled drugs.

The Controlled Substance Act of 1970 (CSA) also provided for necessary funding for the prevention and treatment of drug abuse through Community Mental Health Centers and Public Service Hospitals. Its provisions also allowed for educational efforts to include drug workshops for professional mental health workers and the development of educational materials for the public school system.

Under the CSA, enforcement authority was transferred to the Department of Justice (DOJ) from the Treasury Department, which shifted the emphasis of narcotic control from a excise tax to a powerful direct control by the DOJ. Another major issue for control was that the CSA separated the enforcement of the law from the scientific evaluation of the various drugs considered for control. The attorney general became responsible for the administration of the control aspects of the law, and the secretary of Health and Human Services (HHS) was responsible for the final decisions on which drugs were to be controlled under the provisions of the CSA. Early on, the secretary of HHS delegated this latter responsibility to the FDA, and the FDA considered the following factors prior to placing a particular drug into the controlled substance category:

1. Scientific evidence of its pharmacological effect, if known.
2. The state of current scientific knowledge regarding the drug or other substance.
3. What, if any, risk there is to the public health.
4. Its psychic or physiological dependence liability.
5. Whether the substance is an immediate precursor of a substance already controlled under this law.

Table 5 summarizes the characteristics and penalties for the illegal manufacturing and illegal distributing of a variety of controlled substances in each of the five schedules. Notice that none of the general prescription drugs are scheduled under the CSA because most general prescription drugs do not possess major psychoactive properties or significant abuse potential as outlined above.

Some special control provisions mandated by the CSA include the following:

1. No prescription for a Schedule II drug can be refilled or called in via telephone. Each time the drug is dispensed it requires a new written prescription. In an emergency a Schedule II drug can be dispensed with an oral prescription.
2. Prescriptions for Schedules III, IV, or IV and V cannot be refilled more than six months after the original prescription has been written by a physician.
3. The label of a drug in Schedule II, III, and IV must contain this

Table 5: Summary of Drug Schedules and Penalties for Violation of the Federal Controlled Substance Act of 1970

Schedule	Abuse Potential	Medical Use	Examples	Maximum Penalties for Illegal Manufacturing or Distribution[a]
I	high	none	heroin, marijuana, LSD, mescaline, opiates, hallucinogens	1st offense 15yr/$25,000/3yr[b] 2nd offense 30yr/$50,000/6yr
II	high	yes	morphine, opium methadone, potent amphetamines, amobarital, cocaine, codeine, secobarbital, methaqualone, meperidine,	1st offense 15yr/$25,000/3yr 2nd offense 30yr/$50,000/6yr
III	less than I and II	yes	less potent amphetamines, some codeine preparations, some barbiturates, paregoric anabolic steroids[c]	1st offense 5yr/$15,000/2yr 2nd offense 10yr/$30,000/4yr
IV	low	yes	most anxiolytics, non-amphetamine anoretics, phenobarbital, chloral hydrate	1st offense 3yr/$10,000/1yr 2nd offense 6yr/$20,000/2yr
V	lower than IV	yes	dilute codiene and opium compounds, dilute narcotic mixtures	1st offense 1yr/$5,000/none 2nd offense 2yr/$10,000/none

[a]Maximum penalties may also include confiscation of property, and the offender may be subject to taxes due to the Internal Revenue Service, as set forth by recent amendments
[b]Maximum prison sentence/maximum fine/mandatory probation period after release from prison
[c]Anabolic steroids added to Schedule III as mandated by the Steroid Trafficking Act of 1990

warning: "Caution: Federal law prohibits the transfer of this drug to any person other than the patient for whom it was prescribed."

4. Manufacturing quotas are placed on the drugs classified as Schedule I or II.

The CSA was constructed to control the manufacturing and distribution of controlled substances and punish the violators of its provisions more harshly than those who were found to be in illegal possession of the drugs. The maximum penalities for illegal possession of all schedules of drugs listed as controlled substances are essentially the same for offenders.

In order to curtail illegal manufacturing and distribution and to monitor the prescribing and dispensing of controlled substances by physicians and pharmacists, the CSA requires annual or periodic registration with the Drug Enforcement Agency (DEA) of everyone who manufactures, distributes, or dispenses any controlled substances. Scientists involved with research on controlled substances must also register with the DEA. The CSA also mandates that the attorney general determine the quantity of controlled substances in Schedules I and II needed for scientific, medical, industrial, and research use, and then to place limits for the production of these substances for all of the companies that manufacture them. All registrants must keep complete records of all controlled substances each time the drugs change hands, retain the records for at least two years, and be prepared for an inspection of these records by the DEA.

It is safe to say that the provisions of the CSA have drastically reduced the volume of most controlled substances that are illegally diverted to the black market and at the same time preserved the use of these drugs for appropriate medical use. Exceptions include heroin, cocaine, and marijuana, which are not made to any significant degree by the nation's pharmaceutical industry. These controlled substances are primarily extracted from plants that can be grown and harvested inside and outside the boundaries of the United States. On the other hand, if a controlled substance is made primarily by the nation's pharmaceutical industry, the CSA provisions make a major difference in the quantities illegally diverted and used inappropriately. As a case in point, the quantity of amphetamines manufactured and diverted prior to the CSA was estimated to be nearly 4 billion doses annually. After the enactment of the CSA, the quantity of amphetamines diverted and inappropriately used was reduced to the point where it was not a significant problem. Now imagine for a moment that the CSA provisions were not law and the generic pharmaceutical industry was allowed to mass-produce each of the dozen or more amphetamines without a production quota or record keeping. It would be almost impossible to comprehend the degree of illegal diversion that could take place. Essentially, the provisions of the CSA have halted this phenomenon.

Abuse of controlled substances can be diminished in the United States by educational efforts, enhanced law enforcement, enhanced judicial efforts, treatment programs, and efforts to restrict the drug supply. What the CSA does for the controlled substances manufactured by the nation's pharmaceutical industry is to attack the supply of these substances in a superior manner and thus reduce the need for the other measures to combat abuse. In effect, if the source of the controlled substance can be controlled and limited, then the number of Americans who will need legal assistance and treatment for drug abuse is greatly curtailed. This distinction is made to demonstrate clearly the difference between controlled substances which can be extracted from plants that grow wild in fields; the source of these drugs is more difficult if not impossible to attack and control. This concept is important for the reader to understand to grasp the rationale behind the reclassification of anabolic steroids as Schedule III controlled substances under the provisions of the CSA discussed later in this chapter.

Precipitating Factors for the Reclassification of Anabolic Steroids as Schedule III Controlled Substances

The first documented study that attempted to quantify the black-market sources for anabolic steroids for athletes and bodybuilders was published by Taylor, indicating that 85 percent of health club athletes surveyed in Florida during the early 1980s obtained their steroids without a prescription from a licensed physician.[22] The sources of anabolic steroids for these athletes are listed in Table 6.

Table 6: Poll of 100 Strength Athletes in Florida — Sources of Anabolic Steroids

Source of Anabolic Steroids	*Percentage of Athletes*
health club owners	38
fellow athletes	20
licensed medical physicians	15
drug company representatives	7
pharmacists	6
nurses	5
coaches/trainers	4
direct drug company orders	2
health food stores	1
bodybuilding magazine ads	1
forged or altered prescriptions	1

Taylor presented this short study at the American College of Sports Medicine's (ACSM) annual meeting in 1984, along with what he felt to be a major preventive medicine solution to this burgeoning problem, namely reclassifying anabolic steroids as controlled substances under federal law.[23] Taylor's presentation ruffled many a feather in the sports medicine world, and there was little if any support at that time for his proposal. Certainly there was no support from the ACSM. Taylor published his first proposal to have steroids reclassified as controlled substances as a letter to the editor in the *Annals of Sports Medicine* in 1984.[24]

This began an uphill battle to educate fellow physicians to the fact that anabolic steroids did meet all of the characteristics of a tightly controlled substance under the provisions of the Controlled Substance Act of 1970. Therefore, with this letter in the *Annals of Sports Medicine*, Taylor structured five tables designed to explain the why athletes and fitness buffs would use anabolic steroids and some of the ways these steroids were psychoactive and addictive.[25] See Tables 7–11.

Table 7: Possible Mechanisms of Anabolic Steroid Actions

1. bind to skeletal muscle receptors and compete for receptor sites of testosterone and cortisone
2. exert their effects on DNA-dependent RNA polymerase triggering protein synthesis in skeletal muscle
3. increase the activity of DNA-dependent RNA polymerase over and above that of physical training
4. increase blood volume, hemoglobin, and hematocrit of normal men and women
    a) directly increasing the pool of erythropoietin-responsive stem cells
    b) indirectly stimulating erythropoietin production
    c) probable other mechanisms
5. increase or maintain bone integrity and calcium balance
6. hasten rehabilitation after muscle and tendon injuries
7. increase "pain tolerance" which may hasten rehabilitation
8. induce a "psychological high" greater than that of corticosteroids
9. cause an increase in "mental intensity"

Table 8: Theoretical Effects of Anabolic Steroids on Endurance

• Increased hemoglobin, hematocrit and blood volume—human studies
• Increased storage of muscle glycogen—animal studies and clinical observation

- Increased muscular strength — human studies
- Positive behavioral effects towards training — human studies and clinical observation
- Decreased body fat — human studies and clinical observation
- Adjunct to hypertransfusion of red blood cells (blood doping) — theoretical
- Increased pain tolerance — human studies and clinical observation
- Change in fuel substrate in endurance running — theoretical increase in fat utilization
- Reduction in "overuse" injuries resulting in more intense training — theoretical and clinical observations
- Boosts T-helper cells and immune system in general — human studies and clinical observation
- Reduces stress fractures — theoretical especially in women
- Enhances healing of tendon injuries — theoretical and clinical observation

---

Table 9: Minor Abnormalities Due to Anabolic Steroid Use in Men

Hypertension	Disturbances in sleep cycles
Acne	Increased appetite
Fluid Retention	Gynecomastia
Abnormal liver function tests	Deepening of the voice
Change in testicular size & function	Increased sebaceous gland secretion
Psychologic disturbances	Viral illness after cessation
Penile enlargement	Increased energy level
Increased libido	Cessation of depression
Changes in hair growth pattern and distribution	Rebound resetting of hormone balance
Epistaxis	Increased aggression
Enhancement of coping mechanisms	Withdrawal loss of libido
Withdrawal depression	

Table 10: Minor Abnormalities Due to Anabolic Steroid Use in Women

Hypertension	Disturbances of sleep cycle
Acne	Increased appetite
Fluid Retention	Reduction of body fat
Abnormal liver function tests	Menstrual disturbances
Psychological disturbances	Increased energy level
Reduction of breast tissue	Deepening of the voice

Clitoral enlargement	Cessation of depression
Epistaxis	Increased aggression
Changes in hair-growth pattern and distribution	Increased sebaceous gland secretion
Viral illness after cessation	Withdrawal depression
Rebound estogenization	Increased vascularity
Ruddiness of face	Withdrawal loss of libido

Table 11: Major Conditions Associated with Anabolic Steroid Use in Humans

Liver
    hepatocellular carcinoma
    peliosis hepatis
    benign liver tumors
    clinical hepatitis

Cardiovascular
    myocardial infarction and death
    acceleration of vascular disease

Psychological
    increased hostility, mental intensity, anger, aggressiveness
    increased desire to excel
    increased libido
    probable enhancement of mental alertness
    psychological dependence and withdrawal symptoms
    decreased inhibition to use other medications
    tendency toward "one-track mindedness"
    tendency toward violence

Shortly after the ACSM's annual meeting, other researchers began to concur with the notion that anabolic steroids were easily obtained on the black market and that licensed physicians were only a small factor in prescribing these drugs to athletic individuals.[26] By 1985, one conservative estimate claimed more than a million regular anabolic steroid users in the United States.[27] More and more fitness-oriented Americans, not only athletes, were using anabolic steroids, and among the male users, anabolic steroids were providing them with the macho body they desired. Of those new users who tried the drugs, very few discontinued the habit due to the addicting influences of the drugs.[28] Taylor described not only anabolic steroid addiction, but expanded on the personality changes in users that the drugs tended to cause both while on the steroids and after the steroids were discontinued, as shown in Table 12.[29]

Table 12: Psychological Changes Induced by Anabolic Steroids

While on the Drugs	*After Drug Use*
Increases in self-esteem, sex-drive appetite, explosive hostility and violence, mental intensity, energy, tolerance to pain, desire to train	Increases in depression, listlessness, apathy, desire for the drug
Decreases in ability to accept failure or poor performance, general tolerance, inhibitions about other drug use	Decreases in self-esteem, sex drive, hostility and violence, desire to train intensely
Other changes, including sleeping disturbances and nightmares	Other changes, including a return to normal sleep patterns and ability to control violent behavior

Taylor followed this article with a book that reviewed the anabolic steroid situation in 1985.[30] This book was presented as evidence in the congressional hearings later in the decade.

In 1987, the debate whether to reclassify anabolic steroids as controlled substances began to intensify due to three major factors:

1. The publication of three papers in the scientific literature which recommended that anabolic steroids be reclassified or that surveyed the possibility among a number of sports medicine experts and legal officials;[31]
2. The continued growth of the anabolic steroid epidemic; and,
3. The indictments and convictions of a few major black-market anabolic steroid dealers, which began to convince federal government officials of the scope of the illegal diversion of these drugs.

Taylor clearly showed that anabolic steroids met the criteria as controlled substances as outlined in the provisions of the Controlled Substance Act of 1970.[32] But there was much debate (primarily due to the lack of knowledge of how the CSA would affect anabolic steroid trafficking) about whether reclassification of these drugs would reduce the use by athletes and fitness buffs,[33] as demonstrated below:

> [Anabolic] steroids probably wouldn't meet the standard of having actual or relative potential for abuse. Just because a drug is used for a nonrecognized purpose does not necessarily denote abuse. (Tom Gitchel, chief of the state

and industry section in the Office of Diversion Control of the Drug Enforcement Agency)

I don't believe in regulating things that can't be enforced. It breeds disrespect for the law. (Dr. James Wright, U.S. Army and anabolic steroid researcher)

I don't think it (the controlled substance reclassification of anabolic steroids) would have an impact on the black market trade at all, but it would let us know which physicians are prescribing steroids for performance enhancement.... I would support such a move. (Robert O. Voy, M.D., chief medical officer and director of sports medicine for the United States Olympic Committee.)

Critics of a status change for anabolic steroids also argued that the federal government could handle the problem through existing agencies and laws. But the anabolic steroid problem was just now beginning to be discussed in federal agencies.[34]

The American Medical Association (AMA) responded to the anabolic steroid epidemic by publishing its official position on the topic, which was later prepared and submitted to the Senate Committee on the Judiciary regarding the rescheduling of anabolic steroids[35] (see Appendix 2). The AMA's official conclusion:

The AMA recognizes that steroid abuse is a significant problem. We must, however, oppose legislation that would schedule steroids under the CSA. *First*, the appropriate method for scheduling a drug is through the established regulatory process. *Second*, anabolic steroids do not meet the statutory criteria for scheduling under the CSA. *Finally*, there are more appropriate approaches to address the problem of steroid abuse. There include enforcement of the recently increased criminal penalty for selling steroids without a prescription, and educating the public concerning the harmful health effects of steroid abuse.

The reader can easily see from the aforementioned variety of opinions of so-called experts that the anabolic steroid situation was a mess at this time. It was clear that both physicians and legislators required much additional education to see the light regarding anabolic steroids and the controlled substance status. So in 1987, Dr. William N. Taylor contructed a nationwide educational lecture series entitled "Drug Issues in Sports Medicine," sponsored by Pfizer Laboratories, directed at the nation's physicians for continuing medical education credits at the hospitals and clinics where they worked. The series, which was published in 1988, became an important method to educate not only sports medicine physicians but all types of physicians, allied health professionals, and drug abuse professionals.[36] Many of these lectures were videotaped by the hospital education programs, and some of the lectures were covered by newspapers, major television documentaries, and medical publications. This lecture series helped raise the "noise level" of the growing anabolic steroid epidemic and the need for federal reclassification of these steroids as controlled substances.

Some physicians began arguing for the reclassification of anabolic steroids as controlled substances. An informal opinion sampling of some 50 physicians attending the February clinical conference of the American College of Sports Medicine in Keystone, Colorado, showed that about three-quarters supported the idea.[37] For instance, Dr. John Lombardo, medical director of the section of sports medicine at the Cleveland Clinic Foundation, argued that controlled substance status would pay off. "If steroids were controlled the onus would be on the producer. When large amounts of legitimately produced drugs are found in an illegal distributor's basement during a drug dealer arrest, then you know it is too easy to divert these drugs. Producing them should carry some responsibility."[38] Some of these concerned physicians began to work within their respective states to have anabolic steroids reclassified by the state as a controlled substance.

The Anti–Drug Abuse Act of 1988

Because of the growing concern over and adverse health effects of anabolic steroids, the federal government and many state governments began work to adopt regulations or enact legislation to reduce the abuse and misuse of the drugs. For example, the Congress passed the Anti–Drug Abuse Act of 1988, which included several provisions to control the misuse of anabolic steroids and human growth hormone. The key provisions of the act that related to the misuse of anabolic steroids and human growth hormone provided for the forfeiture of specified property of an individual convicted of a violation of the Federal Food, Drug and Cosmetic Act if such a violation was punishable by imprisonment for more than one year. Violators became subject to imprisonment for up to three years or a fine or both if they (1) distributed anabolic steroids or (2) possessed anabolic steroids with the intent to distribute for any use in humans other than the treatment of disease on the order of a physician.

This federal law was weakened by the fact that anabolic steroids were still just general prescription drugs and the FDA had no authority to require drug manufacturers to submit production data to the agency. Since the FDA did not receive production data on anabolic steroids, they could not correlate anabolic steroid distribution with its production. The nature of anabolic steroid production was such that manufacturers would produce relatively large amounts of a specific steroid in one time period, then cease production of that particular steroid for a while. Therefore, it was impossible to correlate accurately anabolic steroid production with its subsequent distribution. In other words, a generic pharmaceutical company could manufacture huge amounts of the steroid and divert it right under the FDA's nose.

Moreover, the amounts of anabolic steroids used for medical purposes could not be determined by the FDA. There was still no federal requirement that (1) physicians report prescriptions for medications other than controlled substances or (2) pharmaceutical manufacturers estimate the number of patients who would use the anabolic steroids.

Another provision of the Anti Drug Abuse Act of 1988 required the Human Resources Division of the United States General Accounting Office (GAO) to obtain information regarding the current estimated use of anabolic steroids among high school students, college students, and the adult population. The GAO also included in its scope of the problem a summary of the health consequences resulting from anabolic steroid use, a report on the policies and regulations developed by sports associations to monitor athletes' use of anabolic steroids, and a report on the legal and illegal anabolic steroids that were produced and distributed domestically and internationally. The GAO *Report on Drug Misuse: Anabolic Steroids and Human Growth Hormone* was submitted on August 18, 1989, to Joseph Biden, Chairman, Committee on the Judiciary, U.S. Senate (see Appendix 3).

Some of the salient findings of the GAO report:

1. According to the Department of Justice, clandestinely manufactured anabolic steroids, smuggled steroids, and legitimately manufactured U.S. anabolic steroids that have been diverted are the sources of the growing numbers of anabolic steroids sold on the black market. Justice officials estimated that the retail sales (as of 1988) of these anabolic steroids reached $300 to $400 million annually. When the estimated number of anabolic steroid users in the United States was estimated to be about one million in 1985, the black market sales were estimated to be about $100 million. By extrapolating the new estimate of sales on the black market, then, it could be estimated that by 1988 the number of anabolic steroid users in the United States had reached three to four million. Federal government estimates for Americans who used and abused other controlled substances of perhaps greater notoriety included "crack" cocaine (500,000) and heroin (500,000). Certainly the anabolic steroid situation was a national epidemic.

2. National and state surveys indicated that somewhere between 7 percent and 11 percent of the American high school eleventh- and twelfth-grade boys had used or were currently using anabolic steroids. This figure represented nearly 500,000 users alone.

3. The manufacturing of anabolic steroids within the United States had increased dramatically since the generic drug law was passed, and the

annual production of anabolic steroids consistently increased every year thereafter. During that same period of time (1980–1988), the prescribed anabolic steroids by licensed physicians had dropped significantly. So where did the majority of U.S. manufactured anabolic steroids go? They were illegally diverted to the black market.

4. According to the FDA's State Law Coordinator, nine states (Alabama, California, Florida, Idaho, Kansas, Minnesota, North Carolina, Texas, and Utah) had already classified anabolic steroids as controlled substances under state laws.

Hearings Before the Committee on the Judiciary, United States Senate

While the GAO report was being written, Senator Joseph Biden continued to work on the anabolic steroid situation to gain further information. He chaired a series of hearings, one on April 3, 1989, in Newark, Delaware, and another on May 9, 1989, in Washington, D.C.[39] The hearings consisted primarily of testimony by professional sports league officials, professional and amateur coaches and trainers, and olympic, professional, and amateur athletes. In Senator Biden's opening statement, four of his major points shed some light on this subject:

> The use of steroids in sports is troubling for a number of reasons. First, steroid abuse threatens the mental and physical welfare of thousands of our fittest, healthiest and brightest young people. Second, as experts have told us, and we will hear today and in future hearings, steroids could become another gate-way drug, a phrase that is now being used. Gate-way drug refers to marijuana, cocaine, and other drugs. If young people accept the idea that using steroids to build their body is okay, they may be all the more likely to try other drugs to alter their minds, as well as their bodies. And, third, using drugs to improve athletic performance undermines our most basic notions of honesty, discipline and hard work as a means for achieving. And it also undermines, quite frankly, our value system, the so-phrase. And finally, the words and deeds of athletes are critical because they are role models for all people, not just athletes, and young people.

> I want to get a clear message to the pushers of the drugs (anabolic steroids), including unscrupulous coaches and doctors who are willing to risk the lives of their athletes and patients in the pursuit of fame and glory, that distributing steroids is wrong and that those who do it face serious penalties. There is one last message that I would like to get across. We cannot continue the notion of plausible deniability in this country. I am in the process of contacting NFL coaches and major college coaches in the Nation. And guess what? We are having trouble getting them to testify. I want to promise you that if they continue to refuse to come and testify, I will see to that this

committee let everybody know why. . . . We cannot continue this notion of plausible deniability — "I do not care how my athlete got so big and got so fast; I am winning with that athlete." They should care.

Throughout the question periods in the hearings, Senator Biden assured those who testified that he was intent on seeing that anabolic steroids were reclassified as controlled substances. And as the testimony reflects, the majority of the league officials, coaches, trainers, athletes, and the AMA did not endorse such a law.

One of the compelling statements of the hearings was that of Diane Williams, former national track champion. Some of quotations from her testimony are included below. She was encouraged to take anabolic steroids for her athletic performance by an Olympic coach who promised her much fame and fortune if she would use the steroids.

I was able to train longer and harder, which ultimately improved my performance. Immediately I developed acne and light pigmentation on my face. I was a woman who suddenly became strong like a man. . . . I had no menstrual period . . . and certain masculine features appeared, like a mustache and fuzz on my chin. My clitoris, which is a penis equivalent, started to grow to embarrassing proportions. My vocal cords lengthened to a deeper voice. And a muscular pattern of hair growth appeared. Steroids affected my sexual behavior. In many cases I was a nyphomaniac. In women, the production of testosterone is quite low and the androgen is synthesized by the adrenal gland and is indirectly responsible for women's sex drive.

My following athletic achievements were a result of the steroid Dianabol. I am currently a collegiate record holder of the women's 100 meters with a time of 10.94. I was second at the Athletic Congress National Championships in Indianapolis, June 1983. I was a bronze medalist as the first world championship in Helsinki, Finland, during the summer. I received my first major commercial endorsement with *Life* magazine. . . . [The coach] supplied me with more Dianabol and furthermore, he charged me a fee of 10 cents to 25 cents a pill, depending on whatever he felt was appropriate. And at the time I had a little bit more money that I made, sponsorship money from winning the bronze medal.

There is approximately 45 to 50 women on a team (who used steroids) . . . 40% of the 1988 team had tried it at least.

And one of the psychological effects that I had at the time is I really believed that I could not run fast after (I stopped taking) steroids. I did not believe that I had the natural ability to run fast. . . . I have really, really been brainwashed by this coach.

Another compelling statement at the hearings was the one by Bill Fralic, who plays football in the National Football League with the Atlanta Falcons. Some exerpts from his testimony:

I believe steroid use is rampant among the NFL, and that includes my own team. It is rampant in colleges, and it is rampant in high schools. Everybody is blind to it because they choose to ignore what is happening in the world of steroids. It is time to stop ignoring the problem and to open the eyes of the naive.

Steroid use in football represents a vicious cycle. I know there are many players in high school, college, and the NFL who want to stop using steroids but they cannot or will not because they do not believe they can be competitive without them.

In our league, random testing (for anabolic steroids) is the only way to stop the steroid madness. . . . Players know they will test just once, at the start of training camp. This allows him to do steroids all off-season, and then about one and a half months, or whatever the steroid is, it varies in time, before training camp testing in mid–July, he can get off of them. Once he tests, he can restart using steroids, and by the time the season opens in September, he is all bulked up.

Some people brag that they have bulked up without steroids, and they even will give you a grocery list of foods they eat to support their claim. I submit that this is a farce. This player in fact may be consuming 10 to 12,000 calories a day, but I would bet everything I had that this consumption is supplementary to his use of steroids and growth hormones. Growth hormones are a frightening development. . . . It (human growth hormone) is another avenue players will take to beat the system.

What this means is the NFL becomes something of a freak show. Eventually, there will be disgrace in the name, much like we have seen disgrace in the Olympics. And what happens if the game ever became clean of steroids? You might see 300-pound players become 270-pound players. You might see 240-pound players shrink to 220 or 215, and so forth. But the game will not change. If anything, the game will be better because there will be less injuries.

Also at the hearings was Steve Courson, who made his fame as the NFL's strongest player when he played for the Pittsburgh Steelers during the "Steel Curtain" period. Some exerpts from his testimony:

Dianabol . . . was the first entry in 1958 of anabolic steroids in American sports. It was not long afterward when this chemical started spreading throughout the various athletic institutions and weight rooms in America. . . . Here we have the beginning of an escalating chemical warfare. After 25 years, there are new drugs which created a dilemma, not only for the sports world, but for society. Most sports medicine researchers all agree that steroid use in strength sports is epidemic.

With these testimonies in mind, is there any doubt that the Committee on the Judiciary (consisting of Senator Biden, Senator Arlen Specter,

Senator Strom Thurmond, and Senator Charles Grassley) would react by proposing a federal bill to reclassify anabolic steroids as tightly controlled substances?

It had been nearly 20 years since the Controlled Substance Act of 1970 had been passed into law. The law was written primarily to place psychoactive drugs like heroin, cocaine, marijuana, amphetamines, barbiturates, LSD, and other hallucinogens under stricter control by the federal government. However, no public official, medical doctor, or drug scientist ever envisioned that macho-medicine drugs (anabolic steroids) that possessed not only strong psychoactive properties but strong psychosexual properties and muscle-building properties would become into epidemic use by Americans in the 1980s. Medical doctors should have predicted it, but they didn't. They were lied to by medical policymakers. But even when one medical doctor predicted the anabolic steroid epidemic six years ago, clearly outlining the abuse potentials, the black market, the violence-producing effects, the addictive effects, the steroid psychosis, and the need for federal reclassification as a controlled substance, the whole "shooting match," this one young medical doctor was shunned by his peers.

Six long years to come to the correct solution regarding anabolic steroids. Why did it take so long? Long enough for thousands and millions of young Americans to get involved, many of whom experienced major adverse effects that are irreversible. Some died due to steroid abuse; in some, these steroids induced an explosively violent temper ('roid rage) and steroid psychosis that destroyed their interpersonal relationships and their marriages; and some committed acts of violent crime, even murders, under the influence the these drugs. Many have created perhaps irreversible atherogenic plaques within their coronary arteries that will cause them premature death due to an early heart attack. Many have leaped from anabolic steroid use to other controlled substances due to the gateway effect. Many girlfriends and spouses have been physically abused by their men who were on anabolic steroids. Many young women have experienced "date rape" or outright rape by a young man under the influence of the psychosis-producing, psychosexual-altering effects of anabolic steroids. Many parents found that their adolescents who took anabolic steroids suffered major personality changes that resulted in family strife from the users' aberrant behavior patterns. All of this because it took six years to have the majority of these steroids removed from the reach of young Americans. To all of the victims of the anabolic steroid epidemic, this author sends his regrets. It was the best effort that this one physician could muster. For the most part, it was a one-physician, one-decade, one-dream type of ordeal that was never supported by the AMA (in fact opposed by the AMA) or any major athletic institution.

The Steroid Trafficking Act of 1990

Although the original draft of the Steroid Trafficking Act of 1990 recommended that anabolic steroids be reclassified as Schedule II controlled substances, the final version of the Act reclassified anabolic steroids in Schedule III. The provisions of the Steroid Trafficking Act of 1990 provides for the following punishments:

1. It increased anabolic steroid trafficking penalties to match the penalties for selling cocaine and other dangerous drugs.
2. It imposed tighter record keeping and manufacturing control regulations to prevent the diversion of legally manufactured anabolic steroids into the illegal black market.
3. It gave the Drug Enforcement Administration the authority and responsibility to investigate violations involving the illegal manufacturing, distribution, or possessing with intent to distribute of anabolic steroids.
4. It required that United States demand-reduction agencies incorporate anabolic steroids in all federally supported drug abuse prevention, education, and treatment programs.

6

The Identification and
Treatment of Self-Users

The reclassification of anabolic steroids as controlled substances will have a great impact on the number of steroid abusers in the United States beginning in 1991. Since anabolic steroids will be treated by the various government agencies as dangerous narcotics, and since the quantities diverted by the pharmaceutical industry will be all but eliminated, the amounts of anabolic steroids that will be available for continued athletic abuse will be small. And the agencies such as the FDA and the AMA who never supported the reclassification of anabolic steroids to the controlled-substance level will now have to restructure their thinking to support the recent legislation. Moreover, the positions of all of the sporting organizations — including professional, olympic, and amateur sports, who have tended to mishandle this situation — will have to alter their policies and treat anabolic steroids as dangerous narcotics. Furthermore, drug testing for anabolic steroids will have to be more competent and pervasive.

But what about all of the present anabolic steroid users who will suddenly have their steroid sources "dry up"? What anabolic steroid–induced adverse effects will they encounter? Is the medical profession, which is still in need of education on this topic, prepared to identify and handle the adverse effects that anabolic steroid self-users may present to their offices or hospitals? Will the relatively few anabolic steroid experts in the United States be able to serve adequately as consultants to establish functional anabolic steroid withdrawal clinics? Will the federal government fund a national anabolic steroid abuse registry to log and track anabolic steroid–related adverse effects? These are just some of the questions that must be addressed in the early 1990s.

The absolute scientific study of drugs abused by a significant portion of the American public is difficult if not impossible to conduct. Researchers cannot employ a hundred volunteers or so, prescribe large doses of a drug, and watch what happens. According to today's medical ethics, this type of research is obviously unethical. The last such effort of this type was conducted by federal government agencies over 20 years ago when researchers gave large doses of LSD to healthy military personnel and documented the adverse effects on videotape. The future collection of information on anabolic steroid adverse effects will probably parallel the documentation procedures of other recently abused drugs such as cocaine and "crack" cocaine. The information will come from case reports, pilot studies from anabolic steroid withdrawal clinics, and a national registry. An anabolic steroid hotline could serve to further the knowledge on the nature and the extent of anabolic steroid–related adverse effects. However, with much of this information still forthcoming, it is important to review the adverse effects that are currently known to occur or believed to occur.

In this chapter the major psychological and physiological adverse effects associated with anabolic steroids will be reviewed. Then some of the methods that may be used to identify and treat anabolic steroid self-users will be presented, even though this topic is certainly in its infancy. Finally a section will address the need for establishing a national anabolic steroid abuse registry.

Major Psychological Adverse Effects

The most prevalent adverse conditions brought on by the self-use of anabolic steroids are due to psychoactive effects on the limbic system of the brain. The *limbic system* is a term loosely applied to a group of brain structures that have a great influence on various autonomic functions and certain aspects of emotion, behavior, and personality. Although medical science's understanding of how these steroids affect the limbic system is in its early stages, it is probable that anabolic steroids bind to various receptor sites within the limbic system directly and cause an alteration in behavior. Also, anabolic steroids may serve as direct neurotransmitters in other areas of the brain. However, even though the absolute mechanisms of how anabolic steroids influence the brain are still unknown, there is no doubt that these steroids are strong psychoactive drugs and that these psychoactive effects arc complicated, interrelated, and multifactored.

The study of the psychoactive nature of anabolic steroids has been influenced by several "macho" factors. First, the major biochemical difference between the male and female genders is due to the strong influence of testosterone and its concentrations in the human body. It has been difficult for many people to accept that the major differences between male and female behavior can be attributed to a single sex steroid throughout life.

Testosterone is not the only difference, but it is the most prominent difference. Second, it has traditionally been more acceptable and macho to look for the physical answers to medical problems and to discount anything psychological (supratentorial) as merely a weak excuse because a physical reason just could not be found. Third, the medical profession tends to be a very "macho" group, especially in their interpersonal relationships with peers. Male physicians would rather believe that their professional machoism is due to their superior training or their superior quality as human beings, rather than the influence of a single sex steroid that by its nature affords the macho personality. Finally, the majority of medical research to date has been conducted by men, and it would have been asking too much if men had been introspective enough to see the influence of testosterone on male behavior. Wouldn't it be interesting if women had conducted most of the research over the years? Then the chances would have been in favor of a more objective view of testosterone's influence on behavior!

Testosterone's macho influence manifests itself in two major ways, which are interrelated to some degree: (1) body size and muscular strength; (2) male-pattern dominance. When testosterone is secreted in higher amounts than normal or when testosterone and or anabolic steroids are ingested or injected enough to raise the total "androgen burden" in the user, a number of macho behavior patterns may arise, and in some people, these patterns can become aberrant, violent, sexually violent, and criminal. Therefore, in the paragraphs to follow, the summary of the psychoactive effects that anabolic steroids can cause will be grouped into one of two categories dealing with machoism: anabolic steroid addiction and "megorexia," and anabolic steroid–induced violence. Any drug that causes increased size and strength, is addicting, and promotes violent acts is macho in a bizzare and distorted fashion.

Aggression and Violence

The ability of testosterone and anabolic steroids to induce aggression and violence is not confined to humans. In animal studies, treatment with anabolic steroids has long been known to cause overaggressive and violent behavior. Serum testosterone levels and anabolic steroid treatments in rodents, ungulates, and primates have been shown to exert a major influence on social rank and dominance, which are often related to fighting.[1] For instance, the treatment of hens with synthetic testosterone has been shown to induce aggressiveness and "henpecking" enough to disrupt the entire social order of the flock.[2] The testosterone-treated hens received the sexual advances of the roosters and were the dominant hens. When the testosterone treatment was discontinued and the testosterone effect waned, the social order of the flock went through a period of chaos, and with time the social rank of the hens returned to its original state. Similar studies have shown that when heifers were treated with anabolic steroids, they fought significantly more often than the controls.[3] The treatment of male or female rodents with anabolic steroids has been shown to cause overaggressive behavior and intense fighting. Anabolic steroids increased the incidence of fighting among both sexes of rodents and increased the fighting intensity of male rodents. Moreover, the treatment of just one pair of rival rodents stimulated intense fighting in both rodents.[4] Male vervet monkeys, whose serum testosterone levels may fluctuate five- or tenfold normally, have been reported to display overaggressive and fighting behavior that correlates with the high testosterone levels.[5]

Some early clinical trials with testosterone therapy revealed a tendency for the steroid to induce aggression and violent behavior.[6] More recently, other researchers have found positive correlations between high testosterone levels and some aspects of aggressive, violent, criminal, and sexually criminal behavior.[7]

A study published in 1980 on 56 normal adolescent males is perhaps the most definitive human study that links high testosterone levels to certain personality traits. These normal 16-year-old adolescent males were studied through a dozen different personality inventories and were shown to exhibit statistically significant bouts of verbal and physical aggression, and to experience a potential for violence, especially in response to provocation or threat, which correlated to elevated testosterone levels.[8] It easily follows, then, that if an adolescent male who already has high testosterone levels and is subject to a more aggressive, hostile, and violent array of behaviors, takes additional anabolic steroids, he will be a candidate for violent and criminal behavior, especially if provoked. And what if several anabolic steroid-using adolescent males form a gang? It is safe to say that in the late 1980s and early 1990s anabolic steroid abuse by adolescent males has been a factor in the overall violence picture in the United States. It has also been a factor in the increase in violent rapes, date rapes, murders, and gang violence.

Perhaps the first scientific link to anabolic steroid–induced violence in steroid-using athletes was by Taylor.[9] He also wrote that anabolic steroid use by athletes could be responsible for a steroid psychosis.[10] In 1986, Taylor coined the term *'roid rage* to describe the explosively violent behavior anabolic steroid users can display.[11] The FDA considered 'roid rage to be a significant adverse effect in its bulletin mailed to physicians in 1987.[12] Then two psychiatrists (Pope and Katz) reported that 12 percent of 33 regular steroid users exhibited psychotic symptoms, and many others exhibited near-psychotic symptoms, mania, and withdrawal depression.[13] In their follow-up studies, Pope and Katz have reported the following effects to be attributable to anabolic steroid abuse: aggression, violent episodes, paranoia, depression, and hallucinations.[14] Other articles that support these types of psychological disturbances have been published in scientific journals.[15]

The quantity of anabolic steroids that may induce major personality change such as 'roid rage and violent steroid psychosis is unpredictable. However, these phenomena are dose-related to some degree. In other words, in any given anabolic steroid user, the higher the dose of these steroids, the more likely he or she will experience major personality changes. But even moderate doses of these anabolic steroids may induce 'roid rage and psychosis in many users. This can be illustrated by the following statements by a mother and father who wrote about how anabolic steroids claimed their son's life[16]:

> On August 7, 1989, we found our beautiful 18-year-old son hanging from a tree by our front door.... We found five bottles of Dianabol (methandrostenolone) in his car after his death.... He began using them (anabolic steroids) the summer before his senior year in high school to prepare himself for football.... He gained thirty pounds in a short time and his muscles began to appear very defined.... We were unaware of the psychological effects of steroid use. We now know that Eric's symptoms and subsequent depression and suicide were a result of withdrawal from the drugs [anabolic steroids].... Eric had exhibited many episodes of abnormal aggressiveness during the year before his death. Once, when someone cut in front of him, Eric flew into a rage, pulled the man over, and beat him up. A week before his death, he pulled two men over near a shopping center and beat one of them. Several times Eric became enraged at his family members over inconsequential events.... There was no way to predict what would set him off. Once, he pounded dents into the hood of the family car. He alternated between rational and irrational thoughts.... Eric was an amazing kid. He never took any other drugs, nor did he drink more than an occasional beer at a party.... We suspected steroid use and advised him to stop.... These drugs are deadly, and we want that fact known.

In the commentary that followed this article, Harrison G. Pope, Jr., M.D., associate professor of psychiatry, Harvard Medical School, and steroid researcher, wrote:

> Given recent evidence that hundreds of thousands of American high school boys have used these drugs, it is alarming to speculate that many other instances of unexplained psychiatric syndromes in young men — aggressiveness, uncharacteristic violence or criminal behavior, paranoid or grandiose beliefs, and suicide — may represent the undiagnosed effects of these common but illicit drugs. It seems important that both professional and lay observers report further cases when possible so that we may improve our understanding of this potentially serious public health problem.

In the late 1980s Drs. Taylor, Pope, and Katz were involved as expert witnesses in some of the first federal court cases involving anabolic steroid-induced criminal violence and murders. Since these cases are now public, a synopsis of one will be presented below to illustrate further that anabolic steroid–induced 'roid rage and psychosis are real phenomena with real sequelae.

One of the more dramatic federal cases involving an anabolic steroid user who committed a brutal murder was that of Horace K. Williams, a 23-year-old former high school football player turned bodybuilder. This case (May 1988) was followed by major newspapers and was the subject of a television documentary program entitled "On Trial," which aired in 1989. Horace, also known as "Ace," was a high school graduate and son of a minister. He had no known history of conduct disorder or major psychiatric problems. He donated some of his time as a youth minister. He had hoped to play college football, and he became interested in weight training and utilized anabolic steroids to "help him out" when he was 18.

Horace's anabolic steroid use and addiction was that of a classical case that can be arbitrarily divided into three phases: early phase, middle phase, and late phase, as testified by William N. Taylor, M.D. Ace's anabolic steroid use will be placed into these phases for illustrative purposes.

TYPICAL EARLY PHASE OF ANABOLIC STEROID USE
1. Usually oral anabolic steroids in low to moderate amounts.
2. Significant muscle mass and strength gains with weight training.
3. Major personality changes, including euphoria, increased self-esteem, increased sense of well-being, increased sex drive, increased appetite, increased aggressiveness, increased desire to train, increased desire for anabolic steroids.

ACE'S EARLY PHASE OF ANABOLIC STEROID USE
1. Oral Dianabol (methandrostenolone) of only 5mg per day for two weeks, then increasing to 25mg per day over the next five weeks.
2. Significant muscle mass and strength gains with weight training.
3. Major personality changes, including "felt great ... more confidence ... able to ask any girl for a date ... always hungry ... would challenge anybody ... spent more time in the gym training."

TYPICAL MIDDLE PHASE OF ANABOLIC STEROID USE
1. "Stacking" both oral and injectable anabolic steroids with increased doses and total anabolic steroid burden.
2. Further increased muscle mass and strength.
3. Major personality changes, including major mood swings, sleeping disturbances, irritability, easily provoked to display temper and violence,

grandiosity, use of recreational drugs, manic episodes, increased desire for anabolic steroids, withdrawal depression, distorted body image.

ACE'S MIDDLE PHASE OF ANABOLIC STEROID USE

1. "Stacked" methandrostenolone (Dianabol) and oxymetholone (Anadrol-50) orally progressing to having his workout partner inject him with testosterone cypionate.

2. Further increases in muscle mass and strength.

3. Major personality changes: "felt special powers . . . had nightmares . . . got mad real easily . . . hit the wall with my fists . . . pulled telephones off the wall . . . threatened people . . . used cocaine occasionally . . . stopped steroids for two weeks and was so depressed I thought I might kill myself if I didn't get back on steroids . . . felt like a wimp off steroids."

TYPICAL LATE PHASE OF ANABOLIC STEROID USE

1. "Stacking" several anabolic steroids together orally and by injection, further increasing total anabolic steroid burden.

2. Further increases in muscle mass and strength.

3. Major personality changes, including manic episodes, grandiose delusions, paranoia, 'roid rage, narcissistic behavior, psychotic symptoms, criminal activity, full-blown steroid psychosis, usually with violent criminal activity or violent sexual criminal activity.

ACE'S LATE PHASE OF ANABOLIC STEROID USE

1. "Stacked" four or more steroids together without any particular schedule; began to inject himself daily.

2. Further increases in muscle mass and strength.

3. Major personality changes: "Had rushes of energy and power . . . could pound the earth with my fists and feel the earth vibrate . . . everyone was watching me . . . everyone was afraid of me . . . everything pissed me off . . . most of my friends stopped being my friends . . . I was in several fights . . . all I thought about was building my body to compete in bodybuilding . . . I was arrested for possession of cocaine . . . I once turned over fifteen cars . . . I wanted to fight everybody . . . I couldn't control my madness . . . I pulled a phone booth out of the cement and threw it . . . I beat up that hitchhiker real bad for no reason . . . out in that field with the hitchhiker I felt I was alone . . . everybody was in the shadows . . . all I could hear was my head buzzing."

During the day that Ace murdered a hitchhiker, he placed a phone call and got a busy signal, flipped into a rage, and grabbed the phone booth in his arms, uprooted it, and tossed it into a parking lot. He was psychotic for hours. Later that evening, Ace picked up a hitchhiker and drove him to a deserted field. He undressed the hitchhiker until he was nude, beat him to death with a board and a lead pipe, scalped him, shaved the hair off of his arms and legs, hung him with rope, and then ran over him repeatedly with his vehicle.

During the late 1980s there were several major federal court cases involving anabolic steroid–induced criminal violence and murder. These cases involved police officers taking anabolic steroids and engaging in police brutality, college football players taking anabolic steroids and committing violent crimes, and bodybuilders and powerlifters taking anabolic steroids and committing bizarre violence. These few cases, however, represent just the tip of a huge iceberg.

Addiction and "Megorexia"

The first reports that anabolic steroids were addictive drugs were by Taylor.[17] Now almost every leading expert in the anabolic steroid field agrees that these steroids are addictive.[18] I believe that for many users, anabolic steroids can be more addictive than cocaine.

Perhaps the most definitive article on the probable addiction mechanisms of anabolic steroids was written by Kashkin and Kleber.[19] They postulated that anabolic steroid dependence and withdrawal was similar to opioid addiction patterns in both the acute and delayed withdrawal phases. During the acute phase of withdrawal from anabolic steroids, when there is a reduction in serum steroid level, there appears to be an acute hyper-adrenergic withdrawal syndrome, which may give rise to a reduction in self-esteem, depression, panic attacks, and suicidal ideation. These acute symptoms seem to be ameliorated by returning to anabolic steroid use, as documented with opioid dependence. The delayed depression syndrome occurs when the serum anabolic steroid levels drop precipitously, giving rise to an intense anabolic steroid craving; this delayed depression phase is also similar to the delayed phase of opioid dependence.

Drug addiction is habituation to the use of a drug to the extent that deprivation gives rise to symptoms of distress, withdrawal symptoms, or an irresistible impulse to take the drug again. In many cases, these irresistible impulses can be set off by daily or frequent experiences that the drug user associates with prior use of that drug. For instance, with cigarettes, the impulse to smoke again may be most intense after meals or after sexual intercourse. For cocaine, the strongest impulse may be at a party where others are using the drug.

But for anabolic steroids, the user's whole life and body image can be wrapped up with the steroid image. Every time the anabolic steroid user enters a gym or goes to the mall or to the beaches, he compares his body image the way it was then (with steroids) to the way he is now. Everywhere the former user goes, he is confronted with the macho image of other steroid users. He naturally compares and comes up feeling like a wimp. He sees himself as a scaled-down version of himself. This distorted body image may be the most difficult hurdle in overcoming anabolic steroid addiction. Continuing to lift weights during and after the acute and delayed withdrawal phases limits the loss in body muscle mass, but the former user knows that the only way to return to his maximum size and strength is via the steroids. No other drug addiction has been so tied up with both a direct psychological and physiological addiction pattern and such a powerful impact on body image. This is why I believe that anabolic steroids may be more addicting than cocaine for many users.

The perception of body image is also distorted for the anabolic steroid user while he or she is taking the steroids. The anabolic steroid user is never large or muscular enough; there is an unquenchable quest to achieve body mass. Even the most muscular steroid users may stare at themselves in a mirror for long periods, posing and assessing, posing and assessing, and so forth. The net result is that he or she perceives that what is in the mirror is too small. In many ways this is similar to the reverse situation, usually seen with anorexia nervosa. Therefore, this distorted body image, which is often induced by anabolic steroid abuse, has been called "megorexia."[20] Megorexia can be very narcissistic in nature and is associated with a voracious appetite and a distorted body image that has both cognitive and affective disorders.

In summary, anabolic steroids abuse can give rise to major pyschological disorders and addiction patterns. The understanding of these psychological problems have yet to be completely unraveled, but it is safe to say that the psychological disorders induced by anabolic steroid abuse are more prevalent and can be more serious than the physical effects to be covered in the next section.

The exact mechanisms by which anabolic steroids cause overly aggressive and violent behavior are unknown.[21] Studies of androgen receptors and direct testosterone implants into the brain have confirmed that anabolic steroids can induce overly aggressive and violent behavior patterns.[22] Autoradiography has been used to map and identify androgen-binding neurons, and it has been postulated that there are three categories of androgen receptors in the brain.[23] These receptors are in equilibrium between the nucleus of the brain cell and the cytoplasm. Two of these receptors can be both activated and transformed by anabolic steroids.[24] Therefore, currently proposed mechanisms imply that anabolic steroids, acting on specific neurons within the limbic system of the brain, can activate and alter the brain's biochemistry, which results in brain impulses that can alter human behavior patterns.

Testosterone and anabolic steroids are powerful psychoactive chemical mediators that provide the human with strong impulses, and together these impulses are "socialized" through time, resulting in a person's overall personality. One simply does not act and react on impulses alone. Social skills, coping skills, and social mores must be learned. During adolescence in both boys and girls, testosterone serum levels are known to be the greatest. This high level of serum testosterone directs many of the mental and physical changes associated with puberty and adolescence. The elevated testosterone levels help provide for accelerated growth and development, awakening of sexual desire, secondary sexual organ maturation, and a variety of brain impulses that must be "socialized" into acceptable behavior. Perhaps three of the more prominent brain impulses that high levels of testosterone regulate are anger, aggressiveness, and libido. In the United States, the adolescent period is longer than in any other country, and the maturing period is often associated with a very difficult socializing transformation. Adolescents make many mistakes during this socialization period, and they are known to act often on impulse. The mistakes may take the form of poor socialization of sexual desire, which may lead to sexual promiscuity and unwanted pregnancies. They may take the form of violent criminal behavior, especially when the adolescent is provoked, due to their strong impulses for aggressiveness and anger, which are provided to a major degree by the elevated testosterone levels.

When an adolescent self-experiments with anabolic steroids, thus elevating the total androgen burden on the brain, his brain impulses become difficult if not impossible to socialize and control. This can give rise to a personality and behavior pattern that is different from what has previously been established. Even seemingly minute stresses can often provoke an anabolic steroid–using adolescent into abnormal and aberrant behavior due to the steroid enhanced brain impulses on libido, anger, and aggression.

To take this a step further, a young adult who begins using anabolic steroids is faced with socializing brain impulses that in many ways may resemble a second adolescent period. The heightened brain impulses, which together may be viewed as machoism, provide for increased libido, anger, and aggressiveness. These impulses may prove to be difficult to socialize for the adult, and they may take on the personal characteristics of mania, hostility, grandiosity, and moodiness. If the total anabolic steroid burden is elevated enough, the adult may lose complete control of these brain impulses, especially when there is the perception of provocation. Anger may give way to 'roid rage and a violent steroid psychosis, during which the user is unable to distinguish between what is right and wrong. Because of the strong libido-impulse enhancement, this violent psychosis may take on a sexual overtone, resulting in rape or date rape. I believe that the anabolic steroid–induced psychoses are a form of temporary mental insanity in most cases, due to the user's inability to distinguish between what is right and wrong and the often very hazy and spotted recollection of his actions. The adult user may function from day to day within the societal boundaries with a high degree of anger, hostility, and moodiness, and then go off like a keg of dynamite due to minor points of contention because of the loss of control of brain impulses that anabolic steroids influence.

It is impossible to predict how much extra male hormone (anabolic steroids) any given person can tolerate. The aberrant behavior can occur at therapeutic doses, and greater in some people. And a user may handle moderate to large doses for some time before the uncontrollable brain impulses appear and are not adequately socialized. Remember that anabolic steroids can activate *and* transform or alter brain receptors to induce these impulses.

With the aforementioned discussion in mind, the term *anabolic* means "to build," and what these steroids can do is destroy the mind of young muscular persons, which may result in severe sequelae. In this manner, *anabolic* is a misnomer. This discussion is not some sort of "Twinkie defense" for aberrant behavior; in other words, "the Twinkie I ate made me do it." The anabolic steroid–induced personality and behavior alterations are real and represent a major social problem.

The altered personalities that are induced by anabolic steroids are not confined to the athletic world. In 1990 a best-selling book about the life of Barry Minkow was published, a true exposé on how an anabolic steroid–altered Minkow swindled Wall Street. Minkow began weight lifting and anabolic steroid use at age 14 and became a hulk. The anabolic steroids heightened his aggressiveness, euphoria, and feelings of invincibility, which made him the wonderboy of Wall Street until his anabolic steroid–induced personality altered his judgment enough to get involved in all sorts of fraudulent and criminal behavior. He built a business empire and swindled sophisticated accountants, lawyers, and Wall Street investment bankers along the way. Minkow's success depended on his anabolic steroid–induced charisma and energy. He made suckers of them all until his scheme was finally unraveled, and he is now serving a lengthy sentence in federal prison.[25]

Major Physical Adverse Effects

An extensive listing of the adverse physical effects that can be associated with anabolic steroid use and abuse are contained in Tables 9–11 in Chapter 5. These lists will not be reproduced here. It should be noted that any or all of these physical effects can be experienced by any given user, depending on the number of anabolic steroids taken, the dosages, and the duration of the steroid use. Some fortunate users may experience few or none of these adverse physical effects, to their knowledge. For instance, unless the user has his blood pressure measured, he may be unaware of a hypertensive condition brought on by the anabolic steroids. The same goes for elevated liver enzymes and abnormal lipid profiles. These physical abnormalities may be ongoing, but unless they are measured, they may be silent for some time. Left unchecked, these abnormalities could culminate with the severe liver and cardiovascular diseases listed in Table 11.

According to current medical knowledge, the most prevalent adverse physical effect seen with extended anabolic steroid use is cardiovascular disease. The self-use of supratherapeutic doses of anabolic steroids ranks as a serious risk factor for coronary artery disease for both men and women users.[26] The potential health risk is alarming in view of the adverse changes in various lipoprotein values which anabolic steroid use causes (negative impact on HDL-C, HDL²-C and apo A-1 levels) and coronary heart disease (CHD) risk.[27] These altered lipoprotein levels are believed to be a marker for atherogenesis which, if they are persistently abnormal, may result in CHD.

Quantifying the risk of prolonged anabolic steroid use to early CHD is difficult. However, I believe that anabolic steroid use is more of a risk of CHD than a similar period of using tobacco. And in the face of a strong family history of CHD or other CHD risk factors, a year or two of anabolic steroid use could cause an acceleration of the CHD process of a decade or more. For instance, if a football player takes anabolic steroids in high school and college and his father had a heart attack in his fifties, then the steroid-using football player may increase his chances of having a heart attack in his late twenties or early thirties. The combination of this atherogenic property with other potential anabolic steroid–related adverse effects, such as fluid retention, hypertension, clotting abnormalities, hostility, and 'roid rage creates a potential for devastating effects on the cardiovascular system.[28]

There are some reasons why medical science has been slow to link CHD, acute heart attack, and sudden death in anabolic steroid users. First, young muscular men who have a heart attack usually die before they can give a medical history to attest to their anabolic steroid habit. Second, the nation's coroners rarely if ever test for anabolic steroids in cases where muscular athletes die suddenly or of unknown causes. Anabolic steroid testing is not usually included in the coroner's toxicology screen. Third, muscular men who have used anabolic steroids in the past to play professional or college football and then later have a premature heart attack may not have known that anabolic steroids have played a major role in the disease process, or they may tend to be dishonest about their previous anabolic steroid use because of their current employment status. Finally, most physicians, including cardiologists, are still not aware that significant anabolic steroid use is a risk factor for CHD and therefore do not question their patients about it.

The reader may remember from an earlier chapter in this book that testosterone was once used to treat heart disease. We now know that prolonged use of anabolic steroids can cause heart disease. What an irony!

Clinical Assessment of Self-Users

With the recent reclassification of anabolic steroids as controlled substances under federal law, it is even more imperative that physicians become more familiar with the common clinical findings that may be associated with anabolic steroid self-use. Recent studies have suggested that roughly 10 percent of the nation's high school boys have used or are currently using these steroids. Therefore, it is highly likely that physicians who examine and treat the adolescent age group will come in contact with anabolic steroid abusers. The more information that the physician can gain regarding clues to anabolic steroid use from the history, physical examination, and laboratory values, the more likely a successful intervention will take place. Unlike many other drugs of abuse, anabolic steroid abuse may give the knowledgeable physician some objective clinical findings. It has been shown that about 40 percent of high school anabolic steroid users become "hard core" steroid users who cycle on and off the steroids five or more times, with each cycle lasting from 6 to 12 weeks.[29]

As with any medical condition or disease, any given user may have none, a few, or several of the clinical findings during any single examination. Other anabolic steroid users may present with most of the clincal findings discussed below.[30]

Table 13: Medical History Clues to Anabolic Steroid Abuse in Adolescent Males or Young Men

- Weight lifting
- Rapid weight gain—25 to 30 pounds of lean body mass gain over a 3- to 6-month period
- Use of other supplements for muscle building
- Personality changes or behavior problems—see previous sections in this chapter for discussion
- New onset of nose bleeds
- Strength or power athlete
- Recent significant increase in appetite
- Use of various prescription drugs to self-treat steroid-related adverse effects, such as tamoxifen, acne medications, diuretics, or anxiolytics

- Rapid gains in neuromuscular strength or speed
- Frequent posing in front of mirrors
- Recent increase in time spent in the weight-lifting gym
- Often reads or subscribes to muscle magazines
- Recent focus on nutrition as it relates to muscle growth
- Frequently attends bodybuilding contests or shows
- Competes in powerlifting or bodybuilding contests
- Employed as a night-club "bouncer," professional wrestler, or male nude dancer
- Is overly muscular and is employed in the armed forces or by law enforcement
- Claims to have used anabolic steroids in the past but has quit
- Seems very knowledgeable about anabolic steroids when asked
- Has an older brother who is a strength or power athlete

Table 14: Physical Findings Common to Anabolic Steroid Abuse in Adolescent Males or Young Men

---

- Good or excellent muscularity
- Very low body fat percentage
- Hypertension
- Signs of fluid retention such a puffiness of the face
- Icteric sclerae—rare
- Early scalp hair thinning or premature male pattern baldness
- Truncal acne—acne is often worse on the shoulders, back, abdomen and typically spares the face or is less severe on the face
- Very prominent veins in the upper extremities
- Striae in the anterior axillary region of the armpit
- Nodularity around the breast area or frank gynecomastia which may be unilateral
- Needle marks, bruising or nodularity in the upper buttocks area from chronic injection of steroids
- Testicular atrophy—unless an androgen-secreting tumor is present, a muscular male with some of the above physical findings and testicular atrophy is essentially diagnostic

---

Table 15: Frequently Abnormal Laboratory Values Common to Anabolic Steroid Abuse in Adolescent Males and Young Men

---

- Elevated red blood cell mass
- Elevated hematocrit
- Elevated BUN and creatinine levels
- Elevated liver function tests—aspartate aminotransferase, alanine aminotransferase, alkaline phosphatase and total bilirubin may be elevated; SGOT is usually greater than SGPT

- Elevated fasting glucose level
- Depressed serum globulin level
- Depressed protein-bound iodine and thyroxine-binding globulin along with normal free thyroxine and triiodothyronine uptake
- Depressed sperm count—counts may be as low as 20 million/ml and can drop to zero
- Atherogenic lipoprotein profile—very low HDL-C values often below 20, elevated LDL-C levels and elevated triglycerides; total cholesterol may be elevated or normal
- Elevated CPK, SGOT or LDH from injection of steroids
- Elevated serum estrogen levels
- Elevated serum testosterone levels if one of the steroids used is a testosterone preparation
- Depressed serum testosterone levels if none of the steroids used is a testosterone preparation

---

If the evidence of anabolic steroid abuse is strong, it may be desirable for the physician to order specific laboratory tests or order an accurate urine drug test for anabolic steroids from a certified laboratory. In any case, definite protocols should be followed. The more knowledgeable the physician is and the more he can identify clinical findings, the more a young male anabolic steroid user is likely to admit the use of the steroids. The physician should relay his findings from the medical history, the physical examination, and the laboratory findings, and indicate that these findings arouse his suspicion of anabolic steroid abuse. Some abusers may confess, and others may deny it.

To confirm his suspicions further, the physician may wish to perform an accurate urine drug test for anabolic steroids. A testing protocol has been established by the United States Olympic Drug Testing/Education Program, and a toll-free telephone number has been established to assist in the anabolic steroid testing of amateur athletes: (800) 233-0393. A sensitive test that employs gas chromatography–mass spectrometry and costs about $100–$150 is available for the detection of both exogenous testosterone use and anabolic steroid use. Currently, there are only four certified laboratories in North America for the detection of anabolic steroids! However, it is possible that a given anabolic steroid user is taking a steroid that is currently not detected by even the certified laboratories or is utilizing one or more methods to mask steroid use, making the results less reliable. Current anabolic steroid testing will be covered in more detail in Chapter 7.

In many cases, it is important for the physician clearly to diagnose anabolic steroid abuse in adolescents and young men, for they may present to the physician's office with other complaints that may be the result of anabolic steroid abuse. If the physician fails to consider anabolic steroid abuse as the cause of the condition under consideration, he may elect, perhaps in error, to prescribe other prescription medications to alleviate the condition. As a case in point, during my national lecture series for physicians, I encountered a nephrologist who made the following comment after the formal lecture in an Atlanta hospital:

> Each year I am referred at least a dozen young football players who have hypertension. These young men are always very muscular, and as I remember, my medical staff, which are women, always make some comment on how good they look with their shirts off. I work them up from head to toe and I can't find any reason for their hypertension. And, yes, most of them did have acne on their chests, shoulders and back. I failed to examine their testicles. But after your lecture and as I look back, I now know that they were on anabolic steroids. I ended up treating them with anti-hypertensive drugs which may have compounded the problem.

After a similar lecture at a major teaching hospital in New England, a dermatologist made the following remark:

> I have treated severe acne in many young, very muscular men who were weight lifters or football players with Accutane. I did not consider that they may have been on anabolic steroids, though now I think they probably were. As you know, Accutane can be toxic to the liver and so can anabolic steroids. In retrospect, this was not a good idea.

Following still another lecture at a major teaching institution in Atlanta, an emergency department physician made the following comment:

> Just last week a young, extremely muscular physician presented to my emergency department with chest pain. He died of an acute myocardial infarction, and even after the autopsy, which included a negative toxicology screen, we could not determine the cause of his atherogenesis and sudden death. I now know that it was probably due to anabolic steroid abuse. Do any of the current medications which are routinely prescribed for an acute myocardial infarction interact with anabolic steroids?

Among the many interesting and important questions and comments which were raised by physicians following these formal lectures was one by an orthopedic surgeon at a major teaching institution in Los Angeles:

> I am in sports medicine and I perform surgery on many athletes. After hearing your lecture, I am now sure that many of these athletes abused anabolic steroids. My question is, are there any drug interactions with the common general anesthetics and anabolic steroids? Should I put a steroid-abusing athlete under general anesthesia? My second question deals with the healing rates of an anabolic steroid abuser. Will the abuse of these substances affect their surgical result?

The potential drug interactions with anabolic steroids and other drugs are, to a great degree, unknown. But it does emphasize the importance of knowing whether anabolic steroids are being abused. If anabolic steroids are being abused, then it is important for the physician to encourage the withdrawal from the drugs and refer the abuser, if necessary, to an appropriate setting for withdrawal. This will be discussed below.

Treatment of Anabolic Steroid Withdrawal

The understanding of anabolic steroid withdrawal and the treatment of this withdrawal are both in their infancy. The initial recognition of anabolic steroid withdrawal symptoms was by Taylor.[31] Other researchers have described psychological anabolic steroid withdrawal symptoms, such as depression, suicidal ideation, and anabolic steroid craving.[32] The psychological addiction to anabolic steroids can be so severe that suicidal depression can occur during withdrawal. Therefore, close professional monitoring may be required during this period to avoid what the user perceives to be life-threatening withdrawal symptoms.[33] A case report of physical withdrawal has also been published.[34] Moreover, the fact that anabolic steroid withdrawal is associated with a significant loss of muscle mass and strength causes the user to perceive a major decline in body image.[35] Anabolic steroid users may also develop very distorted body images.[36]

With the treatment of anabolic steroid dependence and withdrawal the professional may have to be prepared to identify and treat the following problems that any given user may develop:

1. Psychological withdrawal which may present as an acute depression ranging from mild in nature to severe suicidal ideation.
2. Physiological withdrawal which may present as an acute hyperadrenergic withdrawal syndrome similar to that seen with acute opioid withdrawal. The user, who is withdrawing from anabolic steroids, may present with nausea, chills, headache, dizziness, diaphoresis, piloerection, rapid pulse rate and elevated blood pressure.
3. Strong anabolic steroid craving.
4. Distorted body image.
5. Perceived or real diminished libido.
6. Impending criminal charges.
7. The user's previous attempts to stop the steroids with little or no success.

The professional must also understand some of the other parameters which may have a bearing on the user's habit:

1. The continued use of anabolic steroids even in the face of the user acknowledging psychiatric adverse effects brought on by his steroid use.

2. The continued use of anabolic steroids despite a severe deterioration in the user's personal life that may have included dealing the steroids to support his habit.

3. The expenditure of substantial time pursuing anabolic steroids and that such drug-related activities have begun to dominate and destroy the user's personal life.[37]

Strategies that may prove to be beneficial in treating anabolic steroid withdrawal include combinations of psychotherapy, psychopharmacology, and urine drug screening. The drugs that may be used in the treatment of the acute hyperadrenergic phsysiological withdrawal and the psychological withdrawal depression are naloxone and alpha²-agonists such as clonidine, followed by antidepressants. Clonidine therapy may also help with anabolic steroid craving, provided the withdrawal period is accompanied with continuing the user's weight-lifting program or athletic-training regimen. Without a continued program of weight training, the user's loss of body mass, strength, and body image will probably be substantial, thus making the craving for anabolic steroids even more intense.

The distorted body image and the resultant perceived decline in body image are major issues of concern with anabolic steroid withdrawal. In treating the withdrawal aspects of other drugs it has been important to remove the user from the setting in which he has used the drugs in the past to reduce the craving for the drug. However, with anabolic steroid withdrawal, removing the user from the weight room to treat the withdrawal symptoms promotes a substantial and rapid loss of muscle mass for the user and a resultant perceived decline in body image. On the other hand, allowing the user to use a weight room where anabolic steroids are being used will also enhance his desire for anabolic steroid use. For this reason, perhaps the best method of treating anabolic steroid dependence and the withdrawal period is by placing the user in an inpatient drug withdrawal center equipped with up-to-date weight-lifting facilities for a few weeks up to several months. Once released from the clinic, the former user should be monitored with urine anabolic steroid screening and other serum laboratory tests that may provide clues of a relapse. This urine screening and associated laboratory analysis would especially be important for those users who have been convicted of felonies and are on probation.

The restoration of the libido of the withdrawing user may also be a challenge. He may complain of a low libido or no libido even after the serum endocrine values are restored to normal levels. It must be remembered that libido is a subjective parameter. It could be normal but is perceived by the former anabolic steroid user as abnormally low. For instance, if an adolescent male begins his anabolic steroid use and becomes a hard-core steroid user during the same period when he is developing and understanding his sex drive, he may think that it is normal for him to experience many ejaculations a day. Anabolic steroid use can provide a young man with an increased sex drive and increased number of ejaculations and erections. Then, months or years later, when this young man withdraws from the anabolic steroids, he may perceive that his sex drive and number of erections and ejaculations are abnormally low when they may be about normal. Therefore, when dealing with the libido aspect of anabolic steroid withdrawal, it is important for the professional to take a detailed sexual history regarding both the anabolic steroid-using phase and the withdrawal phases. The treatment of a true loss of libido may prove difficult. It is entirely possible that long-term anabolic steroid use could tend to burn out those brain receptors responsible for the brain impulses that affect libido.

As of this writing, there have been no guidelines published to instruct the professional as to which anabolic steroid users will suffer major withdrawal phenomena. However, it has been this author's experience that most anabolic steroid users will experience some degree of withdrawal depression which is clinically significant. Major withdrawal depression has been found to be over 15 percent.[38] Most anabolic steroid users attempt to self-treat the withdrawal depression by returning to anabolic steroid use.[39] Some users have attempted, with some success, to "wean" themselves from the steroids by utilizing a prolonged tapering technique. Physicians have treated other forms of steroid addiction by a similar prolonged tapering regimen with success. Anabolic steroid tapering may be indicated for those users who have become addicted to large doses of various anabolic steroids. In other cases, the use of synthetic gonadotropin releasing hormones during the withdrawal phase to reinstitute the normal hypothalamic-pituitary-testis axis may prove to be beneficial.

There is no doubt that as the reclassification of anabolic steroids as controlled substances nationwide begins to extinguish the illicit anabolic steroid black market sources, an increase in user withdrawal symptoms will rise. Significant numbers of users could seek medical attention to alleviate withdrawal sequelae. It is hoped that several drug rehabilitation clinics will expand their facilities with both knowledgeable professionals and appropriate weight-lifting equipment to handle this situation. From these clinics could come a wealth of information, and if this information is published, it could prove to be very helpful in the future.

A National Anabolic Steroid Abuse Registry

Any professional who is currently an expert on anabolic steroid abuse and is willing to serve as a consultant to other physicians, the press, or the public should quickly realize the national scope of this problem. There are thousands of case studies in physicians' offices across the country. Local physicians in one city are finding anabolic steroid–related adverse conditions that reflect what local physicians are finding in other cities. Yet in the standard medical textbooks used to teach medical students and residents, the anabolic steroid topic receives very little, if any, attention. Much of what is in the major medical textbooks, which deal with the diagnosis and treatment of disease, is outdated and incorrect regarding anabolic steroids. Most physicians currently seeing patients on anabolic steroids do not recognize it and are not prepared to handle the situation if they do recognize it. And altering standard medical textbooks is a relatively slow process.

Perhaps the best method to solve the issue of how best to accumulate and broadcast anabolic steroid abuse information is via a national anabolic steroid abuse registry. Since anabolic steroids have been reclassified recently as controlled substances, federal money could be available for such a project. This type of project could be funded by private money as well. In this manner the true incidence and severity of the various types of adverse effects can be known and documented to discourage the use of these substances for those who may be tempted to try them in the years ahead.

7

The Limits of
Urine Drug Testing

In this final chapter the current limits of utilizing urine drug testing for anabolic steroid detection will be explored. Current anabolic steroid detection does have its merits and its limits. After a brief historical discussion, the basic principles regarding steroid detection will be discussed, and then some of the loopholes of steroid testing will be pointed out. Due to the impact of the Steroid Trafficking Act of 1990, steroid detection is likely to spread beyond the traditional athletic arena into the workplace, so this topic will be covered briefly. Finally, some recommendations will be made to minimize anabolic steroid use and abuse in college and professional sports.

During the mid-1970s there were various types of detection techniques proposed by investigational groups for accurately screening anabolic steroids in athletes. These methods included gas chromatographic, mass spectrometric and radioimmunoassay techniques.[1] The radioimmunoassay technique was selected to screen for anabolic steroids in Olympic athletes prior to the 1983 Pan American Games due to two major reasons. First, studies utilizing the gas chromatographic and mass spectrometric methods showed that it could be possible to detect the metabolites of specific anabolic steroids in the urine,[2] but the studies were incomplete. Second, the principal disadvantage of using the gas chromatographic and mass spectrometric methods was the length of time required for each specimen analysis. Thus, the radioimmunoassay was selected, even though it was known to be inaccurate and inadequate at the time. Therefore, there was really no accurate anabolic steroid testing performed on Olympic athletes prior to the 1983 Pan American Games. Moreover, the United States Olympic Committee occasionally used the "sink method" for anabolic steroid detection, which was advising Olympic athletes that there was a test for these steroids, collecting their urine specimens, and then pouring them down the sink. This "sink method" was apparently adopted to dissuade anabolic steroid use and to appease the American public.

During the 1983 Pan American Games the current form of anabolic steroid detection was used for the first time to screen Olympic-caliber athletes. The result was that dozens of American Olympic athletes and hopefuls withdrew from the games due to a variety of undocumented injuries and vague illnesses after the testing results of the first day indicated positive anabolic steroid tests in a few American athletes who had already competed. It will never be known how many Olympic records set prior to the 1984 Olympic Games were set by anabolic steroid–using athletes. There were probably many.

Basic Principles of Current Anabolic Steroid Detection

The current methodology for the detection of anabolic steroid metabolites in the urine of athletes employs a computerized gas chromatograph–mass spectrometric combination. Previously determined "steroid maps" serve as an absolute fingerprint of what a particular steroid's metabolites look like in the urine. One or more of these unique metabolites are used as proof that a particular anabolic steroid has been metabolized by an athlete. When one or more of these unique steroid metabolites is present, this type of screen is one of the most accurate tests available in modern medicine.

But there are current limits to this type of testing for the following reasons:

1. If a particular anabolic steroid does not metabolize to a unique metabolite which can be identified in the urine, there is no basis for a positive test. Of the 27 anabolic steroids which are now controlled substances (see Appendix 1), only a few have ever been identified well enough in an athlete's urine for subsequent disqualification or disciplinary actions. It has been this author's experience that athletes are currently using a few of the anabolic steroids of which there seems to be no unique urine metabolite found.

2. The identification of testosterone use by the athlete is complicated by the fact that it is the natural male sex hormone which is secreted normally by every athlete. Through unpublished studies, it was determined that a metabolite of testosterone which appears in the urine in a fairly constant concentration is epitestosterone. Apparently, in normal urine specimens, the ratio of testosterone concentration compared with epitestosterone

concentration is approximately 1:1. An arbitrary ratio of 6:1 has been adopted by the International Olympic Committee to infer that exogenous testosterone has been used by the athlete. It has been known by competitive athletes for some time that by simply injecting epitestosterone parenterally or into the urinary bladder itself blocks the detection of exogenous testosterone use. For instance, prior to the 1991 Cotton Bowl a University of Texas football player was found to have a vial of epitestosterone in his possession along with a needle and syringe. With the aforementioned discussion, one can speculate on why he possessed epitestosterone. It is a chemical compound and not a drug. It has no indicated medical use.

3. There are some drugs which can be taken by an athlete who has been selected for anabolic steroid testing which actually mask the detection of the steroids. One drug has been identified as a common prescription drug, probenecid. Probenecid apparently slows or stops the excretion of anabolic steroid metabolites; it may also bind to a unique anabolic steroid metabolite in the urine making the total molecular weight (unique steroid metabolite-probenecid compound) so heavy that it does not appear in the anabolic steroid range of the mass spectrograph. There are probably several other drugs which "mask" anabolic steroid detection which have yet to be identified by the International Olympic Committee.

4. There are a number of other anabolic and growth-stimulating synthetic hormones, which athletes are currently using, that cannot be detected by current drug testing techniques. Some of these genetically-engineered synthetic hormones include human growth hormone, growth hormone releasing hormone, somatomedin-C, leutininzing hormone releasing hormone, and erythropoetin.

5. There is no way to rule out some sort of sabotage dealing with the ingestion of a detectable anabolic steroid during the events surrounding a national or international athletic competition. For instance, a food or drink product could be "laced" or "doctored" with an oral anabolic steroid which gives rise to a positive urine anabolic steroid test without the athlete's knowledge. A few Winstrol tablets placed into a soft drink a day or two before drug testing could give a positive anabolic steroid test for stanozolol without enhancing the athlete's performance.

6. There are athletes who have used diuretics prior to anabolic steroid testing in order to dilute the urine specimen enough that the concentrations of the anabolic steroid metabolites are too low to be detected. As a result, diuretics were officially added to the banned substance list by many national and international sports organizations. However, some of the diuretics

cannot be detected. For example, ethacrynic acid is a diuretic which can dilute the urine enough to make recent anabolic steroid use undetectable, but it is excreted primarily in the feces. It is very difficult, if not impossible, to detect ethacrynic acid by urine testing.

7. There are limits to how long a particular anabolic steroid can be detected by urine testing after the athlete discontinues the use of that steroid. The limits vary. The anabolic steroid which has the longest detection time (a few months) is nandrolone decanoate and the steroid which has the shortest detection time (a few days) is perhaps oxandrolone. This phenomenon can be a major hurdle for the urine detection of anabolic steroids. For instance, a high school football player can abuse anabolic steroids for years and make himself a "macho" hulk of a person. With only a few exceptions, high school athletes are never tested for anabolic steroids. After this football player receives his college football scholarship and learns of the techniques to "beat" anabolic steroid testing, he has had a major advantage for athletic performance, size and strength without ever being tested. Those anabolic steroids which he took in high school have long been excreted, and are entirely undetectable by college steroid tests.

8. Current anabolic steroid testing is expensive ($100–$200) per specimen and there are only three laboratories in the United States which have been certified by the International Olympic Committee. In short, accurate anabolic steroid testing is expensive and there are inadequate facilities certified to handle extensive anabolic steroid testing programs.

9. There is little published scientific literature which gives instructions on how to set up and certify an anabolic steroid testing facility. Some of the scientists most closely involved with this issue have felt that if they published in detail their detection methods, then athletes would disect the information and discover newer methods to cheat the system. The downside to this philosophy is that few new laboratories can be set up quickly enough to handle a significant increase in urine specimens. Besides, the knowledgeable athlete is already cheating the system.

10. There is some work that is ongoing with anabolic steroid testing research that utilizes the athlete's entire endocrine system for analysis. Bringing this type of blood and urine evaluation to market may never happen due to its complexity and the invasiveness of blood testing of athletes. The downside to this type of approach further indicates that too many athletes are cheating the current methodology.

It is for the reasons listed above that I felt that the anabolic steroid epidemic could not be simply tested away. Anabolic steroid testing has a place in athletics, medicine and law, but it has not been and will not be in the near future a major ingredient in curbing the anabolic steroid epidemic. The major curbing factor will be the extinguishing the black market supplies of the steroids that the Steroid Trafficking Act of 1990 should accomplish.

Impact of the Steroid Trafficking Act of 1990 on Steroid Testing

By reclassification of anabolic steroids as Schedule III controlled substances, the federal government has paved the way for widespread anabolic steroid testing, including the federal workplace. Anabolic steroid testing will impact

1. Professional sports organizations who have been slow to incorporate efficient steroid testing policies. In effect, the new federal law overrides a weak philosophy of a sports organization in dealing with this issue.

2. Armed forces personnel who are already subject to urine drug testing. The federal reclassification of anabolic steroids to the controlled substance status will probably make steroid testing policies similar to that of other narcotics.

3. Law enforcement personnel who are already subject to urine narcotic testing.

4. Criminals who commit violent crimes and violent sexual crimes as it becomes federal law to test for narcotics in felons.

5. College athletic programs which already have some anabolic steroid testing in place. New policies for steroid testing will probably parallel the protocols in place for other dangerous narcotic drugs.

6. Preemployment physical examinations where narcotic screening is already in place.

7. All government employees who are already subject to narcotic screening.

8. Airline pilots and other public transportation employees who are already screened for narcotics.

9. Medical examinations where anabolic steroid abuse is suspected or must be ruled out.

10. Coroner examinations and toxicology screens for cause of death.

11. Psychiatric examinations where narcotic screening is indicated for the diagnosis and treatment of psychiatric illnesses.

12. Emergency examinations where narcotic screening is used diagnostically.

13. Drug rehabilitation clinics and hospitals where narcotic screening is utilized for diagnostic and follow-up purposes.

14. Research centers that are studying the effects of anabolic steroids on mental and physical medical conditions.

The reader can see from this list that there will probably be a shortage of certified steroid-testing facilities in the very near future. To fill this gap, it is probable that regional or hospital-based steroid-testing facilities will need to be established.

Cleaning Up Professional and Amateur Athletics

If drug testing for anabolic steroids is to have any major deterrent effect on the elite amateur, college, or professional athletes of this country, certain criteria must be structured and adhered to that take into account the limits of this testing discussed in a previous section. Thus far, the types of steroid-testing procedures adopted by both amateur and professional athletic organizations have had little impact on reducing anabolic steroid use by participating athletes. Some of the criteria listed below are squarely confronted by organizations that feel that these procedures are in conflict with an individual's constitutional rights. Therefore, these suggestions do not necessarily parallel my beliefs, but they are offered to clearly indicate what has to be done if anabolic steroid testing of college and professional athletes is to have any impact.

To be effective, the following guidelines should be considered for anabolic steroid testing policies for amateur and professional athletes:

1. The potential for testing both during the season and in the off-season.
2. The potential for random selection of athletes included in team sports.

3. The potential for short-notice or totally unannounced testing.

4. The construction of programs designed to deliver strict disciplinary actions, rehabilitation, and education.

5. The funding of ongoing research to improve the current anabolic steroid detection techniques.

It is my opinion that one or more major legal challenges to the current systems for anabolic steroid testing of athletes is likely to cause the demise of the entire program. There are some flaws in the present system, and when wealthy or soon-to-be-wealthy athletes learn how to retain the steroid-testing experts who are willing to help them in their defense, the current system will not survive without major improvements and publication of these improvements. It is beyond the scope of this book to discuss many of the flaws that deal with the protocols which have been adopted by various sports organizations for their anabolic steroid testing. However, a recent book by Robert Voy, M.D. details much of the political inconsistencies and outright cover-ups of anabolic steroid testing at the international and national level for Olympic-caliber athletes.[3]

Afterword

This book concludes a decade of my study and work on the issues that have surrounded the entire history of the macho medicines, anabolic steroids. I have learned that when medicine, sports, and politics collide, it is not a pretty sight. People who do a little work with this subject quickly become so-called experts, and original ideas and theories are often stolen. Moreover, these Johnny-come-lately experts voice their opinions without studying the entire scope of the issues. I had always hoped that medicine would be able to rise above personal egos and go beyond the prevailing concept of "If it is not my idea, I won't support it, even if it makes sense." But it hasn't. Most of the current concepts on the psychological effects of anabolic steroids are mine, and I will take credit for the original theories and earliest publications. The concept of reclassifying anabolic steroids as controlled substances was mine, and I will take credit for that too. And I have documented these original ideas in both scientific publications and books — a record that should withstand the test of time. Future medical students will not have to be lied to, as I was, because the subject of anabolic steroid abuse was too political to handle.

The reclassification of anabolic steroids as controlled substances under federal law made sense to me in 1983. Why did the proposal never make sense to the American Medical Association, the United States Olympic Committee, the United States Food and Drug Administration, the American College of Sports Medicine, the National Collegiate Athletic Association, and various professional and amateur sports associations? Why did they never support my proposal? Was it because they were uneducated to the issues? No. They heard my lectures, or they selected me as an expert witness or as a consultant on the topic. It was because their senses were blinded by macho things like money, power, and professional ego. They were wrong, and I had the guts to persevere. My philosophy won.

93

The philosophical mind is not what people would call a healthy bouyant mind. That "healthy mind" takes life as it finds it and troubles no more about that. None of us start life as philosophers. We become philosophers sooner or later, or we die before we become philosophical. The realization of limitation and frustration is the beginning of the bitter wisdom of philosophy, and of this, that "healthy mind," by its innate gift for incoherence and piecemeal evasion and credulity, never knows.

—*H. G. Wells,* The Mind at the End of Its Tether

Final Plea: Expand the 1970 Controlled Substance Act

In a recent congressional hearing on the topic of whether synthetic human growth hormone should be reclassified as a controlled substance under federal law, I was invited to testify. Dr. Robert Voy and I represented the United States Olympic Committee's Drug Control Program in proposing that synthetic human growth hormone should be reclassified. I'll never forget the fact that Congressman Henry Waxman, Chairman of the Subcommittee on Health and the Environment, took my book *Hormonal Manipulation: A New Era of Monstrous Athletes* in hand and announced to the panel of physicians and officials who represented the pharmaceutical companies who manufactured synthetic human growth hormone, "You lied to us about the effects of steroids; we will not let this happen with human growth hormone."

As part of the Steroid Trafficking Act of 1990, human growth hormone is treated in many ways as a controlled substance (see Appendix 1). But officially it is not a controlled substance. Recent medical publications have continued to show that synthetic human growth hormone can greatly increase muscle mass and selectively reduce body fat, making the abuse potential great. Moreover, some physicians continue to prescribe the hormone for purposes which are outside of the accepted and legal medical indications.

The time will come when the Controlled Substance Act of 1970 will be expanded to include all genetically engineered synthetic hormones that contribute to the growth and development of the human body or that have direct abuse potential in athletic settings.[1] Several of these synthetic hormones which are being abused by famous athletes of today and will be abused by those of the future include (1) synthetic human growth hormone, (2) synthetic human growth hormone releasing hormone, and (3) synthetic somatomedin–C.

95

None of these synthetic hormones, which have the potential to enhance human athletic performance, muscle mass, and ultimate adult height, have a current detection method. Moreover, no method is on the horizon. If we don't make controlled substances out of the synthetic growth hormones that regulate the growth and development of the human body, then why control the use of any drugs? These synthetic human growth hormones are basically nothing short of being the biochemical "fertilizers" for human growth, which can distort the norms for ultimate adult height and afford suprahuman muscle mass and strength and can be converted by a fortune on the athletic field. What a pity! Whatever happened to the natural athlete?

Appendix 1

United States Senate

COMMITTEE ON THE JUDICIARY

WASHINGTON, DC 20510–6275

September 28, 1990

Dr. William Taylor
1125 Tall Pine Trail
Gulf Breeze, Florida 32561

Dear Dr. Taylor:

The illegal use of anabolic steroids is a major drug abuse problem in this country. A recent report by the Department of Health and Human Services confirms the results of the Judiciary Committee's two-year investigation into steroid trafficking and abuse. Steroids are dangerous drugs that threaten the physical and mental health of hundreds of thousands of young people.

With your help, I have called attention to this problem through a series of hearings on steroid abuse in amateur and professional sports. As a result of these hearings, I introduced S.1829, the Steroid Trafficking Act of 1989. This legislation would attack the steroid problem by adding steroids to schedule II of the Controlled Substances Act. This change would boost the penalties for steroid trafficking, impose tight production controls on pharmaceutical companies and incorporate steroid prevention and treatment programs in our national drug abuse strategy.

The reason that I am writing to you is that the full Senate will take action on S.1829 in the near future. Although the bill enjoys broad support, it is important that leaders in the amateur and professional sports industry, coaches, athletes and others take a strong stand against the use of performance-enhancing drugs.

I have enclosed a copy of the report that summarizes the findings of the Judiciary Committee's investigation along with a transcript from the steroid hearings.

I hope I can count on your support as this bill overcomes the final hurdle to becoming law. If you have any questions or need additional information, please do not hesitate to contact me.

Sincerely,

Joseph R. Biden, Jr.
Chairman

Enclosures

Calendar No. 787

| 101st Congress
2d Session | SENATE | Report
101–433 |

THE STEROID TRAFFICKING ACT OF 1990

August 30, 1990.—Ordered to be printed

Filed under authority of the order of the Senate of August 2 (legislative day, July 10), 1989

Mr. Biden, from the Committee on the Judiciary, submitted the following

REPORT

[To accompany S. 1829]

The Committee on the Judiciary, to which was referred the bill (S. 1829), having considered the same, reports the bill, as amended, and recommends that the bill do pass.

CONTENTS

I. Purpose

The purpose of the proposed legislation is to amend the Controlled Substances Act to further restrict the use of steroids. By designating anabolic steroids as a schedule II controlled substance, the bill would crack down on illegal steroid use in four ways:

39–010

2

(1) it would increase steroid trafficking penalties to match the penalties for selling cocaine and other dangerous drugs;

(2) it would impose tight record-keeping and production control regulations to prevent the diversion of legally produced steroids into the illicit market;

(3) it would give the Drug Enforcement Administration the authority and responsibility to investigate violations involving the illegal production, distribution, or possession with intent to distribute steroids; and

(4) the bill would require U.S. demand reduction agencies to incorporate steroids in all federally supported drug abuse prevention, education, and treatment programs.

This legislation would also amend the Food, Drug, and Cosmetic Act to restrict the illegal distribution of human growth hormone which is chemically distinct from steroids.

II. Legislative History

Senators Biden, Simon, and Levin introduced S. 1829, the Steroid Trafficking Act of 1989, on November 1, 1989. This legislation was the result of a year-long investigation by the committee into the problem of steroid abuse in America. S. 1829 builds on the provisions authored by Senator Biden in the Anti-Drug Abuse Act of 1988, which made the illegal sale of steroids a felony, punishable by 3 years imprisonment.

Despite enactment of the steroids provisions in the 1988 drug bill, illegal steroids trafficking remains a major drug problem in the United States. In one blatant example, a Mexican firm, United Pharmaceuticals of Mexico, mailed a solicitation to U.S. citizens giving them directions to a hotel across the border where they could go to buy steroids. The company urged its customers to "tell your friends that here in Mexico there is no prescription necessary to obtain steroids." To crack down on steroid trafficking through the mails, Senator Biden introduced S. 466 on February 28, 1989. S. 466 makes the distribution of steroids through the mail a criminal offense. By adding steroids to schedule II of the Controlled Substances Act, S. 1829 would incorporate the prohibition on steroids shipments through the U.S. mail as proposed in S. 466.

The committee held 2 full days of hearings on the problem of steroid abuse, focusing on the problem of steroid abuse in amateur and professional sports. Chairman Biden convened the first hearing at the University of Delaware, in Newark, DE, on April 3, 1989. The hearing featured testimony from world-class athletes Evelyn Ashford, Diane Williams, and Pat Connolly, Ashford's coach and a former U.S. Olympian. According to two-time Olympic gold medalist Evelyn Ashford, approximately 50 percent of the female medalists in the 1988 summer games used steroids. Her desire to be No. 1 led Diane Williams, former U.S. national champion and winner of the bronze medal in the 1983 world championship in the 100 meters, to use steroids from 1981 to 1984. Now steroid-free, Diane Williams' testimony included stories of physical and mental anguish associated with her steroid abuse.

Testimony from a panel of sports medicine experts reinforced the evidence of steroid use among amateur and professional athletes

3

and warned the committee about the adverse physical and psychological effects linked to steroid use. Dr. Charles Yesalis, a professor at Pennsylvania State University and a leading expert on the prevalence and consequences of steroid abuse, testified about the behaviors, attitudes, and perceptions—consistent with psychological dependence—exhibited by a significant percentage of high school athletes who use steroids. The committee also heard testimony regarding the strong connection between steroid abuse and psychiatric disorders from Dr. David Katz, recognized as one of the leading medical experts on the psychological effects of steroid use. Dr. Katz warned in his testimony that individuals should pay special attention to the phenomenon of steroid use and psychotic episodes, depression, and mania.

Other witnesses at the hearing included: Dr. Edward Langston, American Medical Association; Pat Croce, conditioning trainer for the Philadelphia 76ers and the Philadelphia Flyers; Mike Quick, captain and all-pro receiver with the Philadelphia Eagles; Otho Davis, head trainer for the Philadelphia Eagles and executive director of the National Athletic Trainers Association; and Dorothy Baker, Delaware representative to the Executive Board of State Chairmen of the U.S. Olympic Committee.

The second hearing on steroids, held on May 9, 1989, in Washington, DC, featured testimony from representatives of professional and college football. Recognized as a sport plagued by alarming levels of steroid use, football has always favored those players that are bigger, bulkier and more aggressive than their opponents. According to Bill Fralic, three-time all-pro offensive lineman and National Football League player representative for the Atlanta Falcons, the pressure to gain that competitive edge begins in high school and is the start of a vicious cycle.

Pete Rozelle, outgoing commissioner of the NFL, testified on the NFL's effort to combat steroid abuse among its players. College football coaches also told of their efforts to prevent steroid use among their players. Bo Schembechler, head football coach and athletic director at the University of Michigan, spoke of his support for random, unscheduled testing, while Joe Paterno, head football coach at Penn State University, admitted that "we are now finding ourselves with a disease that is spreading." The hearing also featured testimony from: Jay Moyer, NFL executive vice president; Chuck Noll, head coach, Pittsburgh Steelers; Joe Purzycki, head coach, James Madison University; Harold Raymond, head coach, University of Delaware; and Marty Schottenheimer, head coach, Kansas City Chiefs.

III. Discussion

Anabolic steroids are synthetic derivatives of the male sex hormone testosterone. Technically referred to as androgenic-anabolic steroid, steroids occur naturally in the human body and are essential in the normal physiological processes of men and women. Androgens are hormones responsible for the development of male sex characteristics, including the growth of facial hair and the deepening of the voice. The term "anabolic" refers to the constructive or

4

building process of tissue. For the purposes of this report, the term "steroid" shall refer to androgenic-anabolic steroid.

Although androgenic-anabolic steroids have been approved for the treatment of numerous medical conditions, including hypogonadism, certain anemias, breast cancer and angioedema, they remain the least prescribed and the least studied of the steroid hormones.[1]

A. STEROIDS: A HALF-MILLION HIGH SCHOOL USERS

Steroid abuse has become a major drug abuse problem in America. As many as 1 million Americans or more have used or are currently using steroids for nonmedical purposes, primarily to increase athletic performance and improve physical appearance.[2]

Most disturbing, however, is the widespread steroid abuse among high school students and other young people. *Steroid abuse by male high school seniors is nearly as widespread as the use of "crack" cocaine.* The most complete study of this subject found that the number of male high school seniors who had used steroids within the previous 30 days was 75 percent of the number of male seniors who had used crack within the last month.[3] Another nationwide study of 12th grade male students found that 6.6 percent had used steroids.[4]

Taken together, these studies suggest that up to 500,000 male high school students use, or have used, steroids. Worse still, more than one-third of the users began using steroids at the age of 15 or younger; two-thirds had started by the age of 16. And the phenomenon is not limited to any one part of the country. Recent reports from Michigan, Texas, and Arkansas have all found that 5 to 11 percent of high school males admit to having used steroids.[5] These four studies also concluded that 1 to 2 percent of high school girls reported steroid use.

The severity of the steroid abuse problem among young people is compounded by the extremely high percentage of "hard-core" steroid users. Approximately 40 percent of steroid users can be considered "hard-core" users.[6] More than 90 percent of the anabolic steroid users who began at age 15 or younger are repeat-steroid users. "Stacking"—or the simultaneous use of different steroids—is a popular and dangerous pattern of steroid use among teenagers. 44 percent of the high school student users take more than one steroid at a time, and almost two out of five have used both oral and injectable steroids.[7]

---

[1] William N. Taylor, *Hormonal Manipulation: A New Era Of Monstrous Athletes* (Jefferson, North Carolina: McFarland & Co., Inc., 1985), p. 10.
[2] William N. Taylor, "Synthetic Anabolic-Androgenic Steroids: A Plea for Controlled Substance Status," *The Physician and Sportsmedicine* 15: 5 (1987): 140–150; and L.N., Burkett and M.T. Falduto, "Steroid Use By Athletes in a Metropolitan Area," *The Physician and Sportsmedicine* 12 (1984): 69–74.
[3] National Institute on Drug Abuse, "Monitoring the Future Study," 1989.
[4] William E. Buckley et al., "Estimated Prevalence of Anabolic Steroid Use Among High School Seniors," *Journal of the American Medical Association* 260 (December 1988): 3441.
[5] M. Johnson et al., "Anabolic Steroid Use in Adolescent Males," *Pediatrics* (in press); and R. Windsor and D. Dimutru, "Anabolic Steroid Use In Adolescents: Survey," *Medical Science Sports Exercise* (in press); and M. Newman, "Michigan Consortium of Schools Student Surveys," Minnesota: Hazelden Research" Services, 1986, as cited in Charles E. Yesalis, J.E. Wright and J.A. Lombardo, "Anabolic-androgenic Steroids: A Synthesis of Existing Data and Recommendations for Future Research, *Clinical Sports Medicine* 1 (1989): 109–134.
[6] Buckley, p. 3443. For purposes of this report, a "hard-core" user is someone who cycles five or more times, with each cycle lasting 6 to 12 weeks.
[7] Ibid.

5

B. PHYSICAL EFFECTS OF STEROIDS

Teens take steroids because they "work." [8] As medical experts now concede, steroids are effective in promoting muscle growth, although early denials of this fact,[9] unfortunately, have discredited subsequent warnings issued by medical experts about the serious physical and psychological consequences of steroid use. This has been a deadly mistake.

The abuse of steroids has been associated with serious physical disorders. Steroids have been linked to fatal liver and kidney failure.[10] An increased risk of cardio-vascular disorders is also associated with steroid use due to the drug's effect on the balance of high density and low density lipoprotein (HDL/LDL), which result in increased cholesterol levels and high blood pressure.[11]

Changes in sexual characteristics and reproductive functions are common in both female and male athletes who take steroids.[12] Common in female athletes who take steroids are menstrual irregularities, shrinkage of the breasts, increased facial hair, male-pattern baldness, deepening of the voice, and clitoral enlargement.[13] The last four effects in women tend to be irreversible.

In men, steroids reduce the production of luteinizing hormone and follical-stimulating hormone by the pituitary. This can lead to lower levels of circulating testosterone, testicular atrophy, oligospermia (low sperm count), and infertility.[14]

Prolonged steroid use may be particularly harmful to young people. Premature fusion of the long bones from steroids use can result in stunted growth in adolescents and preadolescents.

In sum, the evidence is clear: steroids are dangerous drugs that can permanently disfigure young users—and, in some cases, can take young lives.

C. STEROIDS AND AGGRESSION: A DEADLY MIX

In our society, which is filled with images of beauty, flawlessness, and excellence, steroids hold the promise of perfection. The promise is shattered, however, when individuals are faced with the brutal reality of steroid abuse: steroids not only cause physical damage but can cause severe psychological disorders. Attempting to strengthen the body, a steroid user can destroy the mind.

The psychological effects associated with steroid abuse include increased aggression, violent episodes, paranoia, depression, and

---

[8] Charles E. Yesalis, J.E. Wright, and J.A. Lombardo, "Anabolic-Androgenic Steroids: A Synthesis of Existing Data and Recommendations for Future Research, *Clinical Sports Medicine* 1 (1989): pp. 109–134.

[9] L.A. Golding, J.E. Freydinger and S. S. Fishel, "Weight, Size and Strength—Unchanged With Steroids," *The Physician and Sportsmedicine* 2 (1974): 39–43.

[10] Gary I. Wadler and Brian Hainline, *Drugs and the Athlete: Contemporary Exercise and Sports Medicine* (Philadelphia: F.A. Davis Co., 1989), p. 65, and John R. Bierly, M.D. "Use of Anabolic Steroids by Athletes: Do the Risks Outweigh the Benefits?" *Postgraduate Medicine* 82 (September 1, 1987): 72.

[11] Bierly, ibid. p. 74.

[12] Robert E. Windsor and Daniel Dumitru, "Anabolic Steroid Use By Athletes: How Serious Are the Health Hazards?" *Postgraduate Medicine* 84 (September 15, 1988): 49, and William P. Morgan, ed., "Erogenic Aids and Muscular Performance" (New York: Academic Press, 1972), p. 381, and Terry Todd, "The Steroid Predicament," *Sports Illustrated* 59 (August 1, 1983): p. 71.

[13] Bierly, ibid. p. 74.

[14] Bierly, ibid. p. 72, and Richard H. Strauss, MD., et al., "Side Effects of Anabolic Steroids in Weight-Trained Men," *The Physician and Sportsmedicine* 11: 12 (December 1983): p. 93, and Windsor, p. 47, and Morgan, p. 381.

6

hallucinations.[15] Despite the drastic and sometimes immediate psychological effects of steroid abuse reported by athletes, very few of these side-effects have been adequately researched.

Countless steroid users, however, provide anecdotal accounts of "roid rages"—the increased aggression and irritability associated with steroid use.[16] Numerous accounts of increased aggression and violence by steroids users have been reported:

Glenn Woolstrum, a former deputy sheriff in Clackamas County, Oregon, was obsessed with weight lifting. Woolstrum took three steroids at the same time: anavar, testosterone, and dianabol. Although Woolstrum was known by many to be a pleasant, gentle man, overnight his personality became aggressive and violent. When Woolstrum asked a store owner if he could use her phone, the owner replied, "I should charge all you cops using this phone. You come in here all the time." The next day, angered by the store owner's remark, Woolstrum went back to the store, ordered her into his car at gunpoint and shot her. Today Leslie Myers, the owner of the store, is paralyzed for life.[17]

At age 13, Mike Keys began weight lifting to build his slender frame. By age 17, Mike Keys stood 5'9", weighed 193 pounds, and injected himself daily with testosterone obtained from the local gym. Never satisfied with the results, Mike continued to take steroids, despite pleas from his family to stop. His grades began to slip, he threw temper tantrums, and his mood swings worsened. According to his parents, on the morning of December 16, 1988, Mike was fine, even cheerful. That evening Blaine Keys discovered his son's body lying next to his weight-lifting equipment—dead from a suicide.[18]

At Harvard Medical School, Dr. Harrison G. Pope, Jr., an associate professor of psychiatry, and Dr. David L. Katz, a psychiatrist, conducted one of the leading scientific studies on mental disorders associated with steroid use.[19] Of the 41 bodybuilders and football players studied, approximately one-third suffered mild to severe forms of mental disturbances. All 39 men and 2 women used steroids, usually obtained from the black market. The researchers concluded that "major psychiatric symptoms may be a common adverse effect of these drugs."[20]

More than 10 percent of Pope's and Katz' subjects experienced psychotic symptoms, and approximately 25 percent of the athletes

[15] Todd, p. 71, and Jodie Slothower, "Mean Mental Muscles: The Psychological Price of Steroids," Health, January 1988, p. 20, and Taylor, "Steroid Use Among Health Club Athletes," p. 158; Bierly, p. 71; Strauss, "Side Effects of Anabolic Steroids in Weight-Trained Men," p. 93; Taylor, Hormonal Manipulation, p. 16; Wadler, p. 66; Windsor, p. 47; and Betsy Carpenter, "A Game of Cat and Mouse: There's a New Olympic Event Pitting Athletes Against Drug Busters," U.S. News & World Report, October 10, 1988, p. 38.
[16] W.J. Annitto and W.A. Layman, "Anabolic Steroids and Acute Schizophrenic Episode," Journal of Clinical Psychiatry 41 (1980): 143; and Montgomery Brower and Carol Azizian, "Steroids Build Mike Keys Up; Then They Tore Him Down," People, March 20, 1989: pp. 107-108.
[17] Sixty Minutes, CBS News, "Beefing Up The Force," November 5, 1989.
[18] Brower and Azizian, ibid. p. 108.
[19] Harrison G. Pope, Jr., and David L. Katz, "Affective and Psychotic Symptoms Associated With Anabolic Steroid Use," The American Journal of Psychiatry 145 (4) (1988): 487-90.
[20] Terrence Monmaney with Kate Robins, "The Insanity of Steroid Abuse: The Drug Can Give Athletes Major Mental Problems," Newsweek, May 23, 1988, p. 75, quoted in Harrison G. Pope, Jr., and David L. Katz, "Affective and Psychotic Symptoms Associated With Anabolic Steroid Use," The American Journal of Psychiatry 145 (4) (1988): p. 487.

7

experienced manic symptoms, including an inflated self-esteem, recklessness, and a feeling of invincibility. Dan, an obsessed steroid user who went from 140 pounds to 270 pounds in 3 years, borrowed $1,500 from the bank to support his steroid habit. Convinced he was immortal, he drove a car at 40 mph into a tree, while a friend videotaped him. Since giving up steroids, Dan's destructive urges have disappeared.

Dr. William Taylor, in his study of the psychological alterations associated with anabolic steroid use, argues that the psychological damage continues even after steroid use has stopped. According to Taylor:

> There is no doubt that the use of anabolic steroids, even in low doses, potentiates certain psychological behavior in men. And with men athletes who are using moderate and larger doses of anabolic steroids, total personality changes may take place, both while on the anabolics and after the anabolics are stopped.[21]

And a yet-to-be-released study—the only controlled study of personality disorders among steroid users ever conducted—will demonstrate that steroid users, like alcoholics have an increased risk of developing personality disorders.[22] Steroid users experience frequent episodes of depression, anxiety, and hostility during cycles of steroid use.

D. STEROIDS ARE ADDICTIVE

The leading study of the addictive nature of steroid dependence cites the following four symptoms: (1) loss of control; (2) continued use despite adverse consequences; (3) tolerance; and (4) withdrawal.[23] Almost every leading expert in the field agrees: steroids are addictive.

In one case a 24-year-old noncompetitive weight lifter sought professional help for his dependence on anabolic steroids.[24] After a year of anabolic steroid use, the patient suffered from severe mood swings and temper outbursts. Two weeks before he was admitted to a hospital emergency room, the man separated from his wife of 5 years. The night before his admission, he had thoughts of suicide. When he attempted to stop taking anabolic steroids, he became depressed and weak; his craving for the "high" he felt when he took the drug was unbearable. After 5 days at the hospital, the man signed out against medical advice.

The perception by the user of anabolic steroids that the drug enables them to become stronger and bulkier is a key element of anabolic steroid dependence. And part of the difficulty in quitting the steroids habit is that users think they look better and perform better when they take the drug.[25] According to leading experts, the

[21] Taylor, *Hormonal Manipulation*, p. 16.
[22] W.R. Yates, P.J. Perry, and K.H. Andersen "Illicit Anabolic Steroid Use: A Controlled Personality Study," *Acta Psychiatrica Scand* 1990 (in press).
[23] Kirk J. Brower, M.D., "Rehabilitation for Anabolic-Androgenic Steroid Dependence," based on a paper presented at the National Consensus Meeting on Anabolic/Androgenic Steroids, in press, pp. 4–5.
[24] Brower, et al., "Anabolic-Androgenic Steroid Dependence", p. 31.
[25] Id.

8

overreliance on the body for self-worth is an element that differentiates anabolic steroid abusers from other drug abusers.[26]

Prominent surveys of male high school seniors who took steroids reveal similar perceptions. More than 50 percent of the users surveyed believed their strength to be above average. Only 27.8 percent of the nonusers felt their strength to be greater than average. Similarly, almost 40 percent of the users felt themselves to be in "excellent" health, compared to 24.1 percent of the nonusers.[27]

Several medical researchers warn that the current trend of anabolic steroid dependence is particularly troubling in adolescent athletes.[28] Adolescents are especially vulnerable to adverse effects because of their developing nervous and skeletal systems. Therefore, the psychological side effects may be intensified in the adolescent because he or she may not have the psychological maturity to cope with the mood changes associated with anabolic steroids.[29] At least one author has suggested that adolescent males may prove to be especially vulnerable to addiction, because its use is associated with low self-esteem, a characteristic common in adolescents.[30]

One study found a shocking attitude among adolescent habitual steroid users [31] who began taking anabolic steroids at a young age: when these users were asked if they would stop using anabolic steroids if it was "proven beyond a doubt" that they would lead to permanent sterility, liver cancer, and a heart attack, approximately 40 to 50 percent responded *that they would "definitely" continue to take anabolic steroids despite the health risks.*

The reported use of anabolic steroids suggests that there may be a psychological and physical basis for anabolic steroid dependence. Although physical dependence has been hyphothesized, few documented cases exist. One theory of physical dependence states that withdrawal symptoms are a response to lower levels of testosterone in the body after anabolic steroid use has stopped.[32] Another theory suggests that anabolic steroids increase opioids, or pleasure producing stimulants, that originate within the brain.

Psychological addiction to steroids includes the desire by some to become bigger and stronger. When an athlete watches his body size and strength decrease during withdrawal, his confidence and self-esteem decrease. Psychological addiction to anabolic steroids can be so severe that suicidal depression can occur during withdrawal. Experts warn that "close professional monitoring is required" during this period to avoid what they perceive to be "life-threatening" withdrawal symptoms.[33]

    [26] Brower, "Rehabilitation", p. 2.
    [27] Buckley, p. 3443.
    [28] Wayne V. Moore, Ph.D., M.D., "Anabolic Steroid Use in Adolescence, *Journal of the American Medical Association* 260 (December 16, 1988): 3486; Windsor and Dimutru, p. 48; and Brower, et al., "Anabolic-Androgenic Steroid Dependence," p. 31.
    [29] Brower et al., "Rehabilitation," p. 32.
    [30] Wayne V. Moore, ibid., p. 3486.
    [31] Charles E. Yesalis, et al., "Anabolic Steroid Use: Indications of Habituation Among Adolescents," *Journal of Drug Education* 19(2) (1989): 103–116.
    [32] Brower, MD., "Rehabilitation," p. 9.
    [33] Brower, "Rehabilitation," p. 10.

9

E. THE FAILURE OF CURRENT EFFORTS TO FIGHT STEROID ABUSE

Current enforcement efforts to control the misuse of steroids are clearly inadequate. Last year, the General Accounting Office conducted a year-long investigation into the steroid problem in America pursuant to the steroid provisions authored by Senator Biden in the 1988 Anti-Drug Abuse Act. Among the major findings in the GAO report is that the illegal steroids trade is a $300 million to $400 million a year industry.

Based on seizures of illicit drugs and other information, the Justice Department believes that the supply of black-market steroids is divided evenly between three sources: clandestine U.S. laboratories; imports smuggled into the United States from foreign countries; and diversions from legitimate U.S. steroid manufacturers.

The U.S. Food and Drug Administration is currently charged with the responsibility for enforcing steroids control laws. However, according to the FDA, only 38 full-time personnel were devoted to steroids enforcement efforts in 1988. In addition, FDA personnel have neither the expertise nor the authority to conduct the complex and time-consuming investigations that are necessary to attack the increasingly sophisticated illegal steroid trade. For example, FDA investigators are not authorized to carry firearms, execute search warrants, or conduct undercover investigations.

The current regulatory scheme is also inadequate to control the diversion of legally produced steroids into the illicit market. The GAO found the steroids-control system ripe for abuse:

The FDA does not require manufacturers to submit information on the amount of steroids produced or sold in the United States.

The FDA does not collect information on the amount of steroids legally prescribed by physicians.

The FDA has no estimate of whether steroid production is increasing or decreasing, whether prescriptions have increased or decreased, nor the amount of diversion occurring in the steroid industry.

This is why S. 1829 is desperately needed legislation. Adding anabolic steroids to schedule II of the Controlled Substances Act would impose tight record-keeping and production controls on steroids. Steroids manufacturers and distributors will be required to comply with production and distribution regulations established by the Attorney General. For example, producers will be required to store steroids in secure facilities. Moreover, distributors will be required to keep detailed records on steroids shipments and make those records available to Drug Enforcement Administration investigators.

S. 1829 will also address the problem of clandestine steroids production and illegal steroids smuggling. By adding steroids to the list of schedule II controlled substances, the Steroid Trafficking Act of 1990 will give the Nation's lead drug-fighting agency—the Drug Enforcement Administration—the jurisdiction to investigate steroids-related offenses. Although DEA is already pressed in its fight against other illegal drug trafficking, DEA is better positioned to commit the resources and expertise necessary to mount an aggres-

10

sive national crackdown on steroid trafficking than are the handful of steroids personnel at the FDA.

In addition, adding steroids to schedule II will significantly increase the penalties for steroid offenses. Under current law, steroid dealers at most face up to 3 years imprisonment, regardless of the quantity involved. Under S. 1829, steroid pushers would face up to 20 years imprisonment and fines of up to $1 million. Similar penalties would apply to illegal steroids smuggling, under the Controlled Substances Import and Export Act (21 U.S.C. 961).

IV. Vote of the Committee

On March 8, 1990, the Committee on the Judiciary by unanimous consent approved an amendment in the nature of a substitute by Senators Biden and Thurmond to S. 1829, and ordered the bill, the Steroid Trafficking Act of 1990, as amended, favorably reported.

V. Text of S. 1829, as Reported

[101st Cong., 1st sess.]

A BILL To amend the Controlled Substances Act to further restrict the use of steroids and human growth hormones

Be it enacted by the Senate and House of Representatives of the United States of America in Congress assembled,

SECTION 1. SHORT TITLE.

This Act may be cited as the "Steroid Trafficking Act of 1990".

TITLE I—ANABOLIC STEROIDS

SEC. 101. STEROIDS LISTED AS CONTROLLED SUBSTANCES.

(a) Adding Steroids to Schedule II of the Controlled Substances Act.—Subdivision (b) of schedule II of section 202(c) of the Controlled Substances Act (21 U.S.C. 812(c)) is amended by inserting at the end thereof the following:

"(22) Anabolic steroids.".

(b) Definition.—Section 102 of the Controlled Substances Act (21 U.S.C. 802) is amended by adding at the end thereof the following:

"(41) The term 'anabolic steroids' means—

"(A) any drug that is chemically and pharmacologically related to the male hormone testosterone and that promotes or purports to promote muscle growth, including any amount of the following chemical designations and their salts, esters, and isomers:

"(i) boldenone,
"(ii) chlorotestosterone,
"(iii) clostebol,
"(iv) dehydrochlormethyltestosterone,
"(v) dihydrotestosterone,
"(vi) drostanolone,
"(vii) ethylestrenol,
"(viii) floxymesterone,
"(ix) formabulone,
"(x) mesterolone,
"(xi) methandienone,

11

"(xii) methandranone,
"(xiii) methandriol,
"(xiv) methandrostenolone,
"(xv) methenolone
"(xvi) methyltestosterone,
"(xvii) mibolerne,
"(xviii) nandrolone,
"(xix) norethandrolone,
"(xx) oxandrolone,
"(xxi) oxymesterone,
"(xxii) oxymetholone,
"(xxiii) stanolone,
"(xxiv) stanozolol,
"(xxv) testolactone,
"(xxvi) testosterone,
"(xxvii) trenbolone, and

"(B) any substance which is purported, represented or labeled as being or containing any amount of any drug described in subparagraph (A), or any substance labeled as being or containing any such drug.

As used in schedule II, such term shall not include an anabolic steroid which is expressly intended for administration through implants to cattle or other nonhuman species and which has been approved by the Secretary of Health and Human Services for such administration, except that if any person prescribes, dispenses, or distributes such steroid for human use, such person shall be considered to have prescribed, dispensed, distributed a steroid in schedule II of this Act.".

(c) EFFECT OF SCHEDULING ON PRESCRIPTIONS.—Any prescription for anabolic steroids subject to refill on or after the date of enactment of the amendments made by this section may be refilled without restriction under section 309(a) of the Controlled Substances Act (21 U.S.C. 829(a)).

(d) EFFECTIVE DATE.—This section and the amendments made by this section shall take effect 90 days after the date of enactment of this Act.

SEC. 102. REGULATIONS BY ATTORNEY GENERAL.

(a) ABUSE POTENTIAL.—The Attorney General, upon the recommendation of the Secretary of Health and Human Services, shall, by regulation, exempt any compound, mixture, or preparation containing a substance in paragraph (41) of section 102 of the Controlled Substances Act (as added by section 101 of this Act) from the application of all or any part of the Controlled Substances Act if, because of its concentration, preparation, mixture or delivery system, it has no significant potential for abuse, and, at a minimum, shall exempt estrogens, progestins and corticosteroids.

(b) DRUGS FOR TREATMENT OF RARE DISEASES.—If the Attorney General finds that a drug listed in paragraph (41) of section 102 of the Controlled Substances Act (as added by section 101 of this Act) is—

(1) approved by the Food and Drug Administration as an accepted treatment for a rare disease or condition, as defined in

12

section 526 of the Federal Food, Drug, and Cosmetic Act (21 U.S.C. 360bb); and

(2) does not have a significant potential for abuse, the Attorney General may exempt such drug from any production regulations otherwise issued under the Controlled Substances Act as may be necessary to ensure adequate supplies of such drug for medical purposes.

(c) DATE OF ISSUANCE OF REGULATIONS.—The Attorney General shall issue regulations implementing this section not later than 45 days after the date of enactment of this Act, except that the regulations required under subsection 102(a) shall be issued not later than 180 days after the date of enactment of this Act.

TITLE II—HUMAN GROWTH HORMONE

SEC. 201. AMENDMENT TO THE FOOD, DRUG AND COSMETIC ACT.

Section 303 of the Federal Food, Drug and Cosmetic Act (21 U.S.C. 333) is amended by inserting a new subsection (e) as follows:

"(e)(1) Except as provided in paragraph (2), whoever knowingly distributes, or possesses with intent to distribute, human growth hormone for any use in humans other than the treatment of a disease or other recognized medical condition pursuant to the order of a physician is guilty of an offense punishable by not more than 5 years in prison, such fines as are authorized by title 18, United States Code, or both.

"(2) Whoever commits any offense set forth in paragraph (1) and such offense involves an individual under 18 years of age is punishable by not more than 10 years imprisonment, such fines as are authorized by title 18, United States Code, or both.

"(3) Any conviction for a violation of paragraphs (1) and (2) of this subsection shall be considered a felony violation of the Controlled Substances Act for the purposes of forfeiture under section 413 of such Act.

"(4) As used in this subsection the term 'human growth hormone' means—

"(A) somatrem, somatropin, and any of their analogs; and

"(B) any substance which is purported, represented or labeled as being or containing any amount of any drug described in clause (A)(i), or any substance labeled as being or containing any such drug; and

"(5) The Drug Enforcement Administration is authorized to investigate offenses punishable by this subsection.".

SEC. 202. CONVICTION OF SECTION 303(e) OF THE FEDERAL FOOD, DRUG, AND COSMETIC ACT.

Section 2401 of the Anti-Drug Abuse Act of 1988 (Public Law 100–690; 102 Stat. 4181) is repealed.

VI. SECTION-BY-SECTION ANALYSIS

Section 1 sets forth the short title of the bill as the "Steroid Trafficking Act of 1990."

13

TITLE I—ANABOLIC STEROIDS

Section 101(a) adds anabolic steroids to schedule II of the Controlled Substances Act (21 U.S.C. 812(c)), the same schedule under which cocaine and opium are controlled. The Controlled Substances Act sets forth specific criteria to determine under what schedule a specific substance should be controlled. The criteria for placing a substance under schedule II include:

(a) The drug or other substance has a high potential for abuse.

(b) The drug or other substance has a currently accepted medical use in treatment in the United States or a currently accepted medical use with severe restrictions.

(c) Abuse of the drug or other substance may lead to severe psychological and physical dependence.

The committee believes that steroids satisfy each of the criteria for control under schedule II. First, steroids have a high potential for abuse. An estimated 1 million Americans use anabolic steroids for nonmedical reasons; 500,000 of these users are highschool children. Second, steroids are indicated for the treatment of certain medical conditions, including specific forms of anemia and reproductive disorders. The committee notes, however, that with the development of new drugs and given the harmful side effects associated with steroids therapy, steroids are the primary or favored pharmacological treatment for a decreasing number of medical disorders. Finally, steroid abuse may lead to severe psychological and physical dependence. As noted in the discussion section, numerous medical and public health experts have found that steroids can lead to severe psychological addiction. For example, Dr. Charles Yesalis, a leading steroids expert at Penn State University, found that 40 percent of the male high school students who use steroids were "hard-core" users. A limited number of studies have also linked steroids abuse to physical dependence. The committee concludes that the abuse potential of steroids is similar to that of cocaine hydrochloride and other so-called hard drugs, and that steroids should be regulated under the safeguards and controls of schedule II substances.

Section 101(b) creates a new subsection (41) of section 102 of the Controlled Substances Act (21 U.S.C. 802), which provides a new definition for "anabolic steroids." To be classified as an anabolic steroid, and drug must be both chemically and pharmacologically related to the male hormone testosterone, and the drug must promote or purport to promote muscle growth. Section 101(b) contains a list of 27 chemicals that are to be considered anabolic steroids under the Controlled Substances Act. The list, however, is not exclusive. Any drug that meets the general definition is paragraph (A) of the new subsection (41), except human growth hormone and subject to the exemptions specified in section 102 of the bill, shall be considered an anabolic steroid. Paragragh (B) of the new subsection (41) expressly provides that counterfeit drugs that are purported, represented or labeled as containing any amount of a drug described in paragraph (A) shall be considered anabolic steroids. However, the term anabolic steroid does not include anabolic steroids that are expressly intended for use in animals and approved for

14

such purposes by the Secretary of Health and Human Services, unless the drug is distributed for human use. In these circumstances, the drug would be considered an anabolic steroid under schedule II.

Section 101(c) sets forth an exemption under section 309(a) of the Controlled Substances Act for prescripitons subject to refill on or after the date of enactment of section 101 of the bill.

Section 101(d) provides that the effective date of section 101 shall be 90 days after the date of enactment. The committee believes that this period provides sufficent time for Federal agencies to implement their responsibilities under this act and for private industry to come into compliance with the requirements of this act.

Section 102(a) requires the Attorney General to issue regulations that exempt any compound, mixture or preparation containing a substance in the new paragraph (41) from the application of the Controlled Substances Act if, because of its concentration, preparation, mixture or delivery system, has no significant potential for abuse. The Attorney General shall base such exemptions on the recommendation of the Secretary of Health and Human Services. At a minimum, section 102(a) authorizes and directs the Attorney General to issue regulations that exempt estrogens, progenstins and corticosteroids from the application of the Controlled Substances Act. These substances shall not be considered anabolic steroids under the new paragraph (41) of section 102 of the Controlled Substances Act. The committee recognizes that many compounds, mixtures and preparations that contain steroids have no abuse potential, such as oral contraceptives. Although these substances shall not be controlled under the Controlled Substances Act, they will continue to be regulated under the provisions of the Federal Food, Drug and Cosmetic Act.

Section 102(b) authorizes the Attorney General to exempt any substance under the new paragraph (41) and any production regulations otherwise issued under the Controlled Substances Act as may be necessary to ensure adequate supplies of such drug for medical purposes. The Attorney General however, may only exempt substances that meet the following criteria: (1) the substance must be accepted treatment for a rare disease or condition; and (2) the substance must have no significant potential for abuse. The committee is concerned that the significant costs associated with the production controls imposed on schedule II drugs may make the production of steroids related-drugs for rare diseases excessively expensive to patients or lead pharmaceutical firms, to stop production entirely. Section 102(b) is intended to balance the need to ensure adequate medical supplies of such drugs with the need to prevent the abuse of anabolic steroids, particularly among young people.

Section 102(c) provides that the regulations required under section 102(a) shall be issued not later than 180 days after the date of enactment. The regulations required under subsection (b) shall be issued not later than 45 days after the date of enactment.

15

TITLE II—HUMAN GROWTH HORMONE

Section 201 amends the Federal Food, Drug and Cosmetic Act (21 U.S.C. 333) to create a felony offense for trafficking in human growth hormone (HGH). Given the separate regime established under title II to control illegal HGH distribution, HGH shall not be considered an anabolic steroid under title I. Specifically, section 201 creates a new subsection 303(e) of the Food, Drug and Cosmetic Act to make it a felony punishable by up to 5 years imprisonment for knowingly distributing, or possessing with intent to distribute, HGH for any use in humans other than the treatment of a disease or other recognized medical condition pursuant to the order of a physican. Paragraph (2) of the new subsection 333(e) of the Food, Drug and Cosmetic Act doubles the penalty for illegally distributing HGH to any person under the age of 18.

The new paragraph (3) authorizes Federal law enforcement agencies to seize and forfeit the proceeds and instrumentalities of illegal HGH distribution in the same manner and under the same procedures as authorized under section 413 of the Controlled Substances Act.

The new paragraph (4) sets forth the definition of "human growth hormone." HGH is defined as somatrem, somatropin and any analog of these substances. The definition also includes any substance that is purported, represented or labeled as being or containing any amount of HGH.

The new paragraph (5) authorizes the Drug Enforcement Administration to investigate violations involving the illegal distribution or possession of HGH and to pursue forfeiture actions under paragraph (3). Given the close link between illegal sales of anabolic steroids and HGH, this provision is needed to ensure that DEA has full authority to investigate and arrest persons for illegal distribution or possession of HGH.

Section 202 repeals section 2401 of the Anti-Drug Abuse Act. This subsection is no longer necessary, given the new and tighter restrictions and penalties contained in titles I and II of this bill.

VII. COST ESTIMATE

U.S. CONGRESS,
CONGRESSIONAL BUDGET OFFICE,
Washington, DC, March 20, 1990.

Hon. JOSEPH R. BIDEN, Jr.,
Chairman, Committee on the Judiciary,
U.S. Senate, Washington, DC.

DEAR MR. CHAIRMAN: The Congressional Budget Office has reviewed S. 1829, the Steroid Trafficking Act of 1990, as ordered reported by the Senate Committee on the Judiciary, March 8, 1990.

CBO estimates that S. 1829, if enacted, would increase costs to the federal government by roughly $250,000 annually, assuming appropriation of the necessary funds. This estimate is based on information provided by the Drug Enforcement Administration (DEA) and the Food and Drug Administration (FDA). S. 1829 would amend the Controlled Substances Act to define certain anabolic steroids as controlled substances. The bill would also modify the

16

criminal penalties for illegally distributing human growth hormone.

Under this bill, the DEA would have primary responsibility for regulating these substances; the FDA has this responsibility under current law. CBO expects that the DEA would need roughly $250,000 annually to issue regulations required by the bill and maintain records in accordance with its regulatory responsibilities under the Controlled Substances Act. If the DEA were also to undertake an active investigatory and enforcement role, costs would be higher. There would be no significant offsetting change in costs to the FDA, because that agency spends little for this purpose.

Enactment of this bill would not affect the budgets of state or local governments.

If you wish further details on this estimate, we will be pleased to provide them. The CBO staff contact is Michael Sieverts, who can be reached at 226-2860.

Sincerely,

ROBERT F. HALE,
(For Robert D. Reischauer).

VIII. REGULATORY IMPACT STATEMENT

In compliance with subsection (b) of paragraph 11 of rule XXVI of the Standing Rules of the Senate, the committee finds that the bill would have a limited regulatory impact.

Manufacturers, producers and distributors of steroids will be required to meet the record-keeping and production control requirements for schedule II controlled substances. These requirements include: registering with the Drug Enforcement Administration; storing and producing steroids in secure facilities; acquiring a production or distribution quota from DEA; and compiling and maintaining records on shipments of steroids. Since DEA already has promulgated regulations concerning the manufacture, production and distribution of schedule II controlled substances, only minor modifications or additions should be required to cover the addition of steroids to schedule II.

The bill requires the Attorney General to issue two specific sets of regulations. Section 102(a) of the bill requires the Attorney General to promulgate regulations to exempt any compound, mixture, or preparation containing a steroid if, because of its concentration, preparation, mixture or delivery system, it has no significant potential for abuse. Section 102(b) requires the Attorney General to issue regulations that exempt certain drugs in the new paragraph (41) of section 102 of the Controlled Substances Act from any production regulations as may be necessary to ensure adequate supplies of the drug for medical purposes. According to the Congressional Budget Office, the cost of issuing the regulations necessary and required under the bill is approximately $250,000.

IX. CHANGES IN EXISTING LAW

In compliance with paragraph 12 of rule XXVI of the Standing Rules of the Senate, changes in existing law made by S. 1829, as reported, are shown as follows (existing law proposed to be omitted

17

is enclosed in black brackets; new matter is printed in italic, existing law in which no change is proposed is shown in roman):

UNITED STATES CODE

TITLE 21—FOOD AND DRUGS

*   *   *   *   *   *   *

CHAPTER 9—FEDERAL FOOD, DRUG, AND COSMETIC ACT

*   *   *   *   *   *   *

§ 333. Penalties.

*   *   *   *   *   *   *

(d) EXCEPTIONS INVOLVING MISBRANDED FOOD.—No person shall be subject to the penalties of subsection (a) of this section for a violation of section 331 of this title involving misbranded food if the violation exists solely because the food is misbranded under section 343(a)(2) of this title because of its advertising, and no person shall be subject to the penalties of subsection (b) of this section for such a violation unless the violation is committed with the intent to defraud or mislead.

(e) ANABOLIC STEROIDS.—[(1) Except as provided in paragraph (2), any person who distributes or possesses with the intent to distribute any anabolic steroid for any use in humans other than the treatment of disease pursuant to the order of a physician shall be imprisoned for not more than three years or fined under title 18, United States Code, or both.

[(2) Any person who distributes or possesses with the intent to distribute to an individual under 18 years of age, any anabolic steroid for any use in humans other than the treatment of disease pursuant to the order of a physician shall be imprisoned for not more than six years or fined under title 18, United States Code, or both.] *(1) Except as provided in paragraph (2), whoever knowingly distributes, or possesses with intent to distribute, human growth hormone for any use in humans other than the treatment of a disease or other recognized medical condition pursuant to the order of a physician is guilty of an offense punishable by not more than 5 years in prison, such fines as are authorized by title 18, United States Code, or both.*

(2) Whoever commits any offense set forth in paragraph (1) and such offense involves an individual under 18 years of age is punishable by not more than 10 years imprisonment, such fines as are authorized by title 18, United States Code, or both.

(3) Any conviction for a violation of paragraphs (1) and (2) of this subsection shall be considered a felony violation of the Controlled Substances Act for the purposes of forfeiture under section 413 of such Act.

(4) As used in this subsection the term "human growth hormone" means—

(A) somatrem, somatropin, and any of their analogs; and

18

    (B) any substance which is purported, represented or labeled as being or containing any amount of any drug described in clause (A)(i), or any substance labeled as being or containing any such drug; and

    (5) The Drug Enforcement Administration is authorized to investigate offenses punishable by this subsection.

    *   *   *   *   *   *   *

CHAPTER 13—DRUG ABUSE PREVENTION AND CONTROL

    *   *   *   *   *   *   *

§ 802. Definitions.

    *   *   *   *   *   *   *

    (40) The term "chemical mixture" means a combination of two or more chemical substances, at least one of which is not a listed precursor chemical or a listed essential chemical, except that such term does not include any combination of a listed precursor chemical or a listed essential chemical with another chemical that is present solely as an impurity.

    (41) The term "anabolic steroids" means—

        (A) any drug that is chemically and pharmacologically related to the male hormone testosterone and that promotes or purports to promote muscle growth, including any amount of the following chemical designations and their salts, esters, and isomers:

            (i) boldenone,
            (ii) chlorotestosterone,
            (iii) clostebol,
            (iv) dehydrochlormethyltestosterone,
            (v) dihydrotestosterone,
            (vi) drostanolone,
            (vii) ethylestrenol,
            (viii) fluoxymesterone,
            (ix) formobulone,
            (x) mesterolone,
            (xi) methandienone,
            (xii) methandranone,
            (xiii) methandriol,
            (xiv) methandrostenolone,
            (xv) methenolone,
            (xvi) methyltestosterone,
            (xvii) mibolerone,
            (xviii) nandrolone,
            (xix) norethandrolone,
            (xx) oxandrolone,
            (xxi) oxymesterone,
            (xxii) oxymetholone,
            (xxiii) stanolone,
            (xxiv) stanozolol,
            (xxv) testolactone,
            (xxvi) testosterone,
            (xxvii) trenbolone, and

19

(B) any substance which is purported, represented or labeled
as being or containing any amount of any drug described in
subparagraph (A), or any substance labeled as being or contain-
ing any such drug.
As used in schedule II, such term shall not include an anabolic steroid which is expressly intended for administration through implants to cattle or other nonhuman species and which has been approved by the Secretary of Health and Human Services for such administration, except that if any person prescribes, dispenses, or distributes such steroid for human use, such person shall be considered
to have prescribed, dispensed, or distributed a steroid in schedule II
of this Act.

*   *   *   *   *   *   *

§ 812. Schedules of controlled substances.

*   *   *   *   *   *   *

Schedule II

(a) Unless specifically excepted or unless listed in another schedule, any of the following substances whether produced directly or
indirectly by extraction from substances of vegetable origin, or in-
dependently by means of chemical synthesis, or by a combination
of extraction and chemical synthesis:

(1) Opium and opiate, and any salt, compound, derivative, or
preparation of opium or opiate.

(2) Any salt, compound, derivative, or preparation thereof
which is chemically equivalent or identical with any of the
substances referred to in clause (1), except that these substances shall not include the isoquinoline alkaloids of opium.

(3) Opium poppy and poppy straw.

(4) Coca leaves and any salt, compound, derivative, or preparation of coca leaves, and any salt, compound, derivative, or
preparation thereof which is chemically equivalent or identical
with any of these substances, except that the substances shall
not include decocainized coca leaves or extraction of coca
leaves, which extractions do not contain cocaine or ecgonine.

(b) Unless specifically excepted or unless listed in another schedule, any of the following opiates, including their isomers, esters,
ethers, salts, and salts of isomers, esters and ethers, whenever the
existence of such isomers, esters, ethers, and salts is possible within
the specific chemical designation:

(1) Alphaprodine.

(2) Anileridine.

(3) Bezitramide.

(4) Dihydrocodeine.

(5) Diphenoxylate.

(6) Fentanyl.

(7) Isomethadone.

(8) Levomethorphan.

(9) Levorphanol.

(10) Metazocine.

(11) Methadone.

20

(12) Methadone-Intermediate, 4-cyano-2-dimethylamino-4, 4-diphenyl butane.

(13) Moramide-Intermediate, 2-methyl-3-morpholino-1, 1-diphynylpropane-carboxylic acid.

(14 Pethidine.

(15) Pethidine-Intermediate-A, 4-cyano-1-methyl-4-phenylpiperidene.

(16) Pethidine-Intermediate-B, ethyl-4-phenylpiperidine-4-carboxylate.

(17) Pethidine-Intermediate-C, 1-methyl-4-phenylpiperidene 4-carboxylic acid.

(18) Phenazocine.

(19) Piminodine.

(20) Racemethorphan.

(21) Racemorphan.

(22) Anabolic steroids.

*   *   *   *   *   *   *

ANTI-DRUG ABUSE ACT OF 1989

(Public Law 100–690)

*   *   *   *   *   *   *

TITLE I—COORDINATION OF NATIONAL DRUG POLICY

*   *   *   *   *   *   *

Subtitle E—Provisions Relating to Certain Drugs

[SEC. 2401. FORFEITURE AND ILLEGAL TRAFFICKING IN STEROIDS.

[Any conviction for a violation of section 303(e) of the Federal Food, Drug, and Cosmetic Act (21 U.S.C. 333(e)), or any other provision of that Act, involving an anabolic steroid or a human growth hormome shall be considered, for purposes of section 413 of the Controlled Substances Act (21 U.S.C. 853), a conviction for a violation of title II of the Comprehensive Drug Abuse Prevention and Control Act of 1970, if such violation of the Federal Food, Drug, and Cosmetic Act is punishable by imprisonment for more than one year.]

*   *   *   *   *   *   *

Appendix 2

Statement
of the
American Medical Association.

to the

Committee on the Judiciary
United States Senate

RE: Scheduling of Anabolic Steroids

April 3, 1989

American Medical Association
535 N. Dearborn Street
Chicago, Illinois 60610

Department of Federal Legislation
Division of Legislative Activities
(312)   645-4775

72

Principal Points

of the

American Medical Association

to the

Committee on the Judiciary
United States Senate

RE: Scheduling of Anabolic Steroids

April 3, 1989

The AMA recognizes and is concerned over the fact that steroid abuse
is a significant problem. Steroids, however, have accepted medical
use in the treatment of several medical conditions, including certain
anemias, hereditary angioedema, and breast cancer. The adverse
health effects associated with steroid misuse include: oligospermia;
temporary infertility; gynecomastia and liver pathology, including
abnormal liver function; cholestatis; peliosis hepatis; hepatic
adenomas; and hepatocellular carcinoma. In addition, steroid abuse
may result in increased irritability and aggressiveness.

Anabolic steroids do not meet the statutory criteria for scheduling
under Schedule I of the CSA. First, anabolic steroids have an
accepted medical use in medical practice. Moreover, anabolic
steroids can be used safely under medical supervision. Second, abuse
of steroids does not lead to physical or psychological dependence as
also is required for scheduling under the other schedules of the CSA.

Scheduling of anabolic steroids would not adequately address the
problem of abuse of these drugs because it would not affect the major
illicit sources of the drug - shipments from foreign countries and
from veterinary supply houses.

The AMA opposes the enactment of federal legislation to schedule
steroids under the Controlled Substances Act (CSA). The preferred
and appropriate method for scheduling or rescheduling a drug is
through the regulatory process already established by existing law.
Using the legislative process to schedule drugs would inappropriately
preempt a well-developed regulatory program designed specifically to
deal with scientific and medical issues.

The existing regulatory mechanism for drug scheduling, which utilizes
the expertise of the Food and Drug Administration and the Drug
Enforcement Administration, has proven to be a highly satisfactory
means of reviewing and evaluating drugs for almost twenty years.

73

More appropriate and effective approaches to combat steroid abuse
are available. These approaches include enforcement of the
recently increased criminal penalty for selling steroids without a
prescription, and educating the public concerning the harmful
health effects of steroid abuse.

74

STATEMENT

of the

AMERICAN MEDICAL ASSOCIATION

to the

Committee on the Judiciary
United States Senate

Presented by

Edward L. Langston, MD

RE: Scheduling of Anabolic Steroids

April 3, 1989

Mr. Chairman and Members of the Committee:

My name is Edward L. Langston, MD. I am a physician specializing in
family practice in Indianapolis, Indiana and I also an alternate delegate
to the American Medical Association's House of Delegates. Accompanying
me is Tom Wolff of the AMA's Department of Federal Legislation. The AMA
is pleased to present this testimony concerning the issue of whether
anabolic steroids should be scheduled under the Controlled Substances Act.

Mr. Chairman, it is important to understand that anabolic steroids do
have an appropriate role in the treatment of several medical conditions,
including certain anemias, hereditary angioedema and breast cancer.
Moreover, they can be safely used by patients under medical supervision.
Thus, while we are very much concerned with abuse of these drugs, we do
not believe that the answer is to legislatively schedule them under the

75

Controlled Substances Act (CSA). We also believe that prior to any further legislation regarding steroids, a thorough evaluation should be conducted of the effect of the steroid provisions of the Anti-Drug Abuse Act of 1988.

Non-Medical Uses and Adverse Effects of Steroids

Anabolic steroids are synthetic androgens, or male hormones, that have been used and abused by athletes for more than two decades to achieve an increase in body mass, muscle tissue and strength. Steroids can easily be obtained on the black market through gymnasiums and mail order sources. Although their prevalence is difficult to assess accurately, their use is believed to be widespread at all levels of athletic activity. Steroid abuse is particularly common among athletes in strength sports (e.g., weight lifters, body builders, shot putters, and discus and javelin throwers). Increased use of anabolic steroids among weight-trained women athletes has been reported, and these hormones have a more significant effect on the muscular development of females than of males.

A number of adverse effects are associated with use of steroids. These effects include: oligospermia; temporary infertility; gynecomastia and liver pathology including abnormal liver function; cholestatis; peliosis hepatis; hepatic adenomas; and hepatocellular carcinoma. Anabolic steroid ingestion by athletes also is associated with an atherogenic blood lipid profile (e.g., elevated low-density lipoprotein cholesterol and decreased high-density lipoprotein cholesterol). In addition, increased irritability and aggressiveness may occur.

76

In women, steroids produce masculinizing effects (e.g., hirsutism, deepened voice, oily skin, acne, male pattern balding, and menstrual irregularities). In children, these drugs may accelerate pubertal changes and limit eventual adult height by causing premature skeletal maturation and closure of the epiphyses.

The adverse effects of steroids are discussed in a 1986 report of the AMA's Council on Scientific Affairs entitled "Drug Abuse in Athletes." A copy of the report is attached to our statement.

AMA Concerns

The AMA recognizes and is concerned over the fact that steroid abuse is a significant problem. Nevertheless, the AMA must oppose the enactment of federal legislation that would schedule steroids under the CSA for the following reasons:

- The preferred and appropriate method for scheduling or rescheduling of a drug is through the regulatory process already established by existing law;
- Anabolic steroids do not meet the statutory criteria for scheduling under the CSA; and
- More effective approaches are available to curb steroid abuse. One approach to deal with steroid abuse, which was adopted in the Anti-Drug Abuse Act of 1988 (P.L.100-690), is to increase criminal penalties for the sale of steroids without a prescription. Another approach is to educate athletes, coaches and trainers concerning the dangers of drug abuse, including steroid abuse. Both of these approaches are more appropriate and effective responses to the problem of anabolic steroid abuse.

77

Regulatory Mechanism for Drug Scheduling

The appropriate avenue for scheduling a drug under the CSA is through the established administrative process rather than by legislation. The CSA authorizes the Attorney General, through the Drug Enforcement Administration (DEA), to initiate proceedings to schedule or reschedule a drug or to remove controls on a drug. However, before a scheduling action can be taken, the Attorney General must request a "scientific and medical evaluation" of the drug from the Secretary of Health and Human Services through the Food and Drug Administration (FDA). The FDA also makes a recommendation as to whether the drug should be controlled (and if so under what schedule) or removed from the schedules. If the DEA concludes that the information provided by the FDA constitutes "substantial evidence" that a drug has potential for abuse, it must initiate proceedings to schedule it. If, however, the FDA recommends that a drug not be controlled, the DEA is not authorized to control it. Finally, if the data provided by FDA constitutes substantial evidence that a drug should be removed entirely from the schedules, proceedings for removal of the drug must be initiated by DEA.

This regulatory mechanism, which utilizes the expertise of the FDA and DEA, has proven to be a highly satisfactory means of reviewing and evaluating drugs for almost twenty years. No convincing reasons exist to forego this appropriate and workable avenue in favor of legislative scheduling. Use of the legislative process to schedule drugs would inappropriately preempt a well-developed regulatory program designed specifically to deal with scientific and medical issues.

78

Statutory Criteria for Scheduling

We believe that anabolic steroids do not meet the statutory criteria for scheduling under the CSA. The CSA provides that in order to be placed in Schedule I, a drug must have a high potential for abuse <u>and have no currently accepted medical use in treatment in the United States</u>. In addition, there must be a <u>lack of accepted safety for use of the drug under medical supervision</u>. In order to be controlled under one of the other schedules of the CSA, a drug must have some <u>potential for abuse that could lead to physical or psychological dependence</u>.

The medical facts do not support scheduling anabolic steroids under the CSA. Anabolic steroids have an accepted use in the treatment of several medical conditions, including certain anemias, hereditary angioedema, and breast cancer. Moreover, anabolic steroids can be used safely under medical supervision. Thus, they do not satisfy the statutory criteria for a Schedule I drug. Scheduling of anabolic steroids in Schedule I would deprive patients of the benefits of this therapy for their legitimate medical needs. Moreover, anabolic steroids should not be scheduled under <u>any</u> other schedule of the CSA since abuse of the drugs does <u>not</u> lead to physical or psychological dependence as is required for scheduling under the Act.

In addition, scheduling of anabolic steroids would not adequately address the problem of abuse of these drugs because it would not affect the major illicit sources of the drug – shipments from foreign countries and from veterinary supply houses. Scheduling would curtail only the relatively small amount of abuse that results from diversion from licit sources.

79

Alternative Approaches

The AMA believes that more appropriate and effective approaches to combat steroid abuse are available. One approach, which was included in the Anti-Drug Abuse Act of 1988 (enacted in November 1988), is increasing the criminal penalty for the sale of steroids without a prescription. This Act provides that persons who distribute steroids or possess steroids with the intent to distribute them without a prescription can be fined and imprisoned for up to three years (six years if the sale involves a minor). (Previously, the maximum penalty was imprisonment for one year and a $1,000 fine.) The law also allows courts to seize property used to support the illegal distribution of steroids and property purchased with the profits from the sale of steroids.

We support these provisions of the Anti-Drug Abuse Act. They should serve to deter the major source of steroid abuse - the widespread distribution of steroids through non-medical channels. In addition, local law enforcement officials, which now have the responsibility for enforcing P.L. 100-690, are more likely than the DEA to have the resources and inclination to address steroid abuse. Rather than create new problems by legislatively scheduling these hormones under the CSA, it makes a great deal more sense to allow this new law to address the issue of anabolic steroid use.

Another more effective means to combat anabolic steroid abuse is to educate athletes, coaches and trainers concerning their many harmful side effects. Many of these persons simply are unaware of the serious adverse effects of these drugs. In addition, physicians need to be made aware of the warning signals of steroid abuse so that they can better recognize

80

and diagnose such abuse and counsel their patients not to use these drugs. We have developed educational materials for physicians which include a discussion of steroid abuse.

Finally, we believe that the Postal Service should conduct a study to determine the extent to which steroids are advertised for sale in periodicals that are shipped through the mail. If the mails are a major source of promoting or providing steroids, further legislation may be needed to prohibit such activities.

Conclusion

The AMA recognizes that steroid abuse is a significant problem. We must, however, oppose legislation that would schedule steroids under the CSA. First, the appropriate method for scheduling a drug is through the established regulatory process. Second, anabolic steroids do not meet the statutory criteria for scheduling under the CSA. Finally, there are more appropriate approaches to address the problem of steroid abuse. These include enforcement of the recently increased criminal penalty for selling steroids without a prescription, and educating the public concerning the harmful health effects of steroid abuse.

Mr. Chairman, I will be happy to answer any questions you or other Members of the Committee may have.

81

REPORT OF THE COUNCIL ON SCIENTIFIC AFFAIRS

Report: B
(I-86)

Subject: Drug Abuse in Athletes: Anabolic Steroids
                and Human Growth Hormone
                (Resolution 57, A-86)

Presented by: John H. Moxley, III, M.D., Chairman

Referred to: Reference Committee E
              (R. Robert Tyson, M.D., Chairman)

----

1   This report, the first in a three-part series on drug abuse by
2   athletes, responds to adopted Resolution 4 (A-84) and to Resolution
3   57 (A-86), "Human Growth Hormone," which was referred to the Board
4   of Trustees for action. Subsequent reports will cover other classes
5   of abused drugs.
6
7   Introduction
8
9   The problem of misuse of anabolic hormones (both steroids and
10 growth hormone) is complex and can be considered from different
11 perspectives:
12
13   (1) Psychological:
14
15   (a) The importance of winning;
16   (b) Placebo effect of drugs.
17
18   (2) Pharmacologic:
19
20   (a) The possibility that these hormones may provide a
21   real physiologic advantage for the athlete;
22
23   (b) The adverse effects of such misuse.
24
25   (3) Ethical:
26
27   (a) The concept of violation of fair play;
28
29   (b) Implicit coercion to use drugs in order to be
30   competitive;
31
32   (c) The concept of hormonal manipulation,
33   particularly in children, to alter body size and
34   build in a manner perceived to be beneficial for
35   athletics or other life endeavors.[1]

Past House Action: A-86:371; A-85:282; A-84:334; A-79:277;
                    I-79:45-47; A-79:277; A-72:261,384

82

CSA Rep. B —

1   General solutions to the problem range from prevention (eg,
2 regulatory action limiting production and/or distribution of drugs)
3 through symptomatic treatment (eg, drug testing of competitors) to
4 cure (eg, motivation of the individual to reject drugs). The
5 personal decision to reject or discontinue drug use is based on the
6 individual's values and reasons for considering drug use. Hence, an
7 ethical argument based on the concept of fair play may be ineffective
8 in an individual who is motivated to win at any physical cost.
9
10   Anabolic steroids and growth hormone will be discussed
11 separately. The following questions will be considered for each:
12
13   (1) Does the drug provide real or perceived benefit for
14   the athlete?
15
16   (2) What are the adverse effects of the drug in this
17   setting?
18
19   (3) Who promotes, distributes, and uses the drug?
20
21   (4) Is abuse of the drug a significant problem?
22
23 Anabolic Steroids
24
25   Anabolic steroids are synthetic androgens that have greater
26 anabolic relative to androgenic activity than testosterone, but in
27 large quantities, these drugs have strong androgenic effects. In
28 general, they are not as useful and effective as earlier thought, but
29 do have legitimate uses in several conditions (eg, certain anemias,
30 hereditary angioedema, breast cancer, and possibly osteoporosis).
31
32   Anabolic steroids have been used by athletes for more than two
33 decades in the belief that they increase body mass, muscle tissue,
34 and strength. More recently, testosterone has been used because it
35 is more difficult to detect in drug screening programs than anabolic
36 steroids. Although studies of these agents have not shown uniformly
37 increased muscular strength, certain benefits to athletic performance
38 seem probable: increased body weight, partly due to fluid retention,
39 may include increase in lean muscle mass. In a continuing program of
40 intensive exercise coupled with a high protein diet, increased
41 muscular strength may be realized in some individuals.
42 In contrast, aerobic capacity is probably not increased beyond that
43 due to aerobic training.[2,3] Increased aggressiveness is also
44 reported among anabolic steroid users, but the degree to which this
45 influences the intensity of training is unknown.[4] It should be
46 noted that small, difficult-to-measure increments in muscular
47 performance or psychological benefit may constitute the difference
48 between winning and losing, particularly at a professional or
49 world-class level. Therefore, these changes may be perceived to be
50 critical to an athlete.

83

1   There are clear adverse effects associated with use of
2   androgenic steroids. The doses and patterns of administration
3   utilized by athletes often differ markedly from those used
4   therapeutically. Athletes have been reported to take steroids
5   cyclically for one to several months followed by a drug-free period
6   up to a year. Doses may be far greater than those considered to be
7   therapeutic, and drugs are sometimes "stacked" (several agents taken
8   simultaneously).[5] Exogenous androgens affect the reproductive
9   system of healthy males: gonadotropin and testosterone secretion
10 are suppressed and oligospermia and temporary infertility may
11 occur. Gynecomastia is common.[6] Agents that are 17 - alkylated
12 compounds (eg. oxandrolone, methandrosteneolone) are associated with
13 liver pathology, including abnormal liver function tests,
14 cholestasis, peliosis hepatis, hepatic adenomas, and hepatocellular
15 carcinoma.[7] Although hepatic effects have been described and
16 documented most often in patients treated for disease, one case of
17 hepatocellular carcinoma has been reported in an athlete who had
18 taken several anabolic steroids to increase skeletal muscle
19 mass.[8] Anabolic steroid ingestion by athletes is also associated
20 with an atherogenic blood lipid profile (eg. elevated low-density
21 lipoprotein cholesterol and decreased high-density lipoprotein
22 cholesterol).[9] Increased irritability and aggressiveness may
23 occur.
24
25   In women, androgenic hormones produce masculinizing effects (eg.
26 hirsutism, deepened voice, oily skin, acne, male pattern balding,
27 menstrual irregularities, increased libido). In children, these
28 drugs may accelerate pubertal changes and limit eventual adult
29 height by causing premature skeletal maturation and closure of the
30 epiphyses.
31
32   Steroids apparently are used at all levels of athletic
33 activity. Although the prevalence is difficult to assess
34 accurately, such use is believed to be widespread.[10] Steroid
35 abuse is particularly common among athletes in strength sports (eg.
36 weight lifters, body builders, shot putters, and discus and javelin
37 throwers). Use among weight-trained women athletes has been
38 reported. Anabolic steroids have a more significant effect on
39 female muscular development than on males. In one study, the women
40 reported typical masculinizing side effects, which they considered
41 an acceptable price for the anabolic benefits.[11] A particular
42 concern is that the wide availability of these agents is likely to
43 make them accessible to adolescents and children, as well as
44 adults.[12]
45
46   Anabolic steroids are easily obtained on the black market
47 through gymnasiums or mail order sources. In a survey of 250 weight
48 lifters, almost half admitted using steroids at some time. Although
49 most steroids were obtained illegally, some athletes claimed that
50 they had been given a prescription for the drugs.[13]

84

CSA Rep. B -

1   In 1985, the Food and Drug Administration (FDA), Federal Bureau
2   of Investigation (FBI), and Department of Justice (DOJ) began a
3   nationwide criminal investigation of black market distribution of
4   anabolic steroids and other drugs purported to enhance athletic
5   performance. Manufacturers and distributors were advised of their
6   responsibility to ensure distribution only to authorized customers
7   and were requested to monitor and report unusual order activity (eg,
8   large or frequent orders, orders by pharmacies for veterinary
9   products). Indictments have been obtained as a result of this
10 effort.
11
12 Growth Hormone
13
14   Human growth hormone (hGH) or somatotropin is a polypeptide
15 hormone secreted by the anterior pituitary gland. GH has widespread
16 metabolic effects, including stimulation of cellular amino acid
17 uptake and protein synthesis, stimulation of lipolysis, and
18 inhibition of glucose utilization in tissue, which tends to increase
19 blood glucose levels. Growth hormone is necessary to achieve normal
20 genetic growth potential. Severe deficiency in childhood results in
21 dwarfism. Human GH is necessary to treat this condition, because GH
22 from other species is ineffective.
23
24   Human pituitary-extracted GH was available from the National
25 Hormone and Pituitary Program and commercial sources until 1985.
26 After the appearance of several cases of Creutzfeldt-Jakob disease
27 believed to have been caused by contaminated pituitary extracts,
28 distribution of the product was halted voluntarily for an indefinite
29 period. Following withdrawal of the pituitary products, a
30 recombinant DNA-derived GH product was approved for marketing in the
31 United States. It is identical to endogenous hGH except for the
32 addition of methionine on the N-terminus of the molecule. This
33 preparation is available commercially.
34
35   The results of hypersecretion of hGH are of particular interest
36 in the context of this report. Uncontrolled hypersecretion in
37 childhood results in gigantism, and in adulthood, acromegaly. The
38 latter condition is associated with glucose intolerance, heart
39 disease, impotence, and bony overgrowth (eg, protruding forehead and
40 jaw, enlarged hands and feet).
41
42   Adverse effects of hGH use by athletes have not been documented
43 but can be predicted on the basis of known effects of endogenous
44 hypersecretion (vide supra). Whether limited exogenous
45 administration may produce beneficial or deleterious effects in
46 healthy athletes is unknown. The effect of hGH administration to
47 normal children is unknown, but might be expected to produce a
48 permanent increase in build and stature. Beyond the physiologic
49 considerations, use in normal children is an ethical problem of
50 far-reaching proportions.[1]

85

1   In contrast to the problem of anabolic steroid abuse, hGH abuse,
2 to the extent that it exists, is a relatively new phenomenon.
3 Reports of its use in athletes are anecdotal;[15] they suggest that
4 hGH is currently favored because of anticipated body growth and
5 increased strength potential and also because it is undetectable in
6 current drug testing procedures. Use is probably limited by the
7 great expense of the product.
8
9   The source of illicit supply is questionable. One physician
10 reportedly obtained supplies of pituitary-extracted hGH simply by
11 mailing prescriptions to companies supplying the product.[16] This
12 account is inconsistent with the companies' stated distribution
13 policies, which required screening of requests and documentation of
14 need. Bogus hGH preparations, animal GH preparations, and foreign
15 products should also be considered as potential illicit sources. To
16 knowledge, there have been no reports verifying that the GH products
17 bought by athletes are in fact hGH.
18
19   Since withdrawal of pituitary-extracted hGH from the US market
20 in 1985, the only U.S. source of hGH is the recombinant DNA
21 product. Although the technology to mass-produce hGH is available,
22 the manufacturer states that it limits production and follows
23 rigorous screening and post marketing surveillance procedures to
24 verify legitimate use in GH-deficient patients.
25
26   In summary, the status of growth hormone abuse is undetermined,
27 but the agent has wide abuse potential, particularly if pharmacologic
28 benefits are shown to result from use in normal athletes. Human GH
29 also may have additional legitimate therapeutic applications for
30 other growth disorders, fractures, burns, and other conditions.
31 Research in these areas has been hampered by the limited supplies of
32 hormone available, but is expected to be undertaken in the future
33 now that it is possible to produce unlimited quantities of the
34 hormone. Increased availability of hGH for other legitimate uses
35 presumably would increase accessibility for illicit use.
36
37 Conclusions
38
39 .   Abuse of anabolic products by athletes differs in the two types
40 of drugs discussed. Anabolic steroids have therapeutic benefits for
41 certain conditions and proven abuse potential among athletes. The
42 abuse of hGH is a recent phenomenon of undetermined extent. Human
43 GH has a clear therapeutic application in growth hormone deficiency
44 and other legitimate investigational uses, and also has great
45 potential for misuse.
46
47   This report responds directly to concerns regarding the abuse of
48 anabolic steroids; future reports will deal with other classes of
49 abused drugs. The report also addresses the issue of the abuse of
50 human growth hormone, which was raised in referred Resolution 57

86

CSA Rep. B -

1 (A-86). Recommendations for AMA action will be developed after
2 completion of all reports on drug abuse in athletes. The following
3 possibilities will be considered in developing the recommendations:
4
5 1. Regulatory action (for anabolic steroids and growth hormone):
6
7   The AMA should continue to endorse current activities of
8   the FDA, FBI, and DOJ directed toward curbing illegal
9   distribution of these drugs. If these efforts are
10   ineffective, the AMA should undertake a study of alternate
11   methods of monitoring and limiting distribution.
12
13   2. Educational action (for drugs with abuse potential):
14
15   The AMA should endorse educational activities at various
16   levels including sports group administrators, coaches,
17   parents, and athletes. Activities suggested for
18   consideration are:
19
20   a) Preparation and distribution of educational
21   pamphlets on drug abuse in athletes
22   emphasizing the adverse effects and limited
23   benefits of such use.
24
25   b) Development of a nationwide network of
26   physicians who would be available to give
27   presentations on this topic to interested
28   community groups.
29
30   c) Preparation of a videotape(s) on drug abuse
31   in athletes for distribution and use by
32   schools, sports programs, parent groups, and
33   community organizations.
34
35   d) Judicious use of the news media and
36   editorials and articles in AMA publications
37   to publicize the AMA's interest and
38   availability to work on this problem.
39
40   The Council on Scientific Affairs recommends the adoption of
41 this report in lieu of Resolution 57 (A-86).

87

CSA Rep. B –

REFERENCES

1. Benjamin M, et al: Short children, anxious parents: Is growth hormone the answer? Hastings Center Rep 1984;14:5-9.

2. Haupt HA: Anabolic steroids: A review of the literature. Amer J Sports Med 1984;12:469-484.

3. American College of Sports Medicine Position Stand on the Use of Anabolic-Androgenic Steroids in Sports. Amer J Sports Med 1984;12:13-18.

4. Mellion MB: Anabolic steroids in athletes. AFP 1984;30:113-119.

5. Tatro DS: Use of steroids by athletes. Drug Newsletter 1985;4:33-34.

6. Limbird TJ: Anabolic steroids in the training and treatment of athletes. Comp Ther 1985;11:25-30.

7. Ryan AJ: Anabolic steroids are fool's gold. Federation Proceedings 1981;40:2682-2688.

8. Overly WL, et al: Androgens and hepatocellular carcinoma in an athlete. Annals Intern Med 1984;100:158-159 (letter).

9. Webb OL, et al: Severe depression of high-density lipoprotein cholesterol levels in weight lifters and body builders by self-administered exogenous testosterone and anabolic-androgenic steroids. Metabolism 1984;33:971-975.

10. Johnson WD: Steroids: A problem of huge dimensions, (special report) Sports Illustrated; 1985;62:38(12).

11. Strauss RH, et al: Anabolic steroid use and perceived effects in ten weight-trained women athletes. JAMA 1985;253:2871-2873.

12. Dyment PG: Drugs and the adolescent athlete. Pediatric Annals 1984;13:602-604.

13. Frankle MA, et al: Use of androgenic anabolic steroids by athletes. JAMA 1984;252:482 (letter).

14. Underwood LE: Report of Conference on Uses and Possible Abuses of Biosynthetic Human Growth Hormone. N Engl J Med 1984;311:606-608.

15. Taylor WN: Hormonal Manipulation. McFarland and Company, Inc., Jefferson, North Carolina, 1985.

16. Taylor WN: Growth hormone: Preventing its abuse in sports. Technology Review 1985;88:14(3).

Appendix 3

United States General Accounting Office

GAO

Report to the Chairman, Committee on
the Judiciary, U.S. Senate

August 1989

DRUG MISUSE

Anabolic Steroids and Human Growth Hormone

GAO/HRD-89-109

United States
General Accounting Office
Washington, D.C. 20548 ·

Human Resources Division

B-235236

August 18, 1989

The Honorable Joseph Biden
Chairman, Committee on the Judiciary
United States Senate

Dear Mr. Chairman:

This report is in response to your November 22, 1988, request for information on the use, distribution, production, and health risks associated
with anabolic steroids and human growth hormone. In accordance with
your request, which parallels the requirements of the Anti-Drug Abuse
Act of 1988, we obtained information on the estimated use of anabolic
steroids among high school and college students and the adult population. We developed information on the (1) legal and illegal distribution
of anabolic steroids and (2) health consequences associated with their
use. We also obtained comparable data, when available, on human
growth hormone.

Background

The Food and Drug Administration (FDA) has approved anabolic steroids, synthetic derivatives of the male hormone testosterone, as prescription drugs, which may be prescribed only by a licensed physician.
Like the hormone testosterone, anabolic steroids have both androgenic
and anabolic properties. The androgenic properties are responsible for
the development of masculine characteristics, such as the growth of
body and facial hair, deepening of the voice, and genital growth during
puberty. The anabolic properties of testosterone promote the retention
of dietary protein and muscle growth.

Anabolic steroids have been approved for the treatment of a small
number of diseases, such as certain anemias, hereditary angioedema,[1]
and breast cancer. These steroids, however, have also been used for non-
therapeutic purposes. The first such use was reported during World War
II, when anabolic steroids were given to German troops to increase
aggressiveness. Based on anecdotal reports, their first use in athletics
was by the Russians in 1954.

Since then, the use of these drugs has increased significantly among athletes. Initially, the use of anabolic steroids was believed to be largely
confined to world class athletes participating in power sports, such as
weightlifting and shotputting. Over the years, however anabolic steroid

---

[1]Recurring attacks of swelling appearing in areas of the skin or mucus membrane.

use has spread to professional, college, and high school sports. Anabolic steroids are taken to enhance performance or body image. Because of the possible competitive advantage and the health risks associated with their use, concerns have been raised about the inappropriate use of these drugs.

Human growth hormone, or somatotropin, is a hormone secreted by the pituitary gland. Body organs depend on growth hormone for proper growth and development. The most apparent effects of growth hormone during puberty are an increase in linear bone growth and in skeletal mass. Overproduction of this hormone in adults results in acromegaly, a disease that almost always shortens the life span of those it afflicts and that is marked by the progressive enlargement of the hands, feet, and face and may affect the major organs of the body, particularly the heart. Athletes use growth hormone because they perceive that it might affect athletic performance. It is suspected that the administration of high dosage levels of synthetic human growth hormone to normal adults, such as athletes, could result in acromegaly.

Objectives, Scope, and Methodology

On the basis of discussions with Committee staff, we focused our work on obtaining, to the extent available, information on the (1) use of anabolic steroids among students, both high school and college, and athletes; (2) health consequences resulting from anabolic steroid use; (3) policies and regulations developed by sports associations to monitor athletes' use of anabolic steroids; and (4) quantity of legal and illegal anabolic steroids that are produced and distributed both domestically and internationally. We obtained similar information for human growth hormone. Additionally, we obtained information from FDA on state laws and regulations to control the misuse of anabolic steroids and human growth hormone.

We reviewed current scientific literature to obtain information on (1) the prevalence of the use of anabolic steroids and human growth hormone and (2) medical consequences resulting from their use. We identified only 15 studies on the prevalence of use of anabolic steroids in the U.S. population; of these studies, 8 focused on use among high school students and 7 on college students and athletes. We did not identify any prevalence studies for human growth hormone use.

We also interviewed FDA and National Institute of Drug Abuse officials, leading researchers in the area, and representatives of medical societies and manufacturers of these drugs to obtain (1) a perspective on the prevalence of steroid and growth hormone misuse and (2) the associated adverse medical consequences.

We interviewed officials of several of the U.S. Olympic Committee's National Governing Bodies, the National Collegiate Athletic Association, and the National Football League to obtain information on monitoring policies and regulations of sports associations for steroid and growth hormone use, such as (1) drug-testing policies and testing results and (2) the prevalence of drug use among athletes.

From FDA, we obtained information on (1) the legal distribution of anabolic steroids and (2) federal and state laws developed to control drug misuse. From the Department of Commerce, we gathered information on the quantity of anabolic steroids imported into the United States. To the extent available, we obtained data on illegal production and distribution of steroids and growth hormone from the Department of Justice.

Results in Brief

Published studies and other information we obtained indicate that anabolic steroids are being misused primarily by high school, college, and professional athletes to enhance their performance and, to a lesser extent, by others participating in sports. A national study found that more than 6 percent of male high school seniors, mostly participants in sports, use or have used anabolic steroids. A more limited study covering five colleges found that about 20 percent of athletes used steroids. Misuse of human growth hormone appears to be a lesser problem.

In view of suspected health risks associated with the misuse of anabolic steroids and indications from the Department of Justice that their misuse is a growing problem, we support federal and state efforts to exercise greater control over their distribution and use.

The information we obtained is summarized below and presented in more detail in appendixes I-VII.

Anabolic Steroid Use Among High School and College Students and Athletes

We identified 15 studies that address the prevalence of anabolic steroid use (see app. VIII); most of these studies were carried out on high school and college students. One study purported to provide results representative of a national sample. Most studies limited the sampling universe to schools from a specific geographic locality, high school, or sex group. These studies showed that male athletes were the primary users of anabolic steroids.

The national study, conducted in 1987, indicates that as many as 6.6 percent of the 12th grade males in the United States use or have used anabolic steroids.[2] According to this and other studies, athletes are the most common users of anabolic steroids among high school and college students. One high school study found that 84 percent of anabolic steroid users participated in sports.[3] According to a 15-year study of college students at five universities, between 15 and 20 percent of the college athletes reported using anabolic steroids.[4]

Less information is available on the prevalence of anabolic steroid use outside of high school and college. The two studies we identified addressed use in relatively small samples of weightlifters. The results show that a high percentage of weightlifters studied use steroids. However, the results cannot be projected beyond the weightlifters included in the studies.

Misuse of Anabolic Steroids Associated With Health Risks

Athletes are reported to consume high dosage levels of anabolic steroids or several steroids at one time. These levels are believed to be greater than those commonly used during medical treatment.[5] Much media attention has been given to the health risks of anabolic steroids among athletes and bodybuilders. No systematic studies of the health risks to athletes have been conducted, however. Thus, information on health risk is lacking.

Studies do exist, however, on the health risks of anabolic steroids in (1) medical use—for example, in the treatment of some rare diseases—and (2) athletes in a limited number of case reports. These studies suggest that anabolic steroids may increase the risk of heart disease; produce liver toxicities; affect sex characteristics and reproductive capacity; cause possible psychological disorders and tendon and ligament injury; and, in children and youth, result in stunted growth.

[2]William E. Buckley and others, "Estimated Prevalence of Anabolic Steroid Use Among Male High School Seniors," Journal of the American Medical Association, Vol. 260 (Dec. 16, 1988), p. 3441.

[3]Mimi D. Johnson and others, "Anabolic Steroid Use by Male Adolescents," Pediatrics, Vol. 83 (June 1989), p. 922.

[4]T. L. Dezelsky and others, "Non-Medical Drug Use Behaviour at Five United States Universities: A 15-Year Study," Bulletin on Narcotics (United Nations publication), Vol. 37 (1985).

[5]Anecdotal reports suggest athletes take doses that are from 4 to more than 100 times greater than the manufacturer-recommended guidelines for approved purposes.

Although some adverse affects are reversible when drug use is discontinued, they can be serious. For example, anabolic steroids may cause changes in the cardiovascular system, such as upsetting the balance of high density and low density lipoprotein (HDL/LDL), an increase in total serum cholesterol levels and blood pressure, increasing the risk of arteriosclerotic disease and possible heart failure. Children's use of steroids may prematurely close the growth centers of the long bones, stunting growth.

Use of Anabolic Steroids Prohibited by Sports Associations

Several sports associations have adopted drug policies that condemn and prohibit the use of anabolic steroids by athletes because of the combination of (1) potential health and safety risks with (2) the potential competitive advantage. Many of the sports associations have implemented drug-testing programs to monitor the use of anabolic steroids among their athletes.

Most of these programs have an announced policy to test athletes competing at scheduled events. According to some experts, the results of such announced tests for anabolic steroid use are poor indicators of true use. Given advance notice, athletes can abstain from the use of these drugs before the test to avoid detection.[6] Although the use of human growth hormone cannot be detected in drug-testing procedures, the sports associations we spoke with—the U.S. Olympic Committee, the National Collegiate Athletic Association, and the National Football League—have also included this drug among their list of banned substances.

Anabolic Steroid Distribution by Manufacturers

Data on the quantity of anabolic steroids produced are not publicly available. From FDA, however, we obtained data on the legitimate distribution of anabolic steroids manufactured in the United States. These data indicate that (1) during the 10-year period 1979 through 1988, U.S. manufacturers distributed 53.2 million grams of anabolic steroids in the United States and abroad; and (2) during 1984 through 1988, hospitals and retail pharmacies in the United States purchased an estimated 26.1 million grams of anabolic steroids. According to Department of Commerce data, 26.2 million grams of anabolic steroids, in bulk rather than dosage form, were imported into the country during 1979 through 1988. Of the total distributed, 92 percent were accounted for by five drugs:

---

[6]According to one expert, detectable traces of oral anabolic steroids are apparent in the urine for 1 to 2 weeks after discontinuing use. Injectable steroids may be present from 1 week to 1 month after use.

Danazol, Testosterone Cypionate, Methyltestosterone, Testosterone Enanthate, and Fluoxymesterone.

In addition to the legitimate distribution, the Department of Justice estimates that on the black market, the annual sales of these drugs is about $300 to $400 million. Justice believes that the source of black market steroids is divided evenly between clandestinely manufactured goods, smuggled products, and diverted legally manufactured products.

Human Growth Hormone

We did not find any studies that document the use of human growth hormone by high school students, college students, or athletes. Reports of its use among athletes are anecdotal and suggest that athletes use growth hormone because (1) they perceive it to increase body growth and strength potential (however, these perceptions have not been confirmed scientifically) and (2) no drug-testing procedure has been developed for its detection in the urine. According to the Council on Scientific Affairs of the American Medical Association, the abuse of human growth hormone, to the extent that it exists, is a recent phenomenon.

The health risks of an oversecretion of human growth hormone in children include abnormal bone growth and dysfunction of the thyroid gland. In adults, oversecretion results in acromegaly, which almost always shortens the person's life span. At this time, there are no reported cases of acromegaly among athletes associated with the use of synthetic human growth hormone.[7]

Between 1985 and 1988 approximately 7,768 grams of synthetic growth hormone were legally distributed for medical purposes in the United States; we were not able to obtain data on the amount produced in this time period. Human growth hormone is much less available on the black market than steroids.

Federal and State Laws on Anabolic Steroids and Human Growth Hormone

Because of the increased interest in the use of anabolic steroids and the potential health risks associated with the use of these drugs, there has been considerable legislative and administrative activity in this area. For example, in 1988, the Congress passed the Anti-Drug Abuse Act of 1988 (P.L. 100-690), which includes several provisions to control the use

[7]Before 1985, human growth hormone was commercially derived through the extraction of the hormone from the pituitary gland of cadavers. In 1985, pituitary extracted human growth hormone was withdrawn from the U.S. market. Synthetic human growth hormone has been marketed since 1985.

of anabolic steroids and human growth hormone. FDA data show that as of June 16, 1989, 25 states have enacted laws or promulgated regulations to control the use of anabolic steroids. Five of these states have enacted laws or promulgated regulations to control the use of human growth hormone.

The Anti-Drug Abuse Act of 1988 provides for the forfeiture of specified property of an individual convicted of a violation of the Federal Food, Drug, and Cosmetic Act[8] involving anabolic steroids or human growth hormone, if the violation is punishable by imprisonment for more than 1 year. The Anti-Drug Abuse Act of 1988 also specifies that violators are subject to imprisonment for up to 3 years or a fine or both if they (1) distribute or (2) possess anabolic steroids with the intent to distribute for any use in humans other than the treatment of disease based on the order of a physician.

Information provided by FDA shows that some states have classified anabolic steroids as controlled substances, and at least one state has promulgated rules regarding the medical profession's responsibility in prescribing, dispensing, or delivering these drugs. Anabolic steroids are regulated as controlled substances under state law in nine states; in addition, six states have legislation pending that would classify anabolic steroids as controlled substances. One state has classified human growth hormone as a controlled substance.

According to FDA, state controlled substances acts are either identical or similar to the federal Controlled Substances Act. The federal act classifies drugs that can be physically or psychologically harmful into categories or schedules based on their potential for abuse, accepted medical use, and whether abuse of the drug may lead to physical or psychological dependence. The schedule under which a drug is placed determines the nature and degree of control exercised to prevent its abuse and diversion. Anabolic steroids and human growth hormone are not classified under the federal Controlled Substances Act.[9]

As arranged with your office, unless you publicly announce its contents earlier, we plan no further distribution of this report until 15 days from

[8]The Federal Food, Drug, and Cosmetic Act (21 U.S.C. 301 et seq.) prohibits specified acts relating to the sale and distribution of misbranded or adulterated articles.

[9]The Attorney General has delegated to the Drug Enforcement Administration the authority for scheduling drugs under the federal Controlled Substances Act.

its issue date. At that time, copies will be sent to the appropriate Senate and House committees and subcommittees; the Attorney General; the Secretary of Health and Human Services; the Secretary of the Treasury; the Commissioner of FDA; and the Director, Office of Management and Budget, and we will make copies available to other interested parties upon request.

The major contributors to this report are listed in appendix IX.

Sincerely yours,

Janet L. Shikles
Director of National and
   Public Health Issues

*Page 9 of the original report is blank.

Contents

Abbreviations

AIDS	acquired immunodeficiency syndrome
DNA	deoxyribonucleic acid
FDA	Food and Drug Administration
HDL/LDL	high density and low density lipoprotein
NCAA	National Collegiate Athletic Association
NFL	National Football League

---

*Page 13 of the original report is blank.

Use of Anabolic Steroids Among High School and College Students and Athletes

We reviewed 15 studies on the use of anabolic steroids among students and athletes.[1] Of these studies, one provides a national perspective on use; the others are limited to a specific geographical locality, school, or sex. Most studies, however, show that athletes are the most common users of anabolic steroids among high school and college students.[2] The national study found that more than 6 percent of male high school seniors, predominately participants in sports, use or have used anabolic steroids. A limited study covering five colleges found that almost 20 percent of athletes used steroids. Because other studies suggest that the misuse of anabolic steroids may pose serious health risks and Department of Justice data indicate that their misuse is a growing problem (see apps. II and IV), we support federal and state efforts to exercise greater control over their distribution and use.

Use of Anabolic Steroids Among High School Students

A national-based study found that 6.6 percent of male 12th graders use or have used anabolic steroids.[3] According to the authors of the study, if this use rate is applied to the national population of males enrolled in secondary schools, it suggests that between 250,000 and 500,000 adolescents in the country use or have used these drugs. In four other studies, while not nationally representative, a similar or higher rate of anabolic steroid use among males was found, with study estimates ranging from 5 percent[4] to 11.1 percent.[5] In three of the four studies, anabolic steroid use was found to be much lower among females, ranging from 1 percent[6] to 2.5 percent.[7]

---

[1] A National Institute of Drug Abuse official informed us that a high school senior survey now in the data collection phase is soliciting information on the use of anabolic steroids.

[2] A listing of studies reviewed on anabolic steroid use by high school and college students and athletes is presented in appendix VIII.

[3] William E. Buckley and others, "Estimated Prevalence of Anabolic Steroid Use Among Male High School Seniors," p. 3441.

[4] Martha Newman, "Hazelden Health Promotion: Michigan Consortium of Schools Student Survey," Minneapolis, Minnesota: Hazelden Research Services, September 1986, p. 30 (unpublished).

[5] Mimi D. Johnson and others, "Anabolic Steroid Use by Male Adolescents," p. 922.

[6] Martha Newman, "Hazelden Health Promotion: Michigan Consortium of Schools Student Survey," p. 30.

[7] Rise Terney and Larry G. McLain, "The Use of Anabolic Steroids in High School Students," Loyola University, Chicago, Illinois, 1988, p. 2 (unpublished).

Athletes Most Frequent User

Among high school students, male athletes were found to be the most frequent users of anabolic steroids. In the five studies we reviewed, information was provided on the use of anabolic steroids and participation in sports activities. A 1988 study of students at an Illinois high school found that 5.5 percent of student athletes of both sexes used steroids; the rate was 6.6 percent among male athletes and 3.9 percent among female athletes. Athletes participating in football (9.3 percent) and wrestling (12.2 percent) had the highest use.[8]

A second study included students from five high schools in both affluent and less affluent school districts in one city. In this study, 10.2 percent of male athletes from affluent school districts used steroids as compared with 2.8 percent of those from less affluent school districts.[9]

In the third and fourth studies, a large percentage of steroid users participated in sports. In the third study, the national study of 12th graders, 65 percent of steroid users participated in sports. In the fourth study, based on a sample of 11th grade male students in six Arkansas schools, 84 percent of steroid users participated in sports.[10] The fifth study was a survey of varsity head coaches from 621 high schools in Michigan; according to the coaches' perceptions, the use of steroids among football players during the period 1985-87 ranged from 11.1 to 13.9 percent.[11]

The most frequent reasons cited for using steroids were (1) to increase strength, size, and speed and (2) to improve athletic performance. In the Arkansas study, 64 percent of steroid users reported that they wanted to increase strength, 50 percent wanted to increase size, and 27 percent wanted to improve physical appearance. In the national study of 12th graders, the largest percentage of users (47 percent) reported that their main reason for using the drug was to improve athletic performance. Another 27 percent of users reported "appearance" as the main reason for using anabolic steroids.

---

[8]Rise Terney and Larry G. McLain, "The Use of Anabolic Steroids in High School Students," pp. 4-6.

[9]Robert Windsor and Daniel Dumitru, "Prevalence of Anabolic Steroid Use by Male and Female Adolescents," Medicine and Science in Sports and Exercise, forthcoming October 1989.

[10]Mimi D. Johnson and others, "Anabolic Steroid Use by Male Adolescents," pp. 921-922.

[11]E. James Swenson, Jr., "Perspectives on Anabolic Steroids: Statewide Survey of High School Varsity Football Medical Coaches," Michigan State University, East Lansing, Michigan, Fall 1987, pp. 1 and 3 (unpublished).

In the Illinois study, 9.4 percent of students reported that they would use steroids if it would help them obtain a college athletic scholarship. Two percent of students also reported encouragement of this use from a coach or faculty member, while 4.8 percent reported encouragement from another person.

Estimates of Use Among College Athletes

We identified only five studies on the extent of steroid use among college students. Two studies on general drug use in a representative sample of the general student body from five universities were carried out over a 15-year period, 1970-84. The first study reported results for 1970 and 1973; the second, for 1970, 1976, 1980, and 1984. In the general student body of the five schools, data for 1970 and 1973 showed that 0 to 2 percent of students had ever used steroids.[12] When data from this study were examined for athletes only, 15 percent of athletes reported using anabolic steroids in 1970. This rate increased to 20 percent for 1976, 1980, and 1984.[13] In 1984, only 1 percent of nonathletes in the study reported steroid use.

The third and fourth studies examined steroid use by sport. In the third study, which was conducted in 1980 and focused on intercollegiate swimmers at six universities, 6 percent of male swimmers reported steroid use.[14] No female swimmers reported use. In the fourth study, involving 2,048 intercollegiate athletes conducted in the fall of 1984 at 11 universities, the national prevalence rate was found to be 4 percent for steroid use in athletes for eight different sports.[15] The highest rate of use was found among male football players (9 percent), followed by male basketball, track, and tennis athletes (each 4 percent); 1 percent of female swimmers reported steroid use.

[12]Brice W. Corder and others, "An Analysis of Trends in Drug Use Behavior at Five American Universities," The Journal of School Health, Vol. 44 (September 1974), pp. 386-387.

[13]T. L. Dezelsky and others, "Non-Medical Drug Use Behaviour at Five United States Universities: A 15-Year Study," pp. 49 and 52.

[14]J. V. Toohey and B. W. Corder, "Intercollegiate Sports Participation and Non-Medical Drug Use," Bulletin on Narcotics (United Nations Publication), Vol. 33 (1981), pp. 23-25.

[15]William A. Anderson and Douglas B. McKeag, "The Substance Use and Abuse Habits of College Student-Athletes," Research Paper No. 1, Michigan State University, East Lansing, Michigan, 1985, pp. 1-3 (unpublished).

The fifth study, published in 1988, provided information on 1,010 male students at three universities.[16] Results from this study also support a higher rate of steroid use among athletes than among nonathletes. Of varsity athletes at two of the three schools in the study, 17 percent reported steroid use. This rate is significantly higher than the 2 percent of all males who reported using steroids in the total survey sample of the three schools.

Use by Weightlifters

For adults who participate in sports activities but are not a part of a college athletic program, few studies have been carried out on anabolic steroid use. We identified two studies of steroid use among weightlifters. One study was based on 250 weightlifters from three gymnasium weight rooms in the metropolitan Chicago area.[17] This study found that 44 percent (110) of the weightlifters reported steroid use at some time. A subgroup of 50 of the 110 weightlifters who used steroids were interviewed in greater detail to obtain information on the pattern, dose, and type of drugs used, as well as the source of the drugs; 40 percent reported drug use for 1 year or less; the rest had been using the drugs for 2 or more years. The majority of users in the subgroup studied obtained their drugs illegally, but 20 percent claimed to have received them by prescription.

The second study was based on a sample of 61 athletes who competed in the 1987 National Championship of the U.S. Powerlifting Federation.[18] Only 45 competitors responded to the survey; of these, 33 percent reported steroid use. As found in studies of high school and college students, the reason given most often for using steroids was to improve athletic performance. The black market was also identified as the primary source for purchasing steroids by 73 percent of the users. In this study, the "black market" was defined as other athletes and gym owners or managers.

[16]Harrison G. Pope, Jr., and others, "Anabolic-Androgenic Steroid Use Among 1,010 College Men," The Physician and Sportsmedicine, Vol. 16 (July 1988), pp. 75-76.

[17]Mark A. Frankle and others, "Use of Androgenic Anabolic Steroids by Athletes," Letter to Editor, Journal of the American Medical Association, Vol. 252 (July 27, 1984), p. 482.

[18]Charles E. Yesalis III and others, "Self-Reported Use of Anabolic-Androgenic Steroids by Elite Power Lifters," The Physician and Sportsmedicine, Vol. 16 (December 1988), pp. 91-94.

Health Risks Associated With the Misuse of Anabolic Steroids

No well-controlled longitudinal studies have been carried out on the health risks to athletes of anabolic steroid use. Consequently, the risks are not well established for consuming massive doses or for consuming multiple steroids at one time ("stacking"), as some athletes have done. There are, however, some case reports documenting medical problems in athletes who have taken high doses. Scientific studies on health risks have been carried out in the treatment of patients who have taken anabolic steroids in normal therapeutic doses. These studies and case reports found that steroids may increase the risk of heart disease and produce liver toxicities, temporary changes in sex characteristics and reproductive functioning, possible psychological disorders, possible injury to tendons and ligaments, and stunted growth in children.

Adverse Effects of Using Anabolic Steroids

Although there has been controversy among researchers about the advantages of anabolic steroid use for athletes and body builders, many researchers and sport medical experts have reported advantages: gains in lean muscle mass, strength, and endurance can be achieved by trained athletes who use steroids and maintain their training and a high protein diet. Experts also report that anabolic steroids do not increase aerobic power or capacity for muscular exercise. These drugs are also reported to increase aggressiveness and tolerance of stress, characteristics considered important in sports.

Currently there are no well-controlled longitudinal studies of the effects of anabolic steroids in athletes, bodybuilders, and teenagers, particularly none that document the effects of taking massive doses, or "stacking." Most of the available information on adverse effects has been reported in the treatment of patients who have taken anabolic steroids in normal therapeutic doses.[1] Some information on adverse effects has also been reported by sports physicians and in a limited number of studies of athletes and bodybuilders.

Most adverse effects have been associated with orally administered anabolic steroids. Orally administered steroids are easier to take and have a shorter detection time in the urine than injected anabolic steroids. In addition, athletes who use anabolic steroids that are injected may risk contracting acquired immunodeficiency syndrome (AIDS) and other diseases, such as hepatitis from infected needles. One case of AIDS in an

---

[1]Anecdotal reports suggest that athletes take doses that are 4 to more than 100 times greater than manufacturer-recommended guidelines for approved purposes.

athlete, who reported using injectable steroids and had no other known AIDS risk factors, has been reported in the literature.

Cardiovascular Problems

Among the most dangerous consequences of taking large amounts of steroids over a prolonged period of time, sports physicians and researchers say, are changes in the cardiovascular system, for example: upsetting the balance of high density and low density lipoprotein (HDL/LDL), elevated blood pressure, and increased total serum cholesterol level. Although these changes are probably reversible, they may result in arteriosclerotic disease and heart failure. According to medical reports, one young athlete had a serious heart attack and two others had strokes possibly associated with steroid use.

Liver Toxicities

Anabolic steroids that are orally administered have been implicated in liver toxicities and in the development of blood-filled cysts (peliosis) and in the formation of benign tumors in the liver. Cases of malignant liver tumors have also been reported in men, including one athlete, using anabolic steroids. In addition, two cases of benign liver tumors have been reported in athletes. Some of these conditions have disappeared once the steroid therapy was discontinued. But deaths have been reported that are associated with tumors and the rupture of the cysts.

Sexual Changes

Changes in sex characteristics and in reproductive functioning are common among athletes who take steroids. Males may suffer from atrophy of the testis, low sperm count, or enlargement of the prostate gland. These side effects are generally considered to be reversible. Males may also develop enlarged breasts, which may not be reversible. One case of prostatic cancer in an athlete who used steroids has also been reported. Females may experience increased hair growth on the face, enlargement of the clitoris, and deepening of the voice. They may also experience a cessation in menstruation. Acne is another common side effect reported in users of both sexes.

Psychological Changes

Sports physicians and athletes report that there are psychological changes when athletes and bodybuilders take steroids. They feel good with increased energy; they are more competitive and have greater capacity to endure pain. They are more irritable, however, and more prone to increased aggressiveness. When the athletes discontinue using steroids, some become depressed and apathetic.

There have been several reports of psychotic reactions. Two physicians nonrandomly solicited responses from 41 bodybuilders and football players who had used anabolic steroids and found 9 who displayed a full affective syndrome[2] and 5 who experienced psychotic symptoms; 5 subjects developed a major depression while withdrawing from steroids.[3] Paranoid psychosis has also been reported in some clinical studies for patients treated for depression with antidepressants and an anabolic steroid. When the steroids were discontinued, the paranoia disappeared.

The behaviors, opinions, and attitudes of a segment of adolescent anabolic steroid users, described in a study to be published in 1989, are consistent with the definition of psychological dependence.[4] In addition, at a 1989 National Institute of Drug Abuse Technical Conference on Anabolic Steroids, information presented supported the possibility of a potential link between using anabolic steroids and psychological dependence. More research is necessary, conference participants acknowledged, to clarify the effects of anabolic steroids on mood and behavior, as well as their potential for psychological dependence.

Tendons and Ligaments

Anecdotal reports from sports physicians suggest that the risk of ruptured tendons and ligaments, as well as tendonitis, is increased when anabolic steroids are used. This results, they believe, from an imbalance between the increased strength of the muscles and the strength of tendons and ligaments, which is not changed by the steroids.

Stunted Growth in Children and Youth

Anabolic steroids may prematurely close the growth centers of the long bones. Pediatricians and sports physicians have reported that prepuberty children and adolescents who take anabolic steroids may be in danger of stunting their growth. Little information exists about the adolescent anabolic steroid user's knowledge of the possible adverse effects of steroids. A study of male, high school students, however, indicates that a segment of the adolescent population is using anabolic steroids without appropriate knowledge about the adverse effects of these

---

[2]An affective syndrome is characterized by excessive mood changes.

[3]Harrison G. Pope, Jr., and David L. Katz, "Affective and Psychotic Symptoms Associated With Anabolic Steroid Use," American Journal of Psychiatry, Vol. 145 (Apr. 1988), pp. 487-489.

[4]Charles E. Yesalis and others, "Anabolic Steroid Use: Indication of Habituation Among Adolescents," Journal of Drug Education, Vol. 19, No. 2 (1989), p. 113 (forthcoming).

drugs.[5] In another study we reviewed, 38 percent of male users initiated anabolic steroid use at age 15 or less.[6]

[5]Mimi D. Johnson and others, "Anabolic Steroid Use by Male Adolescents," p. 924.

[6]William E. Buckley and others, "Estimated Prevalence of Anabolic Steroid Use Among Male High School Seniors," p. 3443.

Sports Associations Prohibit the Use of Anabolic Steroids by Athletes

Because of the possible competitive advantage and health risks to the athlete, several amateur and professional sports associations have placed anabolic steroids on their lists of banned drugs. A recent review of drug testing in sports noted that an adequate methodology for detecting anabolic steroids in the urine was not used in a drug screening program until the 1976 Montreal Olympic Games.[1] Since then, the U.S. Olympic Committee and other sports associations have implemented drug-testing programs for these drugs.

Most of these programs have announced policies to test athletes competing at scheduled events. According to some experts, the results of such announced tests for anabolic steroid use are poor indicators of true use. Given advance notice, athletes can abstain from the use of these drugs before the test to avoid detection.

U.S. Olympic Committee

We contacted seven of the U.S. Olympic Committee's National Governing Bodies concerning their testing policies for anabolic steroids: The Athletic Congress; U.S. Amateur Boxing Federation; U.S. Cycling Federation; U.S. Modern Pentathlon; U.S. Swimming, Inc.; U.S. Weightlifting Federation; and USA Wrestling. No athlete has had a confirmed positive test for anabolic steroid use, according to the U.S. Boxing Federation, U.S. Modern Pentathlon, and USA Wrestling, since testing was implemented. The U.S. Cycling Federation reported one positive urine test during 1987 (280 tested) and 1988 (300 tested). The U.S. Swimming, Inc., reported one positive urine test between 1978 and 1988.

The Athletic Congress and the U.S. Weightlifting Federation have had more positive urine tests. According to The Athletic Congress, since 1983, 12 Athletic Congress athletes have tested positive during activities sponsored by the U.S. Olympic Committee or The Athletic Congress. In the 785 urine tests conducted in 1988, no U.S. athletes were found to be positive for anabolic steroids. Athletes who tested positive were suspended from domestic and international competition for life, with the exception of one athlete. In this case, the athlete appealed the suspension, and an appeals board upheld the appeal because of irregularities in the procedures used to ship and test the urine sample.

In response to a resolution submitted by the Athletes' Advisory Committee asking for random out-of-competition drug testing, The Athletic Congress has established a year-round drug testing program. The program

---

[1]Gary I. Wadler and Brian Hainline, Drugs and the Athlete, F. A. Davis Company, 1989, p. 195.

requires the top 25 performers in each event during a ranking year, as well as athletes receiving financial assistance through any amateur sports organization, to be subject to random year-round drug testing, which includes testing for anabolic steroid use. This program was scheduled to begin in July 1989.

The U.S. Weightlifting Federation reported that 39 urine samples of 1,300 tested were positive for anabolic steroids during 1984-88. In 1984, 9 percent of the 132 urine samples tested were positive. Since 1984, the number of samples found positive decreased substantially. By 1988, only 3 of the 518 samples tested (less than 1 percent) were found to be positive.

National Collegiate Athletic Association

The National Collegiate Athletic Association (NCAA) has implemented two drug testing programs, the Post-Season Testing Program and the Off-Season Anabolic Steroid Testing Program. The Post-Season Program is the association's primary testing program. This program provides for random testing of athletes either before, during, or after participation in an NCAA championship or in any postseason football game certified by the NCAA. In 1988, less than 1 percent of athletes tested in this program were found positive. The Off-Season Program is a voluntary program for institutions with a football program. Preliminary program test results provided to us by NCAA officials show that 3.3 percent of 546 football players tested positive in 1988.

National Football League

A National Football League (NFL) official told us that between 6 and 7 percent of 2,600 players tested were found to be positive for the use of anabolic steroids in 1987 and 1988. In a recent hearing before the Senate Committee on the Judiciary, the NFL Commissioner testified that in 1987 and 1988 pre-season testing steroid use had been "solidly documented" in 6 to 7 percent of NFL players. In 1989, the NFL announced a new testing policy for anabolic steroids and related substances. This policy specified that all NFL players will be tested for anabolic steroids and related substances, as well as "masking agents," which are used to try to suppress steroid detection. Testing will be conducted in 1989 pre-season training camps or after if a player reports late for training camp.

A positive result will prohibit the player from participating in his team's activity for a minimum of 30 days. In addition, the player will be subject to frequent reasonable-cause testing in the future. A player who has previously tested positive for steroids is also subject to reasonable-cause

160   Appendix 3

testing. If a player tests positive on a second test during the season, the player will be suspended for the rest of the season.

Distribution of Anabolic Steroids

During the 10-year period 1979-88, U.S. manufacturers distributed 53.2 million grams of anabolic steroids domestically and abroad. During the same period, an additional 26.2 million grams of these drugs were imported into the country.

According to the Department of Justice, clandestinely manufactured goods, smuggled products, and legitimately manufactured U.S. products that have been diverted are the sources of the growing numbers of anabolic steroids sold on the black market. Justice officials estimate the retail sales of these drugs on the black market to reach approximately $300 to $400 million yearly.[1] They report that over 4 years of investigation, the retail prices for anabolic steroids have increased. They support this finding with price lists confiscated from the black market, one from 1985 and one from late 1988, that show, for example, the price of one anabolic steroid, Maxibolin, was $25 in 1985 and $42 in 1988.

Legal Distribution of Anabolic Steroids

Data on the amount of anabolic steroids produced are not publicly available.[2] However, FDA did provide us with distribution data covering a 10-year period beginning in 1979 for 14 approved anabolic steroids manufactured by various companies under 25 brand and generic names. FDA advised that data for 1988 are incomplete because all manufacturers have not sent distribution data for that year; therefore, conclusions based on these data are understated.

During 1979-88, manufacturers distributed 53.2 million grams of anabolic steroids. The smallest annual quantity of steroids distributed during the period was about 386,000 grams in 1979 (see fig. IV.1). Since then, the distribution of anabolic steroids increased until 1985, when 7.8 million grams were distributed; distribution for 1986 and 1987 was lower, and distribution data for 1988 are incomplete.

[1]Includes human growth hormone, which is found on the black market to a much lesser extent than anabolic steroids.

[2]Appendix VII provides information on the difficulties in obtaining anabolic steroids production data.

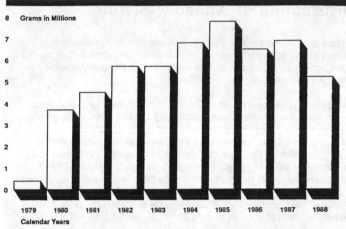

Note: Data for 1988 do not include data from all manufacturers (the data include anabolic steroids that are manufactured domestically and distributed in the United States and abroad).

Source: Manufacturers' annual reports submitted to FDA.

Figure IV.1: Distribution of Anabolic Steroids (1979–88)

Five drugs accounted for 92 percent of the anabolic steroids distributed between 1979 and 1988. In order of the greatest quantity distributed, these were Danazol, Testosterone Cypionate, Methyltestosterone, Testosterone Enanthate, and Fluoxymesterone (see fig. IV.2). Danazol, Methyltestosterone, and Fluoxymesterone are oral anabolic steroids; Testosterone Cypionate and Testosterone Enanthate are injectable. The distribution of Danazol is highest (40.2 million grams) because it is the drug of choice to treat endometriosis and fibrocystic breast disease, two common diseases that affect women.

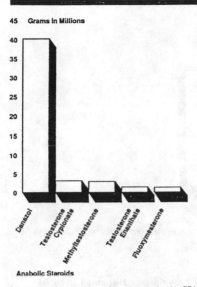

45   Grams in Millions

Anabolic Steroids

Source: Manufacturers' annual reports submitted to FDA.

Figure IV.2: Top Five Anabolic Steroids Distributed (1979–88)

During the 5-year period 1984-88, hospitals and retail pharmacies purchased an estimated 26.1 million grams of anabolic steroids.[3] During the
same 5 years, about 7.1 million prescriptions were dispensed for anabolic steroids. However, since 1984, the number of prescriptions has
declined. About 500,000 fewer prescriptions were written in 1988 than
in 1984 (see fig. IV.3).[4]

[3]These data were based on IMS America, Ltd.'s, audit of pharmacies and hospitals.

[4]Data were based on IMS America, Ltd 's, prescription audit.

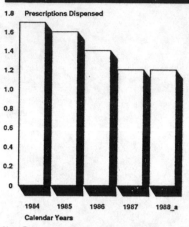

1.8   Prescriptions Dispensed

Calendar Years

Note: Prescription data include only what is prescribed by the physician and what is dispensed by the pharmacist.
ªData for 1988 do not include information for December.
Source: IMS America, Ltd's, national prescription audit.

Figure IV.3: Anabolic Steroid Prescriptions Dispensed (1984–88)

Imports of Anabolic Steroids

The United States imports anabolic steroids from various countries. Between 1979 and 1988, the United States imported 26.2 million grams, totaling $20.6 million. According to a Department of Commerce official, these imports were in bulk rather than dosage form. The amount imported over a 10-year period, beginning with 1979, is shown in figure IV.4.

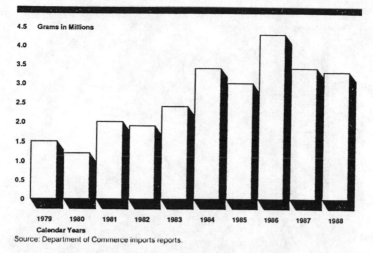

Source: Department of Commerce imports reports.

Figure IV.4: Anabolic Steroids Imported by the United States (1979–88)

The top four countries exporting steroids to the United States were, in order, Mexico, Germany, the Bahamas, and the Netherlands (see fig. IV.5).

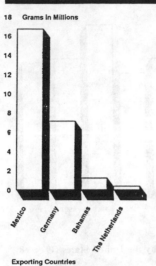

Source: U.S. Department of Commerce imports reports.

Figure IV.5: Top Four Countries Exporting Anabolic Steroids Into the United States (1979–88)

Black Market Major Supplier

Information provided by the Department of Justice documents the existence of a growing black market traffic in anabolic steroids. In January 1985, FDA asked the Office of Consumer Litigation in the Department of Justice's Civil Division to coordinate a national investigation into the black market distribution of anabolic steroids because of the potential health risks associated with the misuse of these drugs. This interagency collaborative effort was motivated by FDA's need for assistance in conducting undercover investigations in the black market trade. Justice's senior litigation counsel and FDA's national anabolic steroids coordinator were designated the focal points for this initiative.

In conducting investigations, confiscating drugs, halting clandestine manufacturing operations, and prosecuting individuals and companies, Justice and FDA have worked with the U.S. Customs Service, the U.S. Postal Service, the Federal Bureau of Investigation, and state and local law enforcement agencies. Since 1985, Justice and FDA officials report that investigators have seen an evolution in illegal trafficking. The evolution began with the diversion of legitimately manufactured domestic anabolic steroids by people without prior criminal activity and moved to: (1) the wholesale smuggling of foreign manufactured products into the United States; (2) the domestic, clandestine manufacture of counterfeit steroid products; and (3) the involvement of criminals.

Drugs get to the black market by several routes. First, drugs can be diverted from the legal market through theft, resale by consumers, or the filling of fraudulent prescriptions. Second, drugs can be counterfeited. These include mislabeled drugs, drugs that are subpotent or adulterated with other substances, or totally bogus drugs that contain none of the substances they purport to contain. These drugs may be produced domestically or smuggled in from other countries. Department of Justice officials report that the proportion of counterfeit anabolic steroids on the black market has increased over the past 4 years. Since 1986, Justice and FDA have uncovered more than 35 different counterfeit drug products and more than 85 different labels used in their distribution.

Confiscated drugs have been manufactured in many countries, including Brazil, France, Italy, Belgium, Canada, Germany, Switzerland, the United Kingdom, and Mexico. According to Justice officials, the majority of confiscations have been made in California.

Based on its drug seizures and other information, Justice believes the supply of black market anabolic steroids is divided about equally between three sources: clandestinely manufactured goods, smuggled products, and diverted legitimately manufactured U.S. products. According to Justice officials, the black market in steroids is of national scope with operations in every sector of the country.

As of April 25, 1989, 440 cases have been generated for investigation as a result of Justice and FDA activities over the past 4 years. Justice conservatively estimates that the total value of the anabolic steroids that have been seized is $16 million.[5]

---

[5]Justice officials provided us with data books derived from reports on drug products that have been seized during investigations. These books contained only a small portion of drugs that were seized and purchased through undercover efforts. Justice uses this information to investigate the black market and to track the many counterfeit drug products; it is not intended to provide a comprehensive catalog of the black market. Thus, we were unable to use the books to provide information on the total quantity and type of drugs found on the black market.

Human Growth Hormone

We did not find any studies that document the use of human growth hormone among high school students, college students, or athletes. Reports of its use among athletes are anecdotal. According to the Council on Scientific Affairs of the American Medical Association, the abuse of human growth hormone, to the extent it exists, is a recent phenomenon.

Production data on human growth hormone were not made available to us by manufacturers. Available distribution information indicates that between 1985 and 1988, 1,553,556 vials or 7,768 grams of human growth hormone were legally distributed in the United States. Small quantities have been found on the black market, but to a much lesser extent than anabolic steroids.

Use Unknown

We were not able to identify information on the extent, if any, of human growth hormone use among high school or college students or among amateur and professional athletes. Anecdotal reports suggest athletes use the hormone because they perceive it to increase body growth and strength potential; athletes believe the hormone (1) prevents the breakdown of muscle after anabolic steroids are discontinued and (2) strengthens tendons and ligaments, thus preventing ruptures or tears. According to researchers and sports physicians, these perceptions that lead athletes to believe human growth hormone might affect athletic performance have not been confirmed scientifically. No studies have been identified that examine an interaction between human growth hormone and anabolic steroids.

According to anecdotal reports, athletes favor growth hormone over steroids because it is undetectable in current drug testing procedures. Even though the use of human growth hormone cannot be detected, the U.S. Olympic Committee, the National Collegiate Athletic Association, and the National Football League have included this drug among their list of banned substances.

Adverse Effects of Human Growth Hormone

Secreted by the pituitary gland, human growth hormone acts as part of the endocrine system to stimulate growth throughout the body. It is particularly active during puberty, contributing to the growth spurt that takes place at that time; deficiency in childhood results in dwarfism. In this rare disease, children fail to grow because the pituitary gland does not produce sufficient growth hormone. Human growth hormone is necessary to treat this disease because growth hormone from other animal species is ineffective. It is estimated that there are about 10,000 to 15,000 cases of dwarfism, which are treated by about 450 pediatric endocrinologists throughout the country.

Although the only approved indication for the hormone is the treatment of dwarfism, FDA officials and other experts state that some ongoing research concerns wound healing, the treatment of Turner's Syndrome in girls,[1] and the treatment of osteoporosis and obesity. The greatest interest is in the possible use of human growth hormone to make short children taller; it has not, however, been approved for this purpose. The administration of the hormone to normal children with short stature is controversial. Some physicians believe psychosocial problems associated with short stature may be reduced with the hormone treatment. Other physicians are uncertain about this treatment, however, since there are short-term risks of abnormal bone growth, dysfunction of the thyroid gland, and creation of antibodies to human growth hormone that have been associated with clinical treatment.[2]

Overproduction of growth hormone in adults may result in acromegaly, a disease that usually becomes obvious in the third or fourth decade of life. It is marked by progressive enlargement of hands, feet, and face. The symptoms may include excessive growth in the skull, other bones, and soft tissue; thickening of the skin; diabetes mellitus; cardiovascular disease; goiters; menstrual disorders in females; decreased sexual desire; and impotence in males. Acromegaly almost always shortens the life span of the persons it afflicts. At this time, there are no reported cases of acromegaly among athletes.

Legal Production and Distribution

Before 1985, human growth hormone was derived commercially through the extraction of the hormone from the pituitary gland of cadavers. Given this source, the availability of the hormone was limited. The National Hormone and Pituitary Program of the National Institutes of Health played an important role distributing the hormone to patients with clinically confirmed dwarfism. According to a National Institutes of

[1] Turner's Syndrome is caused by a genetic defect in females that is characterized by such symptoms as short stature, webbed neck, sterility, and heart problems.

[2] Representatives from Genentech, Inc., one of the manufacturers of human growth hormone, told us that they actively discourage the use of their product for the treatment of short-stature children and that the company is not filing for additional approval from FDA to use this drug for this purpose.

Health official, close to 90 percent of the available hormone was distributed by the program, which treated between 2,300 and 2,500 patients over a 20-year period.

In 1985, the distribution of the pituitary-extracted hormone was halted after several children died after being treated with extracted hormone. Their deaths were caused by Creutzfeldt-Jakob disease, a slow virus that affects the nervous system; it was believed that the disease resulted from the use of contaminated pituitary extracts. Since the withdrawal of pituitary extracts from the U.S. market, two recombinant deoxyribonucleic acid (DNA)-derived human growth hormone products have been approved by FDA for marketing in the United States and are available commercially. These synthetic growth hormones are produced by two pharmaceutical companies: Genentech, Inc., which began marketing it under the trade name Protropin in 1985, and Eli Lilly and Company, which began marketing it under the trade name Humatrope in 1987. The human growth hormone produced by both companies must be administered by injection.

We were unable to obtain data on the production of Protropin and Humatrope; we did, however, obtain information on the distribution of both drugs since their commencement of marketing. According to annual reports to FDA, 1,553,556 vials or 7,768 grams of human growth hormone have been distributed domestically by Genentech and Eli Lilly.[3]

The distribution of synthetic growth hormone differs greatly from that of anabolic steroids, for which no known controls exist. Both manufacturers of the hormone have voluntarily developed distribution controls for their product.

A Genentech representative told us that all patients being treated with Protropin receive the drug through Caremark, a home health care company, or a hospital pharmacy on the basis of a prescription. According to Genentech, Protropin is not available from an ordinary retail druggist. Genentech said that its distribution system enables the company to identify by age, diagnosis, and dosage 91 percent of the patients who receive the product. This is made possible through Caremark's required recordkeeping and Genentech's annual post-marketing surveillance study of 63 percent of the patients being treated with Protropin.

---

[3]According to Genentech representatives, the usual average dosage of human growth hormone required for a child of 30 kilograms is 0.3 mg per kg per week or 1.8 vials per week, or a total of 93.6 vials per year. Each vial contains 5 mg of human growth hormone. The usual average dose required for a 50 kg teenage boy is 0.3 mg per kg per week or 3 vials per week, or a total of 156 vials per year.

Lilly has also developed a system of control similar to that of Genentech. Both Genentech and Lilly believe that the potential for diversion of legally produced human growth hormone is significantly smaller than that for anabolic steroids.

Black Market Supply

The amount of growth hormone sold on the black market is unclear. It appears, however, that the amount confiscated is significantly smaller than that for anabolic steroids. According to the data provided by Justice and FDA, at least 115 vials of drugs purporting to be synthetic human growth hormone were confiscated on 13 different occasions during October 1985 and December 1988. At least 14 vials of genuine Protropin were confiscated on eight different occasions, with five occurring between 1985, when the drug was first distributed, and May 1987. In November 1988, a total of 48 vials labeled as Protropin, although none contained it, were confiscated on three occasions. Human growth hormone produced by Lilly has also been found on the black market by Justice and FDA investigators. A total of 53 vials of human growth hormone produced for research purposes were seized between October and December of 1988.

In addition to the synthetic hormone, small quantities of pituitary-extracted somatotropin (which had been withdrawn from the U.S. market) were seized from the black market. In 1983 and 1985 three vials of counterfeit Asellacrin, an extracted growth hormone produced by Serono Laboratories, Inc., were confiscated. Also in 1985, 28 vials of a genuine extracted growth hormone, called Crescormon, distributed by Pharmacia Inc., were confiscated.

Genentech representatives believe that the following factors contribute to limiting the unauthorized distribution of human growth hormone: (1) the knowledge regarding the use of recombinant DNA technology necessary to make human growth hormone is not widely diffused even in the pharmaceutical industry, (2) the costs of constructing a facility to produce growth hormone illegally are prohibitive, and (3) their rigid distribution controls make the availability of their product on the black market difficult.

The Civil Division of the Department of Justice acknowledges the efforts that the manufacturers have made to control the distribution of their products; however, FDA and the Civil Division take the position that the currently manufactured human growth hormones are drugs that are being abused by athletes and are being traded on the black market. Justice officials estimate that human growth hormones are selling on the black market for $500 to $1,500 per unit.

Justice officials said that the fact that the federal government has been able to buy some of the drugs on the black market leads them to conclude that there is enough trade in these products to justify penalties for the illegal distribution or possession of these drugs similar to penalties that apply to anabolic steroids under the Anti-Drug Abuse Act of 1988 (see p. 37).

Federal and State Governments Increase Control Over the Use of Anabolic Steroids and Human Growth Hormone

Because of concern over the possible health effects of anabolic steroids and human growth hormone, the federal and many state governments either adopted regulations or enacted legislation to reduce the misuse of these drugs. For example, in 1988, the Congress passed the Anti-Drug Abuse Act of 1988 (P.L. 100-690), which includes several provisions to control the misuse of anabolic steroids and human growth hormone. According to FDA, as of June 16, 1989, 25 states had enacted laws or promulgated regulations specifically concerning the distribution of anabolic steroids, and 5 of these states had enacted legislation specifically concerning the distribution of human growth hormone. In addition, 26 states are considering a total of 61 bills intended to provide more effective control over the use of these drugs.

Federal Legislation

The key provisions of the Anti-Drug Abuse Act of 1988 that relate to the misuse of anabolic steroids and human growth hormone are in sections 2401 and 2403. Section 2401 provides for the forfeiture of specified property of an individual convicted of a violation of the Federal Food, Drug, and Cosmetic Act involving anabolic steroids or human growth hormone if such a violation is punishable by imprisonment for more than 1 year.

Under section 2403, which applies only to anabolic steroids, violators are subject to imprisonment for up to 3 years or a fine or both if they (1) distribute or (2) possess steroids with the intent to distribute for any use in humans other than the treatment of disease based on the order of a physician. Violators who distribute, or possess with the intent to distribute, to a person under 18 years of age are subject to imprisonment for up to 6 years.

State Laws on Anabolic Steroids

According to FDA, the 25 states that have enacted laws or promulgated regulations dealing with anabolic steroids are Alabama, Arizona, Arkansas, California, Colorado, Connecticut, Florida, Georgia, Hawaii, Idaho, Indiana, Kansas, Louisiana, Minnesota, New Hampshire, New Mexico, North Carolina, North Dakota, Ohio, Oklahoma, South Carolina, Texas, Utah, Virginia, and Washington.

These laws and regulations vary in the nature and level of control exercised to prevent abuse. For example, some states have enacted legislation or promulgated rules classifying anabolic steroids as controlled substances; at least one other state has promulgated rules specifying the medical profession's responsibility in prescribing, dispensing, or delivering these drugs. Accordingly, the penalties associated with the violation of these laws or regulations also vary by state.

According to FDA's State Law Coordinator, 9 of the 25 states (Alabama, California, Florida, Idaho, Kansas, Minnesota, North Carolina, Texas, and Utah) have classified anabolic steroids pursuant to categories or schedules under their controlled substances acts. FDA indicates that the states' controlled substances acts are either identical or similar to the federal Controlled Substances Act. The federal Controlled Substances Act classifies drugs that can be physically or psychologically harmful into categories or schedules on the bases of the potential for abuse, accepted medical use, and potential for physical or psychological dependence as a consequence of abuse. The federal Controlled Substances Act classifies drugs into five categories or schedules. The schedule under which a drug is placed determines the nature and degree of control exercised to prevent its abuse and diversion. Schedule I controlled substances (1) have a high potential for abuse, (2) have no accepted medical use in the United States, and (3) may lead to severe psychological or physical dependence. Schedule II through V controlled substances have accepted medical uses and abuse potentials correlated to their assigned schedule number, with Schedule II the most dangerous and Schedule V the least. Anabolic steroids and human growth hormone are not currently classified under the federal Controlled Substances Act.

According to FDA, state penalties for the illegal manufacture, distribution, and possession of anabolic steroids vary from misdemeanors to felonies and may result in the imposition of a range of fines and terms of imprisonment, and in some states, the distribution of anabolic steroids to minors may result in harsher penalties. In addition, in one state, a physician's unauthorized distribution of anabolic steroids may violate regulations governing the practice of medicine in that state and may result in revocation or suspension of that physician's license to practice medicine.

According to FDA, 26 states have pending legislation dealing with anabolic steroids.[1] Proposed legislation in six of these states would classify anabolic steroids as a controlled substance.

[1]Some of the 26 states already have laws regulating the use and distribution of anabolic steroids.

State Laws on Human Growth Hormone

According to FDA, Arkansas, Idaho, Ohio, Texas, and Washington have enacted legislation or adopted regulations to control the illegal distribution and possession of human growth hormone. Under the Arkansas law, any person who distributes, or possesses with intent to distribute, human growth hormone for any use in humans other than the treatment of disease at the order of a physician is guilty of a felony. The penalty may be harsher for distribution to a minor. The Ohio law prohibits administering human growth hormone for the purpose of enhancing athletic ability. Physicians who violate this law are subject to reprimand, probation, or license suspension or revocation.

According to FDA, Idaho classified human growth hormone, along with anabolic steroids, under its controlled substances act. The Texas law prohibits medical practitioners from dispensing, delivering, or administering human growth hormone or causing human growth hormone to be administered except for a valid medical purpose and in the course of professional practice. Medical practitioners or pharmacists cannot prescribe, dispense, or deliver human growth hormone without a written prescription that meets the requirements of the Texas Pharmacy Act.

The FDA State Law Coordinator told us that the Washington law prohibits practitioners from prescribing, administering, or dispensing human growth hormone for the purpose of manipulating hormones to increase muscle mass, strength, or weight, or for the purpose of enhancing athletic ability without a medical necessity to do so. The law also requires that patient medical records, including the diagnosis and purpose for prescribing, administering, or dispensing, be completed and maintained. Under the Washington law, any person in illegal possession of more than eight 2-cubic-centimeter bottles of human growth hormone is guilty of a felony.

According to FDA, legislation regarding human growth hormone was also introduced in 1989 into the legislatures of California, Delaware, Florida, Maryland, Nebraska, Ohio, Pennsylvania, Rhode Island, Texas, and Washington.

Requirements for Reporting Distribution Data to FDA

According to FDA officials, FDA has no authority to require drug manufacturers to submit production data to the agency. However, FDA
requires firms that market FDA-approved drugs to submit distribution
data in their annual reports submitted in compliance with the Records
and Reports section of the Federal Food, Drug, and Cosmetic Act, section
505(k).

The annual reports are required to be submitted within 60 days of the
anniversary date of FDA's approval of the drug for marketing rather
than on the basis of a calendar or fiscal year. Because drugs that were
marketed before 1938 are exempt from the premarket approval and
report submission requirements of the act, the distribution data available from FDA may not reflect the total anabolic steroid distribution in the
United States. Additionally, the data the manufacturers submit to FDA
should include both domestic and foreign distribution, but no requirement asks for separate identification of the two; most manufacturers
submit only the total amount distributed. FDA does not verify the accu-
racy of these data.

Since FDA does not receive production data, FDA officials stated they
could not correlate steroid distribution with production. The officials
indicated that the nature of drug production is such that manufacturers
would very likely produce relatively large amounts of a specific drug
product in one time period, then cease production of that particular
product until the supply is exhausted. Therefore, production data may
not correlate well with distribution data.

The amount of steroids used for medical purposes cannot be precisely
estimated. According to FDA, there is no federal requirement that
(1) physicians report prescriptions for medications other than for controlled substances or (2) manufacturers estimate the number of patients
who would use a drug.

Studies on Anabolic Steroid Use Among High School Students, College Students, and Athletes

Studies on Use Among High School Students

Bosworth, E., and others. "Anabolic Steroids and High School Athletes." Abstract. Medical Sciences, Sports, Exercise, 20 (May 25, 1988), S3.

Buckley, William E., and others. "Estimated Prevalence of Anabolic Steroid Use Among Male High School Seniors." Journal of the American Medical Association, 260 (Dec. 16, 1988), 3441-3445.

Corder, Brice W., and others. "Trends in Drug Use Behavior at Ten Central Arizona High Schools." Arizona Journal of Health and Physical Education, Recreation, and Dance, 18 (1975), 10-11.

Johnson, Mimi D., and others. "Anabolic Steroid Use by Male Adolescents." Pediatrics, 83 (June 1989), pp. 921-924.

Newman, Martha. "Hazelden Health Promotion: Michigan Consortium of Schools Student Survey." Minneapolis: Hazelden Research Services, September 1986 (unpublished).

Swenson, E. James, Jr. "Perspectives on Anabolic Steroids: Statewide Survey of High School Varsity Football Medical Coaches." East Lansing: Michigan State University, Fall 1987 (unpublished).

Terney, Rise, and Larry G. McLain. "The Use of Anabolic Steroids in High School Students." Chicago: Loyola University, May 1988 (unpublished).

Windsor, Robert, and Daniel Dumitru. "Prevalence of Anabolic Steroid Use by Male and Female Adolescents." Medicine and Science in Sports and Exercise, forthcoming October 1989.

Studies on Use Among College Students

Anderson, William A., and Douglas B. McKeag. "The Substance Use and Abuse Habits of College Student-Athletes." East Lansing: Michigan State University, 1985 (unpublished).

Corder, Brice W., and others. "An Analysis of Trends in Drug Use Behavior at Five American Universities." The Journal of School Health, 44 (September 1974), 386-389.

Dezelsky, T. L., and others. "Non-Medical Drug Use Behaviour at Five United States Universities: A 15-Year Study." Bulletin on Narcotics (United Nations publication), 37 (1985), 49-53.

178   Appendix 3

Pope, Harrison G. Jr., and others. "Anabolic-Androgenic Steroid Use Among 1,010 College Men." The Physician and Sportsmedicine, 16 (July 1988), 75-81.

Toohey, J. V., and B. W. Corder. "Intercollegiate Sports Participation and Non-Medical Drug Use." Bulletin on Narcotics (United Nations publication), 33 (1981), 23-27.

Studies on Use Among Weightlifters

Frankle, Mark A., and others. "Use of Androgenic Anabolic Steroids by Athletes." Letter to Editor, Journal of the American Medical Association, 252 (July 27, 1984), 482.

Yesalis, Charles E. III, and others. "Self-Reported Use of Anabolic-Androgenic Steroids by Elite Power Lifters." The Physician and Sportsmedicine, 16 (Dec. 1988), 91-100.

Major Contributors to This Report

Human Resources Division Washington, D.C.

Janet L. Shikles, Director of National and Public Health Issues,
  (202) 275-5451
Albert B. Jojokian, Assistant Director
Beryce W. MacLennan, Mental Health Advisor
Rose Marie Martinez, Assignment Manager
Millie D. Baskin, Evaluator-in-Charge

Chapter Notes

Chapter 1. The First Fifty Years

1. Ncwerla, G. J. The history of the discovery and isolation of the male hormone. *New England J. Med.,* 1943; 228(2): 39–47.

2. Weil, A. The history of internal secretions. *M. Life* 32:73–97, 1925.

3. *The Works of Aristotle,* translated by A. Thompson, vol. 4, book 9. London: Oxford Univ. Press, 1910.

4. *The Extant Works of Aretaeus, the Cappadocean. On Gonorrhea.* Translated by F. Adams. London: Syndenham Society, p. 346, 1954.

5. Rolleston, H. *The Endocrine Organs in Health and Disease: With a historical overview.* London: Oxford Univ. Press, p. 390, 1936.

6. Willis, T. *Cerebri Anatome: Cui accessit nervorum descripto et asus.* London: J. Flesher, p. 456, 1664.

7. Hunter, J. *A treatise of the blood, inflammation, and gunshot wounds.* London: Nicol, p. 224, 1974.

8. Berthold, A. A. Transplantation der Hoden. *Arch. f. Anat. Physiol, u. Wissensch. Med.* 1949; 42–46.

9. Brown-Sequard, C. E. Du role physiologique et therapeutique d'un suc extrait de testicules d' animaux d'apres nombre de faits observes ches l'homme. *Arch. de Physiol.* 1889; 1:739–746. Brown-Sequard, C. E. Experience domonstrant is puissance dynamogenique ches l'homme d'un liquide extrait de testicules d' animaux. *Arch. de Physiol.* 1889; 1:651–658.

10. de Kruif, P. *The Male Hormone.* New York: Harcourt, Brace and Company, 1945.

11. Salomon, F., R. C. Cuneo, R. Hesp, and P. H. Sonksen. The effects of treatment with recombinant human growth hormone on body composition and metabolism in adults with growth hormone deficiency. *New England J. Med.,* 1989; 321(26): 1797–1803.

12. McGee, L. C. The effect of injection of a lipoid fraction of bull testicle in capons. *Proc. Inst. Med.,* 1927; 6:242.

13. See note 10.

14. Gallagher, T. F., and F. C. Koch. The testicular hormone. *J. Biol. Chem.,* 1929; 84:495.

15. David, K., E. Dingemanse, and J. Freud. Uber krystallinisches mannliches

181

Hormon aus Hoden (Testosteron), wirksamer als aus Hard oder aus Cholesterin bereitetes Androsteron. *Ztschr. f. Physiol. Chem.*, 1935; 233:281.

16. Ruzicka, L., A. Wettstein, and H. Kaegi. Sexualhormone VIII Darstellung von Testosteron unter Anwedung gemischter ester. *Hevl. Chim. Acta.,* 1935; 18:1478. Butenandt, A., and G. Hanisch. Uber Testosteron, Umwandlund des Dehydro-androsterons in Androstendiol und Testosteron; ein Weg zur Darstellun des Testosterons aus Cholesterin. *Ztschr. f. Physiol. Chem.*, 1935; 237:89.

17. See note 10.

18. Hitler's final days recalled by physician. *Am. Med. News.* 1985; October 11, 14.

19. Hamilton, J. B. Treatment of sexual underdevelopment with synthetic male hormone substance. *Endocrinology*, 1937; 21:649–654.

20. Barahal, H. S. Testosterone in male involutional melancholia. *Psychiatric Quarterly*, 1938; 12:743–749.

21. Goldman, S. F., and M. J. Markham. Clinical use of testosterone in the male climacteric. *J. Clin. Endocrin.,* 1942; 2:237–242.

22. Guirdham, A. Treatment of mental disorders with male sex hormone. *British Med. J.*, 1949; January 6: 10–12. Danziger, L., and H. R. Blank. Androgen therapy of agitated depressions in the male. *Medical Annals of the District of Columbia,* 1942; 11(5):181–183. Davidoff, E., and G. L. Goodstone. Use of testosterone propionate in treatment of involutional psychosis in the male. *Archives of Neurology and Psychiatry*, 1942; 48:811–817.

23. Edwards, E. A., J. B. Hamilton, and S. Q. Duntley. Testosterone propionate as a therapeutic agent in patients with organic disease of the peripperal vessels: preliminary report. *New England J. Med.,* 1939; 220:865.

24. Bonnell, R. W., C. P. Pritchett, and T. E. Rardin. Treatment of angina pectoris and coronary artery disease with sex hormones. *Ohio State Med. J.,* 1940; 37(6):554–556.

25. Lesser, M. A. The treatment of angina pectoris with testosterone propionate. *New England J. Med.,* 1942; 226(2):51–54.

26. Hamm, L. Testosterone propionate in the treatment of angina pectoris. *J. Clin. Endocrinol.,* 1942; 2:325–328.

27. Lesser, M. A. The treatment of angina pectoris with testosterone propionate: further observations. *New England J. Med.,* 1943; 228(6): 185–188.

28. Lesser, M. A. Testosterone propionate therapy in one hundred cases of angina pectoris. *J. Clin. Endocrinol.,* 1946; 6:549–557.

29. Levine, S. A., and W. B. Likoff. The therapeutic value of testosterone propionate in angina pectoris. *New England J. Med.,* 1943; 229:770–772. Walker, T. C. The use of testosterone propionate and estrogenic substance in treatment of essential hypertension, angina pectoris and peripheral vascular disease. *J. Clin. Endocrinol.,* 1942; 2:560–568. McGavack, T. H. Angina-like pain; a manifestation of male climacterium. *J. Clin. Endocrinol.,* 1943; 3:71–80. Opit, L. The treatment of angina pectoris and essential hypertension by testosterone propionate. *Med. J. Australia,* 1943; 1:546. Opit, L. The treatment of angina pectoris by testosterone propionate. *Med. J. Australia,* 1943; 2:173. Sigler, L. H., and J. Tulgan. Treatment of angina pectoris by testosterone. *New York State J. Med.,* 1943; 43: 1424–1428. Strong, G. F., and A. W. Wallace. Treatment of angina pectoris and peripheral vascular disease with sex hormones. *Canad. Med. Assoc. J.*, 1944; 50: 30–33.

30. Waldman, S. The treatment of angina pectoris with testosterone propionate. *J. Clin. Endocrin.,* 1945; 5:305–317.

31. Curtis. J. M., and E. Witt. Activities of the Food and Drug Administration in the field of sex hormones. *J. Clin. Endocrin.*, 1941; 1:363–365.

32. Simonson, E., W. C. Kearns, and N. Enzer. Effect of methyl testosterone treatment on muscular performance and the central nervous system of older men. *J. Clin. Endocrin.*, 1944; 4:528–534.

33. Shelton, E. K., and A. E. Varden. Use of methyl testosterone in the treatment of premature infants. *J. Clin. Endocrinol.*, 1946; 6:812–816. Shelton, E. K., A. E. Varden, and J. S. Mark. Experimental use of testosterone compounds in premature infants. *J. Clin. Endocrinol.*, 1947; 7:708–713.

34. Kugelmass, N. Androgenic arrest of familial enuresis in 75 children. *J. Clin. Endocrinol.*, 1946; 6:823–825.

35. McCullagh, E. P., and R. Jones. Effect of androgens on the blood count of men. *J. Clin. Endocrinol.*, 1942; 2:243–251.

36. Freeman, H. The treatment of a case of impotence with a combination of pituitary gonadotropin and testosterone. *J. Clin. Endocrinol.*, 1941; 1:593–594.

37. Hotchkiss, K. S. Effects of massive doses of testosterone propionate upon spermatogenesis. *J. Clin. Endocrinol.*, 1944; 4:117–120.

38. Butler, A. M., N. B. Talbot, E. A. MacLachlan, J. E. Appleton, and M. A. Linton. Effect of testosterone propionate on losses incident to inadequate dietary intake. *J. Clin. Endocrinol.*, 1945; 5(8):327–336.

39. Bassett, S. H., E. H. Keutmann, and C. D. Kochakian. Effect of injections of testosterone propionate on a male subject with nephrotic syndrome. *J. Clin. Endocrinol.*, 1943; 3:400–404.

40. Hamilton, J. B. Significance of sex hormones in tanning of the skin of women. *Proceedings Soc. Experimental Biology Med.*, 1939; 40:502–503.

41. Mazer, C., and M. Mazer. The treatment of dysfunctional uterine bleeding with testosterone propionate. *Endocrinology*, 1939; 24(5):599–602.

42. Kurzrok, L., C. H. Birnberg, and S. Livingston. The treatment of female menopause with male sex hormone. *Endocrinology*, 1939; 24:347–350.

43. Freed, S. C. Therapeutic use of testosterone in aqueous suspension. *J. Clin. Endocrinol.*, 1946; 6:571–574.

44. Salmon, U. J., and S. H. Geist. Effect of androgens upon libido in women. *J. Clin. Endocrinol.*, 1943; 3:235–238.

45. See note 10.

Chapter 2. The Search for Medical Applications

1. Council on Pharmacy and Chemistry, A.M.A.: The present status of testosterone propionate: Three brands, Perandren, Oreton and Neo-Hombreol not acceptable for N.N.R. *J. American Med. Assoc.*, 1939; 112:1449.

2. de Kruif. P. *The Male Hormone.* New York: Harcourt, Brace and Company, 1945.

3. Taylor, W. N. *Anabolic Steroids and the Athlete.* Jefferson, N.C.: McFarland & Company, Inc., Publishers 1982.

4. Goldman, B. *Death in the Locker Room.* South Bend, Ind.: Icarus Press, p. 1, 1985.

5. Ibid.

6. Fruehan, A. E., and T. F. Frawley. Current status of anabolic steroids. *J. American Med. Assoc.*, 1963; 184(7):527–532.

7. See note 3; Wright, J. E. *Anabolic Steroids and Sports.* Natick, MA: Sports Science Consultants, 1978.

8. See note 3.

9. See Wright, note 7.

10. Kory, R. C., M. H. Bradley, R. N. Watson, et al. A six-month evaluation of an anabolic drug, Norethanoxolone, in underweight persons. II. Bromsulphalein retention and liver function. *Ann. Internal Med.,* 1959; 26:243–248.

11. Brochner-Montensen, K., G. Steffen, and J. H. Thaysen. The metabolic effect of new anabolic 19-nor-steroids. Metabolic studies on patients with chronic Rheumatoid Athritis during combined therapy with prednisone and anabolic steroid. *Acta Medica Scandinavica,* 1959; 165(3): 197–205.

12. Bradshaw, J. S., W. E. Abbot, and S. Levey. The use of anabolic steroids in surgical patients. *Am. J. Surg.,* 1960; 99:600–607.

13. Kennedy, B. F. Effect of androgenic hormone in myleofibrosis. *JAMA,* 1962; 182:116–119. Gardner, F. H., and D. G. Nathan. Androgens and erythropoesis. III. Further evaluation of testosterone treatment of myelofibrosis. *N. Engl. J. Med.,* 1966; 274:420–426.

14. Martins, J. K. Use of nandrolone phenpropionate in refractory anemias. *Curr. Ther. Res.,* 1961; 3:513–519. Khahl, N., and A. H. Ibrachim. The treatment of aplastic anemia with anabolic steroids. *Acta Paediatr.* 1962; 51:201–208. Sanchez-Medal, L., and J. Pizzuto. Effect of oxymetholone in refractory anemia. *Arch. Internal Med.,* 1964; 113:721–729. Sanchez-Medal, L., A. Gomez-Leal, and L. Duarte-Zapata. Anabolic therapy in aplastic anemia. *Blood,* 1966; 28:979. Allen, D. M., M. H. Fire, T. F. Necheles, et al. Oxymetholone therapy in aplastic anemia. *Blood,* 1968; 32:83–89. Silink, S. J., and B. G. Firkin. An analysis of hypoplastic anemia with special reference to the use of oxymetholone ("Adroyd") in its therapy. *Aus. Ann. Med.,* 1968; 17:224–235. Daiber, A., L. Herve, I. Con, et al. Treatment of aplastic anemia with nandrolone decanoate. *Blood,* 1970; 36:748–753. Craddock, P. R., F. A. Hunt, and M. C. Rozenberg. The effective use of oxymetholone in the therapy of thalassaemia with anemia. *Med. J.. Aust.,* 1972; 2:199–202.

15. Chestnut, C. H., W. B. Nelp, D. J. Baylink, et al. Effect of methan-drostenolone on post-menopausal bone wasting as assessed by changes in total bone mineral mass. *Metabolism,* 1977; 26(3):267–277.

16. Doyle, A. E., N. B. Pinkus, and J. Greene. The use of oxandrolone in hyperlipidemia. *Med. J. Aust.,* 1974; 1:127–129.

17. Moore, D. C. Studies of anabolic steroids: V. Effect of prolonged oxandrolone administration on growth in children and adolescents with uncomplicated short stature. *Pediatrics,* 1976; 58(3):412–424.

18. Johnson, L. C., and J. P. O'Shea. Anabolic steroids: Effects on strength development. *Science,* 1969; 164:957–959. Casner, S. W., R. G. Early, and B. B. Carlson. Anabolic steroid effects on body composition in normal young men. *J. Sports Med. Phys. Fitness,* 1971; 11:98–100. Johnson, F. L., G. Fisher, L. J. Silvester, et al. Anabolic steroid: Effects on strength, body weight, oxygen uptake and spermatogenesis. *Med. Sci. Sports,* 1972; 4:43–45. Fahey, T. D., and C. H. Brown. The effects of an anabolic steroid on the strength, body composition and endurance of college males when accompanied by a weight training program. *Med. Sci. Sports,* 1973; 5:272–276. Win-May, M., and M. Zmya-tu. The effects of anabolic steroids on physical fitness. *J. Sports Med. Phys. Fitness,* 1975; 15:266–271.

Hervey, G.R., I. Hutchinson, A. V. Knibbs, et al. "Anabolic" effects of methandiaone in men undergoing athletic training. *Lancet*, 1976; 2:699–702. Fowler, W. M., G. W. Gardner, and G. H. Egstrom. Effect of an anabolic steroid on physical performance of young men. *J. Appl. Physiol.*, 1965; 20:1038–1040. O'Shea, J. P., and W. Winkler. Biochemical and physical effects of an anabolic steroid in competitive swimmers and weight lifters. *Nutr. Rpts. Intern.*, 1970; 2:351–362. O'Shea, J. P. The effects of an anabolic steroid on dynamic strength levels of weight lifters. *Nutr. Rpts. Intern.*, 1971; 4:363–370. Bowers, R. W., and J. P. Reardon. Effects of methandrostenolone (Dianabol) on strength development and aerobic capacity. *Med. Sci. Sports*, 1972; 4:54. Ariel, G. The effect of an anabolic steroid on skeletal muscle contractive force. *J. Sports Med. Phys. Fitness*, 1973; 13:187–190. Ward, P. The effect of an anabolic steroid on strength and lean body mass. *Med. Sci. Sports*, 1973; 5:277–282. Golding, L. A., J. E. Freydinjer, and S. S. Fisher. Weight, size, and strength—unchanged with steroids. *Phys. Sports Med.*, 1974; 2:39–43. Stanford, B. A., and R. Moffatt. Anabolic steroid: Effectiveness as an ergogenic aid to experienced weight trainers. *J. Sports Med. Phys. Fitness*, 1974; 14:191–197. O'Shea, J. P. Biochemical evaluation of effects of stanozolol on adrenal, liver and muscle function in man. *Nutr. Repts. Intern.*, 1974; 10:381–388. Freed, D. L. J., and A. J. Banks. A double-blind crossover trial of methandieonone (Dianabol, Ciba) in moderate dosage on highly trained experienced athletes. *Br. J. Sports Med.*, 1975; 9:78–81. Ljungquist, A. The use of anabolic steroids in top Swedish athletes. *Br. J. Sports Med.*, 1975; 9:82. Hervey, G. R. Are athletes wrong about anabolic steroids? *Brit. J. Sports Med.*, 1975; 9:74–77. Johnson, L. C., E. S. Roundy, P. E. Allsen, et al. Effect of anabolic steroid treatment on endurance. *Med. Sci. Sports,* 1975; 7(4):287–289.

Chapter 3. The Period of False Dogma

1. Freed, D. L. J., and A. J. Banks. A double-blind crossover trial of methandieonone (Dianabol, Ciba) in moderate doses on highly trained experienced athletes. *Br. J. Sports Med.*, 1975; 9:78–81.

2. Hervey, G. R., I. Hutchinson, A. V. Knibbs, et al. "Anabolic" effects of methandiaone in men undergoing athletic training. *Lancet*, 1976; 2:699–702.

3. Personal communications, Tony Fitton to W. N. Taylor, M.D.

4. Ljungquist, A. The use of anabolic steroids in top Swedish athletes. *Br. J. Sports Med.*, 1975; 9:82.

5. Ryan, A. J. Anabolic steroids: The myth dies hard. *Physician and Sportsmed*, 1978; March:3.

6. See note 5; Personal communications, D. C. Hanley, M.D., to W. N. Taylor, M.D.

7. Johnson, L. C., and J. P. O'Shea. Anabolic steroids: Effects on strength development. *Science*, 1968; 164:957–959.

8. Wright, J. E. *Anabolic Steroids and Sports*. Natick, MA: Sports Science Consultants, 1978.

9. American College of Sports Medicine: Position statement on the use and abuse of anabolic-androgenic steroids in sports. *Med. Sci. Sports*, 1977; 9:11–13.

10. Taylor, W. N. *Anabolic Steroids and the Athlete*. Jefferson, N.C.: McFarland & Company, Inc., Publishers, 1982.

11. Haupt, H. A., and G. D. Rovere. Anabolic steroids: a review of the literature. *Am. J. Sports Med.,* 1984; 12(6):469–484.

Chapter 4. The Period of Enlightenment and Reeducation

1. American College of Sports Medicine: Position stand on the use of anabolic-androgenic steroids in sports, revised. *Sports Med. Bull.*, 1984; 19(3): 13–18.

2. Moxley, J. H. Drug Abuse in Athletes: Anabolic Steroids and Human Growth Hormone. AMA, Report of the Council on Scientific Affairs, Resolution 57, A-86, December 1986.

3. Taylor, W. N. *Hormonal Manipulation: A New Era of Monstrous Athletes*. Jefferson, NC: McFarland & Company, Inc., Publishers, 1985; Taylor, W. N. Synthetic anabolic-androgenic steroids: A plea for controlled substance status. *Physician & Sportsmedicine*, 1987; 15(5):140–150.

Chapter 5. The Reclassification as Schedule III Controlled Substances

1. Oakley, R. *Drugs, Society & Human Behavior*. St. Louis: C. V. Mosby Co., 1983.

2. See note 1.

3. See note 1.

4. See note 1.

5. Alcohol and health: new knowledge, National Institute on Alcohol Abuse and Alcoholism, Publication No. (ADM) 75-212, U.S. Department of Health, Education and Welfare, Washington, D.C., U.S. Government Printing Office, 1975.

6. See note 5.

7. See note 1.

8. Postmarketing surveillance vs. phase III, Medical News. *J. American Med. Assoc.*, 1981; 245:21.

9. *A Prognosis for America*. Washington, D.C.: Pharmaceutical Manufacturers Association, 1977.

10. See note 9.

11. The GAO drug lag report: new perspectives on an old controversy. *Drug Therapy*, September 1980.

12. Legislation, regulation, drug lag, and new drugs. *The Drug Year*, 1979; 241:13.

13. Hings, M. I. C. Industry cited for drug delay. *New York Times*, February 4, 1982, D1.

14. Rockwell, L. H. Prescribing science and safety for the 1980s. *Private Practice*, 1981; 12:22.

15. *HHS News*, U.S. Department of Health and Human Services, December 8, 1980, 80–89.

16. See note 1.

17. See note 1.

18. Schmeckebier, L. F. The bureau of prohibition. Service Monograph No. 57, Institute for Government Research, 1929, Brookings Institute.

19. Senate Committee on the Judiciary: The illicit narcotic traffic. Senate Report No. 1440, 84th Congress, 2nd Session, 1956.

20. Depressant and stimulant drugs, Part 166, Title 21, Code of Federal Regulations, Washington, D.C., 1966, Food and Drug Administration.

21. Congressional Record, House of Representatives, House Bill H9170, September 24, 1970.

22. Taylor, W. N. The last word on steroids: Medicine can't ignore the issue. *Muscle & Fitness*, 1984; February, 88v.

23. Taylor, W. N. Effects and actions of human growth hormone. Presented at symposium on drugs in sports, American College of Sports Medicine annual meeting, San Diego, May 24, 1984.

24. Taylor, W. N. Are anabolic steroids for the long distance runner? Letter, *Annals of Sports Medicine*, 1984; 2(1):51–52.

25. See note 24.

26. Burkett, L. N., and M. T. Falduto. Steroid use by athletes in a metropolitan area. *Physician & Sportsmed.*, 1984; 12(August):69–74; Zurer, P. S. Drugs in sports. *Chemical & Engineering News*, 1984; April 30:69–78.

27. Taylor, W. N. Super athletes made to order. *Psychology Today*, 1985; May:64–66.

28. See note 27.

29. See note 27.

30. Taylor, W. N. *Hormonal Manipulation: A New Era of Monstrous Athletes.* Jefferson, NC: McFarland & Company, Inc., Publishers, 1985.

31. Taylor, W. N. Synthetic anabolic-androgenic steroids: A plea for controlled substance status, commentary. *Physician & Sportsmed.*, 1987; 15(5):140–150. Cowart, V. S. Would controlled substance status affect steroid trafficking? *Physician & Sportsmed.*, 1987; 15(5):151–154. Cowart, V. Classifying steroids as controlled substances suggested to decrease athletes supply, but enforcement could be a major problem, Medical News & Perspectives. *J. Amer. Med. Assoc.*, 1987; 257(22):3029.

32. See Cowart, Classifying steroids, note 31.

33. See Cowart articles, note 31.

34. See Cowart, Would controlled . . .?, note 31.

35. Moxley, J. H. Drug abuse in athletes: Anabolic steroids and human growth hormone. AMA, Report of the Council on Scientific Affairs, Resolution 57, A-86, December 1986.

36. Taylor, W. N. Drug issues in sports medicine, part 1: Steroid abuse & non-steroidal anti-inflammatory (NSAID) selection in athletic/active patients. *J. Neurological & Orthopaedic Med., & Surg.* 1988; 9(2):159–164. Taylor, W. N. Drug issues in sports medicine, part 2: Growth hormone abuse & anti-hypertensive drug selection in athletic/active patients. *J. Neurological & Orthopaedic Med. & Surg.*, 1988; 9(2): 165–169.

37. See Cowart, Would controlled. . .?, note 31.

38. Ibid.

39. Steroids in Amateur and Professional Sports—The Medical and Social Costs of Steroid Abuse. Hearings before the Committee on the Judiciary, United States Senate, 101st Congress, 1st Session (S. Hrg. 101-736). U.S. Government Printing Office, Washington, D.C., 1990.

Chapter 6. The Identification and Treatment of Self-Users

1. Taylor, W. N. Synthetic anabolic-androgenic steroids: A plea for controlled substance status, commentary. *Physician & Sportsmed.*, 1987; 15(5):140–150.

2. Allee, W. C., N. C. Collias, and C. Z. Lutherman. Modification of the social order in flocks of hens by the injection of testosterone propionate. *Physiol. Zoology*, 1939; 12(4):412–440.

3. Buoissou, M. F., and V. Gaudioso. Effect of early androgen treatment on subsequent social behavior in heifers. *Hormones & Behavior,* 1982; 16 (June): 132–146.

4. Simon, N. G., R. E. Whalen, and M. P. Tate. Induction of male-typical aggression by androgens by not by estrogens in adult female mice. *Hormones & Behavior*, 1985; 19 (June):204–212. Van De Poll, N. E., F. de Jonge, H. G. van Oyen, et al. Failure to find sex differences in testosterone activated aggression in two strains of rats. *Hormones & Behavior*, 1981; 15 (March):94–105. Kurischko, A., and M. Oettel. Androgen-dependent fighting behavior in male mice. *Endokrinologie*, 1977; 70 (September):1–5. Van de Poll, N. E., S. van Zanten, and F. H. de Jonge. Effects of testosterone, estrogen and dihydrotestosterone upon aggressive and sexual behavior of female rats. *Hormones & Behavior,* 1986; 20 (December): 418–431.

5. Steklis, H. D., G. L. Brammer, M. J. Raleigh, et al. Serum testosterone, male dominance, and aggression in captive groups of vervet monkeys (Cercopithecus aethiops sabaeus). *Hormones & Behavior*, 1985; 19 (June):154–163.

6. Vest, S. A., and J. E. Howard. Clinical experiments with the use of male sex hormones. *J. Urology*, 1983; 40 (January):154.

7. Persky, H., K. D. Smith, and G. K. Basu. Relation of psychological measures of aggression and hostility to testosterone production in man. *Psychosomatic Medicine*, 1971; 33 (May):265–277. Kreuz, L. E., and R. M. Rose. Assessment of aggressive behavior and plasma testosterone in a young criminal population. *Psychosomatic Medicine,* 1972; 34 (July–August):321–332. Ehrenkrants, J. E., E. Bliss, and M. H. Sheard. Plasma testosterone: correlation with aggressive behavior and social dominance in man. *Psychosomatic Medicine,* 1974; 36 (November–December):469–475. Doering, C. H., H. K. Brodie, H. C. Kraemer, et al. Negative effect and plasma testosterone: a longitudinal human study. *Psychosomatic Medicine*, 1975; 37 (November–December):484–491. Rada, R. T., D. R. Laws, and R. Kellner. Plasma testosterone levels in the rapist. *Psychosomatic Medicine,* 1976; 38 (July–August):257–266.

8. Oleweus, D., A. Mattsson and D. Schalling, et al. Testosterone, aggression, physical, and personality dimensions in normal adolescent males. *Psychosomatic Medicine,* 1980; 42 (March):253–269.

9. Taylor, W. N. Are anabolic steroids for the long distance runner? (letter). *Annals of Sports Med.*, 1984; 2(1):51–52. Taylor, W. N. Effects and actions of human growth hormone. Presented at symposium on drugs in sports, American College of Sports Medicine annual meeting, San Diego, May 24, 1984. Taylor, W. N. *Hormonal Manipulation: A New Era of Monstrous Athletes.* Jefferson, NC: McFarland & Company, Inc., Publishers, 1985. Taylor, W. N. Super athletes made to order. *Psychology Today*, 1985; (May):63–66.

10. Taylor, W. N. *Anabolic Steroids and the Athlete.* Jefferson, NC: McFarland & Company, Inc., Publishers, 1982.

11. See note 1.

12. Anabolic Steroid Abuse. *FDA Drug Bulletin*, 1987; 17(3):27.

13. Pope, H. G., and D. L. Katz. Bodybuilders psychosis. *Lancet*, 1987 (April 11):863.

14. Pope, H. G., and D. L. Katz. Affective and psychotic symptoms associated with anabolic steroid use. *American J. Psychiatry*, 1988; 145(4): 487–490.

15. Taylor, W. N., and A. B. Black. Pervasive anabolic steroid use among health club athletes. *Annals of Sports Med.,* 1987; 3(3):158. Taylor, W. N. Influences of synthetic androgenic/anabolic steroid self-use on human behavior. *J. Osteopathic Sports Med.,* 1987; 1(2):19–25. Yates, W. R., P. J. Perry, and K. H. Andersen. Illicit anabolic steroid use: A controlled personality study. *Acta Psychiatrica Scand.*, 1990 (in press). Pope, H. G., and D. L. Katz. Homicide and near-homicide by anabolic steroid users. *J. Clinical Psychiatry*, 1990; 51(1):28–31. Brower, J. K., F. C. Blow, T. P. Beresford, et al. Anabolic-androgenic steroid dependence. *J. Clinical Psychiatry*, 1989; 50(1):31–33. Elofson, G., and S. Elofson. Steroids claimed our son's life. *Physician & Sportsmedicine*, 1990; 18(8):15–16.

16. See Elotson and Elotson, note 15.

17. See note 9.

18. The Steroid Trafficking Act of 1990 (see Appendix 1, p. 7).

19. Kashkin, K. B., and H. D. Kleber. Hooked on hormones? An anabolic steroid addiction hypothesis. *JAMA*, 1989; 262(22):3166–3170.

20. Taylor, W. N. Drug issues in sports medicine, part 1. *J. Neurological & Orthopaedic Medicine & Surgery,* 1988; 9(2):159–164.

21. Sheridan, P. J. Androgen receptors in the brain: what are we measuring? *Endocrine Reviews*, 1983; 4(2):171–178.

22. Davidson, J. M. Neurohormonal bases for male sexual behavior. *International Rev. Physiol.* 1977; 13 (February):225–254.

23. See note 21.

24. Ibid.

25. Akst, D. *Wonder Boy: Bary Minkow—The Kid Who Swindled Wall Street*, New York: Charles Scribner's Sons, 1990.

26. Strauss, R. H., J. E. Wright, G. A. Finerman, et al. Side effects of anabolic steroids in weight-trained men. *Physician & Sportsmed*, 1983; 11 (December):86–98. Costill, D. L., D. R. Pearson, and W. J. Fink. Anabolic steroid use among athletes: changes in HDL-C levels. *Physician & Sportsmed*, 1984; 12 (June): 112–117. Peterson, F. E., and T. D. Fahey. HDL-C levels in five elite athletes using anabolic-androgenic steroids. *Physician & Sportsmed*, 1984; 12 (June):120–130. Cohen, J. C., W. M. Faber, A. J. Benade, et al. Altered serum lipoprotein profiles in male and female power lifters ingesting anabolic steroids. *Physician & Sportsmed.*, 1986; 14 (June):131–136. Webb, O. L., P. M. Laskarzewski, and C. J. Glueck. Severe depression of high-density lipoprotein cholesterol levels in weight lifters and body builders by self-administered exogenous testosterone and anabolic-androgenic steroids. *Metabolism*, 1974; 33 (November):971–975. Kantor, M. A., A. Bianchini, D. Bernier, et al. Androgens reduce HDL-2 cholesterol and increase hepatic triglyceride lipase activity. *Med. Sci. Sports Exerc.*, 1985; 17 (August): 462–465. Moffatt, R. J., M. B. Wallace, and S. P. Sady. Effects of anabolic steroids on lipoprotein profiles of female weight lifters. *Physician & Sportsmed.*, 1990; 18 (September):106–115.

27. Freedman, D. S., S. R. Srinivasan, and C. Shear. The relation of apoproteins

A-1 and B in children in parental myocardial infarction. *New England J. Med.,* 1986; 315(12):721–726. Maciejko, J. J., D. R. Holmes, B. Kottke, et al. Apolipoprotein A-1 as a marker of angiographically assessed coronary artery disease. *New England J. Med.,* 1983; 309(7):385–389.

28. See Taylor, Effects and actions, note 9.

29. Buckley, W. E., et al. Estimated prevalence of anabolic steroid use among high school seniors. *JAMA*, 1988; 260(12):3441.

30. Taylor, W. N. Observations from many patients who are self-using anabolic steroids. Hough, D. O., and R. O. Voy. When to suspect steroid abuse. *Patient Care,* 1990 (August 15):129–140.

31. See Taylor, Are Steroids ... runner?, note 9.

32. See notes 15, 19; Brower, K. J. Rehabilitation for anabolic-androgenic steroid dependence, based on a paper presented at the National Consensus Meeting on Anabolic/Androgenic Steroids, in press.

33. See Brower, note 32.

34. Tennant, F., D. L. Black and R. O. Voy. Anabolic steroid dependence with opioid-like features. *New England J. Med.* 1988; 319:578.

35. See Taylor, *Hormonal Manipulation* and Super athletes, note 9.

36. See note 20.

37. See note 19.

38. See note 13.

39. See note 1.

Chapter 7. The Limits of Urine Drug Testing

1. Holder, F. W. Anabolic detection and enforcement. *Br. J. Sports Med.,* 1975; 9:98–99. Ward, R. J., C. H. L. Shackleton, and A. M. Lawson. Gas-chromatographic–mass spectrometric methods for the detection and identification of anabolic steroid drugs. *Br. J. Sports Med.,* 1975; 9:93–97. Brooks, R. V., R. G. Firth, and N. A. Summer. Detection of anabolic steroids by radioimmunoassay. *Br. J. Sports Med.,* 1975; 9:89–92. Hempl, R., and L. Starka. Practical aspects of screening anabolic steroids in doping control with particular accent to nortestosterone radioimmunoassay using mixed antisera. *J. Steroid Biochem.,* 1979; 11:933–936. Peterson, N. J., A. R. Midgely, and R. B. Jaffe. Regulation of human gonadotropins. III. Luteinizing hormone and follicle stimulating hormone in sera from adult males. *J. Clin. Endocrinol. Metab.,* 1968; 28:1437–1478. Wheeler, M. J., P. Woodrup, and D. Watson. Comparison of radioimmunoassay methods for human luteinizing hormone. *Clin. Biochem.,* 1975; 8:23–32. Ward, R. J., A. M. Lawson, and C. H. L. Shackelton. Metabolism of anabolic steroid drugs in man and the marmoset monkey. I. Nivelar and orabolin. *J. Steroid Biochem.,* 1977; 8:1057–1063.

2. See Ward, Gas-chromatographic, note 1.

3. Voy, R. O. *Drugs, Sport and Politics.* Champaign, IL: Human Kinetics Publishers, 1990.

Final Plea: Expand the 1970 Controlled Substance Act

1. Taylor, W. N. Super athletes made to order. *Psychology Today*, 1985; May:63–66. Taylor, W. N. Synthetic HGH should be classified as a controlled substance to prevent abuse. *Genetic Engineering News*, 1986; 6:4. Taylor, W. N. Will synthetic human growth hormone become the peril of genetic engineering? *Annals of Sports Medicine*, 1986; 2:197–199. Taylor, W. N. Synthetic human growth hormone: A call for federal control. *Physician & Sportsmed*, 1988; 16(3): 189–192.

Index

habit forming 41
hallucinogens 51
Halotestin 18, 21
Hamilton, Dr. J. B. 9, 11
Hamm, Dr. 12
Hanley, Dr. Dan 26, 27, 35
Harrison Act 48
Hatfield, Dr. Fred 36
Haupt, Dr. Herbert 33
healing rates 55
health food stores 4
heart attack 77, 81
hemoglobin 19, 54, 78
heroes 2
heroin 51, 60, 64
Hervey, Professor G. R. 25, 31, 35
Hitler, Adolf 8, 9
hormonal manipulation 15
hormone hunters 7, 16
horses 18
hostility 56, 75, 76
human growth hormone (HGH) 4, 6, 7, 35, 37, 44, 59, 60, 63, 88, 95
Hunter, John 5
hyperlipidema 22
hypertension 11, 55, 77, 80
hypodermic syringe 47
hypogonadism 9, 10

immune system 55
impotence 5
insomnia 55
Internal Revenue Service 51
International Olympic Committee 88, 89
involutional melancholia 10

Johnson, Dr. Levon C. 27, 29, 31
Jones, Dr. Arthur 27

Katz, Dr. David 71
Kefauver-Harris Amendment 42, 43
Keynon, Dr. A. T. 7
Koch, Dr. Fred 7, 8

Lamb, Dr. David 28
Land of Bimini 1
Laqueur, Ernst 8
legend drug 41
Lesser, Dr. Maurice A. 11, 12
libido 11–13, 55, 56, 62, 75, 83
limbic system 67
lipoprotein values 77, 79
liver abnormalities 56
liver function tests 55, 79
livestock 18
Lombardo, Dr. John 34–36, 59
lysergic acid (LSD) 48, 51, 64, 67

McGee, Lemuel C. 7
"macho image" 67, 74
male climacteric 10
Male Hormone, The 15
mania 69, 72, 75
marathon runners 13
marijuana 48, 51, 61, 64
Maxibolin 18, 21
medical antipathy 3, 15, 22
"medical dynamite" 15
"megorexia" 68, 73, 74
menopause 14
menstrual disturbances 55
mental disorders 10, 11, 56
mental intensity 54, 56, 57
meperidine 51
mescaline 51
Mesue, Johannes 5
methadone 51
methamphetamines 9
methandriol 18
methaqualone 51
methenolone 21
methyl testosterone 18
Minkow, Barry 76
misbranding 40
morphine 51
movie stars 2
Muscle & Fitness magazine 36
muscle sparing effect 14
muscular performance 13, 14
muscular strength 15
Myagen 18, 21
myelofibrosis 22

About the Author

William N. Taylor, M.D., is currently the Medical Clinic Director at the Sports/Spa & Clinic at Sandestin in Destin, Florida. He serves on the Board of Advisors for the American Academy of Sports Physicians and is a Fellow of the American College of Sports Medicine. Dr. Taylor is also Sports Medicine Editor for *Powerlifting-USA* magazine and is a contributing editor for *Muscle & Fitness* magazine. For the past three years he has been a lecturing consultant on the topic of anabolic steroid abuse for major league baseball. He is a consultant for the Consultant Resource Group for the Office of Substance Abuse Prevention of the United States Department of Health and Human Services.

Dr. Taylor was selected as a physician crew chief for the United States Olympic Committee's Drug Control/Education Program during the quadrennium 1984–1988. He has also been an expert witness for the FDA in federal court and has been selected to testify before Congress regarding anabolic steroid and growth hormone abuse. He has appeared in several major television documentaries dealing with the topic of anabolic steroid abuse, including ABC's "20/20" and videotaped programs for the United States Department of Education.

As an anabolic steroid researcher, Dr. Taylor has published several articles for both the scientific and lay press. He has written two previous books that deal with the use and abuse of anabolic steroids and growth hormones: *Anabolic Steroids and the Athlete* (1982) and *Hormonal Manipulation: A New Era of Monstrous Athletes* (1985). He was the first person to recognize and publicize that anabolic steroids should be reclassified as controlled substances nationally, and his lecture series "Drug Issues in Sports Medicine" was instrumental in promulgating this necessary change in federal law.

Dr. Taylor's educational background includes a B.S. in chemistry from the University of West Florida (1975), an M.S. in chemical and polymer engineering from the University of Tennessee (1976), and an M.D. from the University of Miami School of Medicine (1981) where he was selected into the national Alpha Omega Alpha Honor Medical Society. He completed a flexible internship in the Pensacola Educational Program in 1982.

After practicing family medicine for several years, Dr. Taylor has focused on preventive medicine and exercise prescription. He has completed 14 marathons, participates in an avid weight-lifting program and aerobic training program, and is a scratch golfer who has competed in statewide amateur golf championships in Florida. He is also a professional model and national spokesman for Palm Beach's athletic-cut men's formal and business attire.